JOHN SURTEES

World Champion

JOHN SURTEES

World Champion

EDITED BY ALAN HENRY

HAZLETON PUBLISHING

PUBLISHER
Richard Poulter

EXECUTIVE PUBLISHER
Elizabeth Le Breton

ART EDITOR
Steve Small

PRODUCTION MANAGER
George Greenfield

HOUSE EDITOR
Peter Lovering

PRODUCTION ASSISTANT
Deirdre Fenney

This first edition published in 1991 by
Hazleton Publishing, 3 Richmond Hill, Richmond,
Surrey TW10 6RE.

ISBN: 0-905138-73-2

Typeset by First impression Ltd, Richmond, Surrey.
Colour reproduction by Masterlith Ltd, Mitcham, Surrey.
Printed in England by Richard Clay Ltd, Bungay, Suffolk.

DISTRIBUTORS

UK & OTHER MARKETS

George Philip Limited
59 Grosvenor Street
London W1X 9DA

NORTH AMERICA
Motorbooks International
PO Box 2
729 Prospect Avenue
Osceola
Wisconsin 54020, USA

Acknowledgements

I would like to offer my thanks to John Blunsden, Ferrari Heritage, Franco Gozzi and Cyril Quantrill for their help with the preparation of this book.

J.S.

Colour and sepia photographs by:
Geoff Goddard – front cover main photograph.
Don Morley – back cover *(top)*, pages 114 *(top)*, 115 *(top)* and 117.
David Phipps – back cover *(bottom)*, pages 118, 119, 120, 121, 122 *(bottom)*, 123, 124 *(bottom)*, 125 and 127.
Nigel Snowdon – page 122 *(top)*.
John Surtees – front cover insets, pages 113, 114 *(bottom)*, 115 *(bottom)*, 124 *(top)*, 126 and 128.
Mick Woollett – back cover main photograph and page 116.

Black and white photographs contributed by:
Classic Bike, Ferrari Heritage, Dave Friedman, Alan Henry, David Phipps, Steve Small, Nigel Snowdon, John Surtees and Mick Woollett.

Contents

Chapter 1
The Early Years

The Surtees story in racing starts with my father. The youngest of two brothers, John Norman Surtees – 'Dad' – didn't enjoy a very happy childhood. Just prior to World War I his father had become very involved in forming shop floor representation in one of the Sainsbury's stores and this had not brought about a very happy household atmosphere.

Obviously the pressures had told on his mother and, for some unaccountable reason – perhaps it was just that – the two boys found themselves in a Salvation Army home. They clearly were not very happy there because, even though they were under age, my father and his elder brother Henry ran away and joined the Army. They ended up in France early in the war where Henry lost his life when the ambulance he was driving was blown up.

My father learned to drive during his time in the services and survived the war intact. After the war, with the break-up of the Ottoman Empire, Britain was given the responsibility of administering the Palestine and Trans-Jordan areas, the Army working alongside the civilian government to establish some form of control.

Father found himself posted out there with plenty of desert and rough-road driving to be done. In the early 1920s he returned to England where he began driving buses, of which there was no shortage, it seems, as many had returned from the battlefields of France. Plenty of these buses were going cheap, which meant that lots of private, pirate companies began to become established. By all accounts, rivalry between the various companies gave rise to Grand Prix-style competition on the road – not a bad start for a competitive person like my father!

That competitive nature and, I suppose, a bit of the inherent Surtees family cussed-ness meant that he couldn't stop there. He didn't like the way things were done, so he upped and left. By this stage he had married Dorothy Cynthia, and I arrived on 11 February 1934 at the home of my mother's sister in a small village called Tatsfield in Surrey, right on the Kent border.

My parents were living where they could at that stage, my father ekeing out a living at whatever work he could get at that time. Just after this, he set up a motor cycle shop to do repairs and sell the odd machine in Tamworth Road, Croydon. Two years earlier, he had enjoyed his first ride on a racing bike when he had acquired a B14 Excelsior-JAP.

I have been able to uncover some details of his first competition outing which, in many ways, was similar to my own, although I didn't lead the race. The event was at the Layhams Farm Mountain Mile grass track, near West Wickham in Kent. This had a one-in-three climb called Bob's Knob, it seems, with a hump near the bottom, a downhill ess-bend and an acute hairpin leading into the bumpy bottom straight.

Dad led on the first lap, gave it too much stick and looped it . . . well, as gracefully as one can in the circumstances. After that, he attached a sidecar to the Excelsior and, for the occasional event, Mother climbed into the sidecar, but then I came along and perhaps spoilt it all!

But Dad still continued racing and was, I suppose, the most successful sidecar rider on the mountain grass tracks when World War II broke out. There wasn't that much opportunity, of course, to race on permanent circuits. Records exist of him racing round the Campbell circuit at Brooklands, and at Crystal Palace, Alexandra Palace, Cadwell Park and Donington Park.

War came again, however, and Graham Walker, then Editor of *Motorcycle* magazine, devised a scheme for recruiting some of the stars of road and grass track racing into the Royal Signals in order to assist with the training of despatch riders as well as the setting up of the necessary workshops.

Dad was by now 38 years old, above the normal age to be recruited, and was one of the first to volunteer. Graham Walker pulled a few strings to ensure he was posted to Catterick where he was made responsible for setting up the workshops and for attempting to bring as much professionalism as possible into training the despatch riders. As he told me later, it was necessary to try and train the lads to have a better than average chance before they were sent out to the front.

At that time we were living in a flat over another shop at Elmers End to which Dad had relocated his business. I suppose some of my earliest childhood memories are of that small shop, and of the waste land which ran alongside the end of the parade. As a lad I recall playing around there, climbing trees, doing all the sorts of things that youngsters do.

I don't really remember what sort of cars and motor cycles he dealt with, but after the war he did mention on numerous occasions that he had had to dispose of a Delage, an SS100 Jaguar and a Bentley on behalf of some friends. He was hard pressed to get £30 apiece for them!

By the time 1939 arrived, my father, along with Eric Oliver, had transferred his affections to 596 camshaft Nortons. There were one or two works racing versions made, but most of those in general use had originally been built for trials – for events such as the International Six Day Trial – normally to be used with sidecars. These featured aluminium crankcases, whereas the few works machines which had been built around 1936 featured crankcases and other parts made from magnesium. Interestingly, I have recently been able to acquire one of these 1936 works engines, which I found tucked away in Australia, with a view to recreating my father's outfit from that period.

By this time my brother Norman and sister Dorothy had arrived on the scene. With myself and Norman sharing my father's two Christian names, Dad became increasingly referred to as Jack.

Although he had gone off to Yorkshire, Dad was keen to keep the family in the south London area where we already lived. With this in mind, he managed to rent a house in Homer Road, Shirley, just outside Elmers End. This arrangement started off quite well until the Blitz started.

My mother hadn't long given birth to my sister Dorothy, so it was rather fortuitous that my father had built up a shelter on the ground floor, because a bomb dropped in the front garden, blowing in most of the front of the house on top of the shelter. My father was then up at Catterick, so you can understand his concern.

So now he decided it was all up and off to Catterick. The only property he could get at the time was a minute flat opposite the barracks. Yes, it was very convenient, but it was incredibly cramped. But it would do until such time as Dad could find something else.

The other prize possession he had taken to Yorkshire was his 596 Norton. This was tucked away in a little lock-up next to the bowling green, which was also quite close to the barracks. This, I suppose, was one of my first recollections of his involvement with racing bikes. I remember during his free moments I would go with him to the lock-up where he would re-oil the bike and just turn over the engine before locking it up again.

It wasn't long before Dad managed to find another home for us. It was a pair of cottages out on the moors near Huddersfield. There had been thoughts of converting them. At least, that is what must have been in the minds of the owners, because a makeshift doorway had been knocked through between them; the jagged, irregular brickwork surrounding it still sticks very clearly in my mind. It was rather a nice place to be, a bit basic, but a haven for a small lad, with the garden full of rubble and general debris.

Dad was keen that our family life should continue as unaffected by the war as was conceivably possible, and he did his level best to keep us occupied. I recall one occasion he returned home with an old laundry box brimful of second-hand Meccano parts, and I had a tremendous time assembling a model crane which I positioned on the garden wall and used to attempt to move small pieces of rubble around. Being out on the moors also developed my intense liking for the countryside and open air.

A short distance away from the cottage was a ravine containing a little stream coming out of the rocks, and a wide assortment of trees and undergrowth. This left a very special impression on me as I spent a lot of time wandering round there, enjoying being in the open air, trying to climb all the trees, and, I suppose, just thinking. It left a lasting impression on me that has developed into a hate for the litter bugs and vandals who plague our lives in these modern times. Sad to say as an Englishman, in this respect the British rank among the worst.

However, the real significance for me of that period is that it instilled in me a feeling of not wanting to make my home within a city or town. To this day, although I have enjoyed some of the world's finest cities, I can't wait to get back out into the countryside. We also briefly lived in York, after leaving Catterick, close to the Rowntree factory with all the benefits for a young lad that that entailed in terms of free samples!

Another thing I was able to amuse myself with was the contents of a number of large cardboard boxes holding Dad's copies of *Motor Cycle* and *Motorcycling* – the two main magazines of the time – and quite a number of old race programmes. Particularly on long winter evenings, I spent much time leafing happily through their pages.

I remember being extremely impressed with one particular photograph of Georg Meier – the first non-British rider, if you don't count Dubliner Stanley Woods, on a foreign machine to win the Isle of Man Senior TT – hurtling down Bray Hill standing on the footrests of his BMW during the 1939 event.

In addition, I was also captivated by details of the little supercharged Benelli four-cylinder which had been developed just prior to the outbreak of war, and the single-cylinder which had won the TT. There were also pictures of people I was to meet and come into contact with such as Harold Daniell on the Norton and Freddie Frith on the Velocette.

I think it's fair to say that, while I've never been one for hero-worship relative to personalities – admiration and respect, yes, but not actual hero-worship – that picture of Georg Meier made an enormous impression on me. Racing forward slightly to more recent years, I was able to transfer some of those memories into a reality in 1989. Having found the Georg Meier machine during the early 1980s, lying in pieces in a number of boxes in the United States, we carefully and painstakingly put the machine together again, making sure it was as authentic as could be.

It was ready for a special day at Brands Hatch in 1989, which was very satisfying because it demonstrated the support of the British motor cycling community for recapturing the thrill and exciting sounds of the classic period. I had helped put on a charity event at Brands Hatch, a very successful event, incidentally, which raised £50,000 for a charity for the disabled and attracted the biggest crowd there since the 1986 British F1 Grand Prix. I was able to put my leg over that very BMW that I had looked at so longingly in the magazines all those years ago, and ride it around Brands Hatch.

On the track at the same time was one of BMW's big rivals, the V4 AJS, ridden by Sammy Miller. I wasn't disappointed in the BMW. It felt super. Having later had the opportunity to drive both the Auto Union and Mercedes-Benz from that same period, I believe that era leading up to World War II was one which, in another life, I would really have loved to have participated in.

We were happy in that little house, but Father was certainly uneasy. There was the question of our long-term schooling and he wanted to get back into a district he was familiar with, to think about what was to be done and where the family budget was to come from when the war was over.

As a result, he took a little time off and went down to see whether he could find a place for us in the area around Shirley and Elmers End. Our old home in Homer Road was not available. It had been rebuilt and was now occupied by another family. But he managed to come up with a council house in Mardel Road which had the additional advantage that it was just opposite Monks Orchard School, ideal for the children.

So the plans were set. Dad would stay at Catterick, getting away as often as he could, and we would all move back down to Mardel Road. It was a basic little house, but it had quite a nice garden leading down to a bird sanctuary in one corner and, from the other, we could get over the fence into the Long Lane woods.

In the garden was a dug-out shelter, and I suppose this was a matter of great excitement to young children of our age. Up in Yorkshire, after our move north, we had not experienced the air raids. On reflection, in some ways, Dad had got his timing a little wrong!

Just as we got settled in, the flying bombs arrived, the incendiary bombs and, of course, the V2s. I remember one day, in our ignorance, going around with a number of other lads, picking up these metal canisters in the woods. They only happened to be unexploded incendiary bombs! You can imagine the reactions of the ARP personnel when they saw these lads arriving with unexploded incendiary bombs. It was certainly the first and last time we did that, and I was shipped back to my mother quite firmly!

I recall looking out of the Anderson shelter watching the flames spurting out of the 'doodlebugs' and I learned, at a very young age, that there was no worry as long as their motors were still running. The only moment to scramble back into the shelter was if you heard the motors stop just before they got to you. I remember peeping out of the shelter and thinking, 'Well, as long as they're still going, there's no problem.' The biggest worry of all – although I don't think youngsters do worry too much at that age – was the V2s, as with those there was just a big explosion. There was no warning with those!

There wasn't a great deal to eat, of course, but Dad would come down from Catterick on his motor cycle combination to see us as often as possible, sometimes officially, sometimes not. I remember him saying on one occasion that he had been stuck up on red tape trying to get machines repaired, or machinery installed to actually get the machines repaired.

From time to time he would speak to the commanding officer, get an official pass, a bag full of cash and come down to London in order to go to people like Claude Rye to get components to assist with the rebuilding of the bikes. Other times, well, he just had to take a chance, scrounge some fuel and get round the problem of the 'red caps' – the Military Police – who would be checking on the legitimacy of such journeys, particularly around the London area.

However, as the machine he was riding was always an Army combination – a big four Norton or perhaps even a V-twin Indian – it would not have been very quick. And it was a long journey. But he would turn up with the odd piece of ham and sometimes tins of Libbys fruit, which was a real treat.

I recall one Christmas he arrived with an enormous ham, the biggest joint we'd ever seen. It was too big for any of the pots we had managed to salvage, so I remember Mum scrubbing out the Burco boiler in order that it could be cooked and everybody enjoyed the great feast.

It was shortly after this trip that a big disaster took place. On the return journey to Catterick late one night, after a day trip down to see us, the pressures of Dad's recent hectic schedule caught up with him. He fell asleep on his motor cycle and crashed down into a quarry.

He was smashed up very badly indeed and ended up in Pinderfields Hospital, Wakefield, with a fractured femur and several other broken bones. They did a good job for him, and it was very convenient that, as soon as he could be moved, he was brought down to Epsom for convalescence. I remember Mother gathering us all up to go over to Epsom on the bus to visit him. He was left with one leg an inch or so shorter than the other and always walked with a limp after that, particularly when he was tired. By this time the war was almost at an end and these injuries meant that he was invalided out of the services.

This left things in a very difficult state. What assets he had had been sold up with his entry into the special scheme. His one remaining asset was his 596 Norton and he lost that. He was in and out of hospital for about 18 months, during which time the last thing anybody was thinking about was that Norton tucked away in the lock-up. Except, of course, the person who owned the lock-up. He decided that the fact he had not been paid the few shillings for rental at that time gave him the right to sell the machine without any form of communication, or attempt to get in contact.

On leave from hospital, Dad turned his mind to getting a business started again. I remember travelling around with him and looking at various shops, until he found one not very far away from where Harold Daniell and Steve Lancefield were operating, in Forest Hill, south London.

The premises were in a bit of a state, but the rent was cheap and, with the promise from a number of his old trading colleagues of machines on a sale-or-return basis, the scene was set. There was no money to fight a legal claim over the Norton, so that had to be written off.

One of the first little machines I recall seeing was a KTT Mk 8 Velocette, given to him by Eric Oliver to sell. Other machines which left a lasting impression on me were a pair of beautiful Rudge Ulsters which came from Les Hall from Balham, a colourful character who specialised in that make. Les had been a sidecar rider himself and these two machines, I understand, had been prepared for the European Six Day Trial just as war broke out, so of course they were never sent, and Rudge disappeared, never to recommence bike production after the war.

I suppose a feature of that period was the warm-hearted camaraderie between neighbouring dealers like Harold Daniell, Halls of Balham and even Eric Oliver, who, although he wasn't a dealer as such, moved the odd machine around. There were a host of people involved. Some had been in the military, others had managed to continue some form of work which had been deemed sufficiently important to avoid their being called up.

I well remember going up as a youngster, and feeling slightly bewildered when I was introduced to Harold and, of course, Steve Lancefield, who was in charge of the tuning side and who turned out the Nortons raced by Johnny Lockett, the Brands Hatch grass track specialist.

Harold was actually the most unlikely sort of person you would ever imagine to be a super champion rider, but, of course, appearances can be deceptive.

Anyway, so Dad began to deal in motor cycles again, he and a number of old colleagues picking up the threads of the business they had all been in before the war. No question about it, those were hard times; in fact, I never quite realised at the time what a struggle he had been through. He was attempting to build up a business on his disability pension. There were times when there wasn't quite as much to eat as there might have been, but by the same token we never really went short. Dad had a real fight on his hands.

Nevertheless, he was still deeply enthusiastic about motor cycle sport and determined to resume competing. To that end, I remember one day going over to Balham with him, to a firm called C.S. Smith, which was quite famous for the manufacture of big ends and bearings for motor cycle engines.

We arrived and were taken down into a cellar at Charlie Smith's premises and found all these bits from a 596 Norton – not quite the same as Dad's original one.

It was spread around the floor in pieces, but it suited Dad because it didn't cost much. He managed to come to an arrangement, swapping this and that, and having the balance on hire purchase. Away we went. All the pieces were taken back and I, of course, as chief cleaner of parts and polisher, set to work cleaning up the parts. In fact I was more of a hindrance than a help.

The year is now 1946 and I had just transferred from the Monks Orchard Primary School to Ashburton School, in Long Lane, Addiscombe. At Easter we all went off to the first post-war race meeting at Cadwell Park. The meeting took place on Good Friday and

Easter Monday. I remember we were all loaded up into the family car, an early 1930s Ford V8, and set off for Cadwell Park, towing the Norton – with a yoke attached to its front forks – and the sidecar, suitably weighed down by the tool boxes, behind us. No trailers or transporters here, of course.

The three children – my brother Norman, sister Dorothy and myself – occupied the dicky seat. We arrived at Cadwell Park very late on the Thursday night and I recall the antics we had trying to set up the tent in which we were going to stay, and being uncertain where we should pitch it.

To our great excitement, we finally got ourselves settled in, only to wake up in the early hours of the morning and find ourselves being washed away. We'd pitched our tent at the base of the valley at the point where the bottom straight turned up onto the Mountain in what was effectively a stream bed. You can guess the rest! The overnight rain resulted in our being flooded out! We were certainly not expert campers.

From then on, we changed our plans. It was a mistake we didn't make twice; thanks to the generosity of Charles Wilkinson, who owned the track at that time, at future Cadwell meetings we were allowed to camp out in a little glass summerhouse quite close to the Esses which the marshals used during the race meeting. This meeting was also the first time that I was to see George Brown, on his beautiful little special HRD which was based on a pre-war TT replica.

I felt a lot of pride watching Dad battle it out with Eric Oliver in the sidecar race on Good Friday and finish second, only to have a disaster take place in the handicap race. Dad had persuaded his old passenger, Frank Lilley, to come back and ride with him, but the back sidecar ball joint, which connected the sidecar to the bike, broke, the sidecar virtually came away from the bike, and they went careering off the track.

It was the first time I had seen my father involved in an accident and, just as worryingly, I saw the effect it had on my mother. Dad and Frank both escaped unhurt. I suppose that was one of the first heart-stopping moments I ever experienced although, as with the incendiary bombs, you don't appreciate or understand the dangers quite as much when you are a kid. Luckily, it wasn't too serious and he repaired the machine in time for the Monday, when he dominated the sidecar scratch race, increasing his lead all the way to win from Eric Oliver.

Later in May the combination was taken down to our local track, Brands Hatch, but on this occasion Dad was partnered by Les Seals, who had previously passengered one of his former rivals, Arthur Horton, who in turn had, I think, been the first British rider to compete in international races prior to the war and use a Continental-style sidecar, on which the passenger got out in front of the sidecar wheel. Second place was again filled by Eric Oliver, with the Seymour brothers, on their beautifully prepared Douglas, coming in third.

Off came the knobbly tyres and on went the racing Dunlops, 300 × 21 front and 350 × 20 rear, just as used on solos (there were no special tyres in those days for sidecars) and it was off to a disused airfield, North Weald. A number of ex-RAF planes were still parked all around and I recall seeing the pictures of the bikes virtually running in and out of the parked aircraft.

Another first! This time from Jack Varlow who, at a later stage, was in fact to passenger my father in some of his races. Other now long-forgotten airfield circuits were at Anstey,

Boreham and Haddenham. There were virtually no permanent road circuits open at this time other than Cadwell Park. Donington Park was no longer in use. Silverstone, which was just starting up, and the other ex-airfields therefore filled the void, despite their being on the whole flat and featureless places.

The 1946 season was also when what I consider an historic meeting took place at Brands Hatch. It was a team challenge event between the Northern Ireland contingent and the resident Brands Hatch brigade, held at the still-unsurfaced Kent track.

The Irish team included Artie Bell (500 pushrod AJS), Peter Gill (BSA), Harry Jackson (350 Velocette), Ernie Lyons (500 Triumph), Rex McCandless (350 Triumph) and Bill Nicholason (350 BSA). Ranged against these were the Brands Hatch team including Charlie Beischer (500 Norton), Jack Difazio (500 Rudge), Harry Ditchburn (350 AJS), Wally Lock (350 AJS), Eric Oliver (500 JAP), Les Schwieso (350 AJS) and Jock West (350 AJS).

Brands Hatch had a narrow 17-15 win in the six-race match event, with Oliver winning three of the races, but Ernie Lyons and Artie Bell created an enormous impression. They turned up with rear suspension fitted, something that nobody had ever considered before for grass track racing. They had telescopic forks in conjunction with swinging arms. It was a McCandless invention made up from Jeep suspension and reminded people of the system used on the Velocette KTT Mk 8s.

So you had the sight of these riders storming confidently through the corners, feet on their footrests, almost running round the outside of the old regulars. This represented a total revolution, after which everybody had to have it. Agencies for the McCandless suspension system sprang up everywhere and it became one of the biggest areas of motor cycle development at that time.

I had stayed at Monks Orchard School until I was 12, then transferred to Ashburton Secondary Modern School where, in the early post-war years, there were very limited resources available. I always remember that, when the football team was being organised, the biggest problem was actually finding a ball!

The school had some very enthusiastic teachers. I remember the headmaster, Mr Stone, assisted by Mr Harding, Mr Neach, the arts master, and Mr Butler, who did his best to make one appreciate the wonders of working with wood. It has been particularly enjoyable in recent years to make contact again with Mr Neach and to follow through some of the developments at the school and, of course, talk about old times.

I recall Miss Rogers, the music teacher, who was a great Vaughan Williams fan. I remember her efforts training the school choir, and the courage she displayed in putting me up to perform a solo piece when we had to appear at the Croydon Centre concert – there was young JS, still with a boy near-soprano voice, singing 'Oh for the Wings of a Dove'.

I took an interest in boxing and athletics, representing the school in the long jump, the 100 yards and the 220. Mind you, I can't say that I was particularly successful at cricket, but I did enjoy football. Being rather speedy on my feet, I was inevitably put out on the right wing and ended up with the nickname 'Bullet'.

On reflection, it's fair to say that I had more speed than skill. It was all rather a question of rushing down the right wing and booting the ball over. Not quite the sort of thing you'd expect to see from Stanley Matthews.

I was not exactly outstanding on the academic side. When it came down to a little engineering, or discussions on the internal combustion engine, I was more in my element, because of my experience with my father. I think I was average in most subjects, but not brilliant at anything.

I was extremely interested in art and I got on quite well with practical mathematics. But my mind kept wandering away to projects I'd seen at my father's shop or other things I'd wanted to start.

Something else, however, was on the horizon. There was talk about the new Series B Vincent. The Series A had already raced with some success. In fact, Ted Friend, who was later to be a works Porcupine AJS rider, had raced one in grass track events and had actually been leading one particular event at Layhams Farm when the exhaust pipe fell off, and Ginger Woods had demonstrated its speed, but poor handling, on the road circuits like Donington Park.

These machines had a reputation of being quick, but hairy. However, the new Series B was to be a totally new machine; designed by Philip Vincent and Phil Irving, it was intended to claim the title of the world's finest motor cycle from the Brough Superior. At least, that was the stated aim.

Father was very excited and I remember going with him to the Vincent factory and being with him when he talked to Mr Vincent and Phil Irving. It was agreed that he would become a Vincent agent for the south-east of England, operating from Forest Hill, and that he would have a bike which he could race himself.

The machine was two engine numbers along from that which was to become the famous 'Gunga Din'. It was a very good thing for Vincents. Lashing on the third wheel of a sidecar put added stress through the frame and engine and helped to sort many teething problems, notably with gearboxes and clutches. These problems were not so prevalent when it was used as a solo.

Dad loved Vincents and at times he would display what I can only describe as an over-abundance of enthusiasm. He would develop an almost blind determination to go ploughing on with any project – and it was quite an uphill struggle to get the Vincent project off the ground. I well recall listening to those problems as a young lad and I'm sure my future was partly influenced by seeing the difficulties that he experienced; on reflection perhaps I should have taken more heed, particularly during my car racing years, relative to the price one can pay for decisions based on over-enthusiasm. Or is it just being a bit of a dreamer?

Basically, though, it was a good life and I certainly have no regrets about that period in my youth. Obviously there were the usual disagreements that arise between parents and their children, but on the whole I cannot imagine any parents doing a better job.

I think it is important to emphasise just what a close relationship I enjoyed with my parents. My brother, sister and I grew up in a really close-knit family environment. Make no mistake, Dad worked very hard indeed. After those initial disappointments when he returned from Yorkshire, he gradually built up quite a reasonable business and a nice family home.

At the time of writing these words, Mother is still alive, of course, but Dad died back in 1972. He was a super person and we were very close. I think that quality of becoming passionately and overwhelmingly involved with any project he turned his hand to, giving it his all, is something that tends to run through much of our family.

Father continued with the Vincent, and at times his 596 Norton, racing through to

1952. He was 46 at the end of the war, which had cost him his prime years, and I think it's fair to say he was the most competitive rider around in 1939, perhaps even in the immediate post-war years. But by this time the likes of Eric Oliver, a good friend of Dad's who went on to win the World Championship in 1949 – with Denis Jenkinson in the chair – and 1950, and other younger rivals were coming along.

Dad's enthusiasm was infectious and it didn't take me long to become hooked on the world of motor cycles. Increasingly, I spent every minute of my spare time at his shop, becoming unofficial chief cleaner, polisher, assistant and bottle washer. During this time I also managed to acquire some bits and pieces of a Wolf motor cycle which my father suggested I try putting together, which I did.

In his dealings at Forest Hill, Dad had come across an old Wallis-Blackburne speedway bike which I used to tinker with, and in 1947, when I was just 13, I had my first rides on this single-gear bike round Brands Hatch, on the cinder path which was used for public access on the outside of the grass circuit. This was at a time when Father was visiting Brands Hatch quite frequently, representing the riders in their dispute with the circuit owners and the ACU over the condition of the track.

Between my first rides on the Blackburne I managed to give it some brakes in the form of an old wheel that I had found in Father's shop for the front, and a friction block running in a V-section rim fastened to the spokes for the rear. That made it a real motor cycle!

We had also moved to a house in Addington, Surrey, where the garden shed was turned over to me for my hobby shop. Projects like finding various silent-block-type engine mounts, again from my father's shop, and turning them into various forms of suspension for my push-bike, plus the building of an aluminium-fuselage model aircraft, were fitted in around the bike work.

The push-bike and the Blackburne were used on the waste land alongside the house. The aircraft project died a rather sudden death when, having exchanged my cricket gear for a little Frog aero engine, I actually got it off the ground only to have it crash straight into a telegraph post and disintegrate.

I recall getting excited when I heard that Father was going to get a supercharged BMW into the Sunderland Road, Forest Hill, shop, perhaps fired by my enthusiasm for Georg Meier. In the event, I was quite disappointed when I discovered it to be a pushrod version of a type developed shortly before the war by a number of privateers. It wasn't really the real thing in my mind, but the black paint, white lining and distinctive BMW badge nevertheless made it something quite special in my eyes.

The 1948 season was to bring quite a few changes into my life. By this stage I had ridden the Wallis-Blackburne single-speed, a Corgi that my mother used for a very short while – I think we all decided it was dangerous – a BSA Bantam which my mother transferred to for general shopping and, briefly, an ex-Birmingham Speedway JAP.

This last-mentioned bike had arrived after one of the more serious disagreements I had with Father. We got involved in the Vincent, which I loved, but I also had a very warm affection for the Norton, and when he decided that he was going to concentrate only on the Vincent and sell the Norton, because of the money situation, I got terribly upset.

The deal he eventually did was for two speedway bikes, and the Norton went. Just to make certain they were all right, the speedway bikes were taken over to the waste land, started up and Dad said, 'Here you are; have a try.'

There was a straight path which went over a rise, down into a dip and up the other side, and on either side the farmer had planted his corn and barley. Well, I climbed on, let in the clutch and the bike took control. I careered across the field and ended up in a heap. I had certainly savoured the JAP's instant power!

I was also to take part in a competition for the first time. The Vincent was entered for the Trent Park speed trials at Cockfosters in north London. There was only a slight curve in the circuit, as it was basically just a straight line, but what it really required was a little ballast.

Dad hadn't asked one of his regular passengers along because they would have had to take time off work. So when we got there it was a case of 'John. In you go!' He won the event, but was disqualified. I was under age. I suppose, since I was only 14, we were pushing our luck just a little!

The Vincent was having more and more time spent on it, and I recall that one of the places where it was given the odd run was the Warlingham Heights, close to where I was born at Tatsfield, and where the police used to do their speedometer checking. Dad would take the bike up there for a few runs up and down, and I recall, just as I was approaching my 15th birthday, being handed the machine very early one morning.

My father said, 'John, be careful, but have a ride!' That was a tremendous thrill. I am not sure how fast I went, but I probably didn't get too far away from my first 100 mph!

However, other things were happening. During the winter, what should come into the shop but a B14 Excelsior-JAP. I think its price tag was £25. Dad had a very special spot for this because, of course, it was the first type of machine he had ever ridden, so it was decided that it should come to yours truly. The Wallis-Blackburne went. My bicycle went and the Wolf, which was at last together, also went.

Finally my 15th birthday came and, with it, thoughts of entering an event. Well, perhaps I shouldn't really have done so, because I didn't have a licence and I suppose I was under age, but some of the grass track meetings were not too fussy.

I first entered the Excelsior for a grass track meeting at Eaton Bray, just outside Luton. Leathers? My father had a spare pair, but they were rather baggy on me as he was quite a large man at that time. But I climbed into them and secured them round my waist with a body belt. Since he was around 13 stone and I could barely tip the scales at ten, I certainly must have looked rather odd on that particular occasion.

This was not a mountain grass track, but a circuit more like those of today, flat and relatively smooth. But it was turned into a mud bath by heavy showers just prior to the start. I must have set a record that day, possibly the only competitor to have slid off on every corner. Mind you, before that I'd been fairly pleased with myself because I think I'd been lying third. But this was a bit of a setback.

I went home, thought all about it, and Dad, while encouraging, said he frankly felt it was too much. He knew from his experience before the war that the bike was a bit of a handful at the best of times, so he felt that I'd better move to something more my size. I was already racing under age but, as a fairly slight youngster, the power of the B14 with the JAP engine was a little too much. I didn't really have sufficient muscle to handle it.

Yes, I have fond memories of that old B14. Granted, it threw me off on almost every occasion I rode it, but it is still a machine that I would like to own today.

I had left school at 15. The plan was that I would work along with Father for a while until I had decided on some future form of education. There was talk of my joining Vincents as an apprentice, but initially I was to find my feet and, I suppose, get some idea of what I wanted to do.

After one or two more rides with the B14, the question came about of what should be the next move. I have already mentioned that, just up the road from our shop in Sunderland Road, was Harold Daniell's base and one day when I was visiting him there on a parts collection what did I see but a Triumph Tiger 70.

I had seen a number of these machines in modified form at the grass tracks and also the odd one in road-race trim, and I had been quite impressed. Perhaps it wasn't quite a coincidence that I had been sent up to collect those parts, for it seems that Dad had also previously seen the machine and actually discussed with Harold the question of its price.

This was all part of giving me my head, I suppose, and letting me decide. I got quite excited and mentioned it to my father on my return. I had had a glance at the label, which said £32. Well, that was a lot of money, certainly beyond my reach and not very easy for Father to find. In the end, however, a deal was struck and the machine actually changed hands for £12, with Dad passing over a few spare parts. Cash was very important. Apart from keeping the family, there was the question of keeping the business running and, of course, our little race programme.

Whereas, during the time he had the Norton, Father had been able to eke out the racing expenses by being pretty sure of coming home with a few shillings in winnings to pay for the next lot of methanol, or the spare parts, with the Vincent he had encountered a number of problems and suffered some retirements. Yes, he got some help from the Vincent factory, but it was placing a strain on the finances and now here was John Junior coming along – but there was lots of encouragement and certainly no hint of resentment.

It was made quite clear that I had to work off the cost of the Triumph. At the time, although I liked the riding, or thought I did, my main interest was just in tinkering around with bikes and spanners. The fact that one rode them was just the product of testing them; one had the satisfaction of preparing them correctly, or suffered the disappointment of having got it wrong.

Although I had met all these famous people and had seen Father riding, I didn't really have any ideas of starting off on a crusade for championships or anything like that. It was purely this relationship with the machinery, and I suppose the racing scene, which attracted me. The test was not really so much of how good you were, but of how well you could actually put your bike together and then compete against the other lads who had done just the same.

In some ways I find it quite sad in these days when the monetary rewards from sport are so very, very high. I don't begrudge the participants their rewards – after all, if the money is there, why shouldn't they have it? – and this is particularly so in motor sport where there is still a risk factor considerably greater than in the majority of other sports.

What I do find disappointing is that people forget that what they are doing is something which, when they started out, they were doing purely for pleasure and enjoyment. It is a pity that the commercial side sometimes clouds what the sport should be all about.

If my father hadn't enjoyed a degree of success – and this was no doubt an added motivation – he wouldn't necessarily have been able to get to the next meeting, and this certainly applied to me in the early stages of my career, particularly once I had started to get into the slightly more expensive business of racing the Vincent in later years.

I obviously put my whole heart into everything I did – except perhaps my original schooling – but it wasn't until considerably later that I set myself the ambition of becoming the best on bikes and, later, the best in car racing.

Before I left school, Father was insistent that I should take more interest in my school work, so I sat for a scholarship at Stanley Technical College in Norwood, but failed. I am rather sorry that I didn't put in more effort when I look back on it, but I was totally absorbed in mechanical matters, and all my father's projects, so that test rather took second place.

Just left to myself I could get on, make good progress and be quite confident. But place a set of questions in front of me amidst a group of other people, and I could be terribly nervous. I suppose, in a way, this tended to make me even more of a loner, certainly putting a stamp on how I would develop in later life.

There was certainly nothing fancy or glamorous about the Surtees racing *équipe* at this time. Mother was, in effect, chief mechanic and caterer, with the three children tagging on, plus obviously Dad and his passenger. In addition to Frank Lilley, others who rode in the chair were Jack Noble and Les Seals, who had been passenger for Arthur Horton (as I have already mentioned) who competed in the Swiss Grand Prix in the late Thirties, setting a pattern which I'm sure Dad and Eric Oliver would have followed if war hadn't broken out.

In later years, other passengers included Charlie Rous, who became a well-known sprint competitor and journalist, and, on one occasion, Denis Jenkinson, who had jumped in the sidecar when Dad took the Vincent down to the Shelsley Walsh hillclimb.

On getting the Triumph 70 back to Palace Green, Addington, Dad was understandably insistent that everything should be totally stripped. Obviously all the lighting and standard mudguards would come off and I would build it up as a racer. I built up the bike with Dad keeping an eye on things over my shoulder, although on the whole he would trust me, saying, 'You just get along and do it yourself.'

The first event I competed in with it was a scramble at Pirbright. It was the only scramble I ever did. At virtually the first bump after the start, I didn't get it quite right. I went straight into a rut, the front forks broke and pitched me over the handlebars. It was a case of '*anno domini*' as far as the forks were concerned, and lack of it on the part of yours truly. I should have got the front wheel well up and avoided that rut in the first place.

Right, I thought, it's grass track racing from now on. However, of more immediate importance was the effect this accident had on my finances. Not only was I paying back to my father the purchase price, but part of our deal together was that I should be responsible for the maintenance and any repairs.

Thankfully, I searched around and a friend of Father's came up with a pair of ex-War Department Teledraulic Matchless forks, and a front hub. I duly fitted these and continued my racing programme. I obtained from Father a dual seat which had come off an Excelsior Manxman, I think, and also a small TT carburettor which I duly fitted to the cylinder head after much painstaking work with an electric drill and a grindstone on the inlet port of the cylinder head. A BTH magneto, again one of the Norton spare parts, was fitted.

I was very proud of it. I competed at grass track events from High Wycombe to Folkestone, not gaining a great deal of success but trying all the time to develop and improve the little bike. I also found myself on the receiving end of a rather distasteful official protest at the Folkestone meeting after finishing second in the novices' race for first-year riders, even though my only other competitive outing up to that point had been at the Trent Park speed trials where I had not really been officially competing.

I think the main thing my rival was protesting was that my name was Surtees, and that my father was a respected member of the motor cycling fraternity. Somebody felt there was a need to go along and have a dig. It is one of those things which, of course, normally springs from jealousy or a grudge. I always find it a shame when such actions enter into sporting activities. It was a great shock to a youngster like me and, for a moment, I found it very disillusioning.

Lots of things would happen in 1950. Brands Hatch would get its first tarmac surface. The MV Agusta, the Remor-designed four-cylinder machine, would appear. Norton would come out with the 'Featherbed', there was the tragedy of David Whitworth being killed and, of course, the very sad accident which ended the career of Artie Bell and no doubt made a great change to the face of the result sheets of that period.

It was a year in which, unbeknown to me, Bob Geeson, a technical boffin with the Metal Box Company, would finish off his little home-made REG and take it off to the Lightweight TT, actually completing the seven-lap event to finish 12th.

It was also the year when I was to become an ex-grass track racer. While I was working in the little shop at Forest Hill, we had a visit from Bill Oliver, who was the uncle of another young rider called Michael O'Rourke; he called at Dad's shop and excitedly reported they were on their way to try the new Brands Hatch tarmac circuit which had recently been completed.

Would I like to come? I looked at Dad, Dad looked at me, and within a few minutes the Triumph Tiger 70 was loaded into his van – knobbly tyres and all – and we were on the road on our way down to Brands.

I went out and did about half a dozen laps. Instantly, I thought, 'This is for me'. John Surtees, road racer, was born.

Once the decision had been made, we had to take stock of what needed to be done to the Tiger 70 to make it as competitive as possible as a road racer. I had already carried out a lightening programme as far as possible, cutting out various bits and pieces with a hacksaw and drilling holes here and there without compromising the basic stiffness of the frame. I fitted a little sprint tank which I unearthed in my father's workshop, and added an Ariel handlebar bend which was fitted with the grips facing downwards.

Some of the work on the engine was obviously outside our scope, so, at Dad's suggestion, we asked Jim Hiscock, a Croydon engineer who had gained considerable success racing 250 Velocettes, to bore out the inlet port and fit a bigger valve. I also changed the saddle, removed the chain case and set the footrests slightly further back into a position similar to that used on the Grand Prix Triumphs.

Lastly, showing how impressionable one can be at that age, I remembered that occasion at the Brands Hatch grass track when the machines with suspension had demonstrated such superiority. It caused me to think about the benefits that might be offered by a sprung hub on my Triumph.

It just so happened that my father had in stock at the time a Tiger 100 equipped with a sprung hub. I thought this was for me. I wondered whether I could do a swap. I broached the subject tentatively with Father and, rather foolishly, as of course I now know, I put this very heavy sprung hub on the back of my little Triumph.

Naturally, the hub wouldn't be working at all with the light weight of the Triumph, but at least I suppose it was good for the ego! My father's reaction was surprisingly mild for one who could be so trenchant, so I subsequently repeated the switch when an even newer Triumph Tiger 100, with an improved version of that sprung hub, eventually came into the shop!

My first race with the heavily revamped Tiger 70 was to be the opening event on the newly surfaced Brands Hatch track, running in an anti-clockwise direction. Father was to ride a Norton sidecar passengered by Charlie Rous, who had taken over from Jack Varlow, Les Seals and his original passenger, Frank Lilley.

As for me, at barely 16 years old, I was on the startline for my first race, the 250 heat. It went surprisingly well. I came third, so I got very excited for the final. By then it had turned into a very damp and dismal day. I found myself coming into the last lap on the heels of Harry Pearce, who would later go on to be head of the McLaren machine shop in the early days of the F1 racing team, on his beautifully prepared Tiger 70.

I thought, 'I can go by him,' and I think I did get alongside. The only problem was that I wasn't with my bike. I had overstepped my abilities and we had parted company. Harry went on to win the race and I had learned another lesson. I suppose if you are going to fall off, it should be early in your career. I certainly practised that theory, as my previous exploits on the grass tracks had shown!

This early promise wasn't destined to continue. Whether it was my standard of preparation, or my inexperience as a rider, with consequent over-stressing, I don't know. I think what I was really encountering was the sort of problems one meets when taking a standard road machine and then thinking about trying to turn it into a racer. I didn't finish many races. I fell off in some, but Dad was normally fairly philosophical about it. He worried in case I hurt myself, of course, but generally it was a case of 'it's up to you, lad.'

To be honest, the Triumph was not the answer and I went through quite a disheartening patch after that Brands Hatch race. I don't think I finished any of my events. I think I either fell off or suffered some sort of mechanical problem. But, as Dad said, it was better to find out the hard way: 'It's up to you, John.'

The big end had been a particular problem, so we consulted with Jim Hiscock over what we could do. At one point we got the money together to get Jim to convert the big end bearing to needle rollers and to fit a larger crankpin.

Again, perhaps rather foolishly, I was absolutely enchanted by the looks of the square aluminium cylinder head and barrel which were fitted to certain special Triumphs. Some of these were made by a company called Conway and Lilley. So I decided to fit the aluminium head and barrel, although we might well have been better off leaving well alone and sticking with the original, as with the iron head we could have used a bigger inlet valve.

This package was readied for a race at Silverstone and, in the initial stages, I felt in high spirits. At last the Triumph seemed to be performing really well. There I was, tucked down, trying to reduce the frontal area round Abbey Curve, and the next moment I was skating down the road.

The big end didn't go, but the con rod did. It let go in a big way. Afterwards, I discovered the majority of those who modified Tiger 70s were, in fact, using Excelsior Manxman con rods. Oh well, it was another lesson learned.

By a fortunate coincidence, my father had taken in a very purposeful, but rather untidy, swinging-arm Triumph fitted with a JAP engine. My eyes lit up at the sight of that engine! Perhaps this was the way out.

Father quickly saw what I had in mind. Even more fortunately, on various visits to the Vincent factory, I had met up with one or two of the lads who were working there, and one of them showed an interest in the Triumph.

So I suggested a deal: a swinging-arm Triumph, complete but a bit tatty, together with a Tiger 70 engine, with aluminium cylinder head and barrel – but in a rather sad state with a rod jammed through the crankcase. A deal was done, so I busied myself fitting the newly acquired JAP engine into my bike.

At about this time, my father had been wandering through the road test department at Vincents when he spotted a partially dismantled Grey Flash – but not painted grey – which had been used for road test and development work in the past, just lying in the corner.

It was painted black, but was to full Grey Flash specification, and fitted with an Albion gearbox, with all the appropriate drilling that one expected on such a model. This machine had been used for test purposes and dealer evaluation, and in fact had just returned from Kings of Oxford where Stan Hailwood, who owned that company, had been trying it out.

Was it for sale? Yes! Father explained that it was for his lad, who was due to join the Vincent company anyway on reaching the age of 17 at the end of the year. Dad, after careful consideration, agreed that we could purchase the dismantled experimental 'Grey Flash' for a nominal price. Of the £2 10s I would earn as a Vincent apprentice, a pound would go towards the cost of the bike. It came back to our base in Forest Hill as a bunch of bits and we built it up into a racer with a view to getting in one or two events before the close of the season.

I remember quite vividly Dad bringing home the boxes, and us going through them to check all the parts. I was quite used to working on Vincents because that is what Father dealt in. Perhaps to his own financial detriment, he turned down the chance of handling the NSU Quickly, or selling Lambretta scooters, because he didn't consider them to be serious motor cycles.

He was at that time probably the largest seller of Vincents and, certainly, the most enthusiastic. His racing had helped sort out the machines, particularly the early bugs connected with the gearbox. Perhaps not enough, as things turned out, for Philip Vincent's tragic accident, which we will refer to later, and which had such dire consequences for the company in the long term, was caused by a gearbox seizure.

The Vincent 'Grey Flash' got its name from the fact that all the bikes were painted a distinctive grey. I had been determined to approach the preparation of the Grey Flash – or the Black Flash, as I should refer to it prior to its respray – in a more scientific way. I had particularly admired the way in which George Brown rode the small-capacity Vincents, and the manner in which he and his brother Cliff had prepared them, and I was now actually to come into competition with him.

George had been stopped from using his speedway specials and was having to race a Grey Flash. In turn, another Grey Flash in the hands of John Hodgkin was also partly supported by the works. The Vincent factory had entered some works machines in the 1950 TT races, but it had been a bit of a hurried affair. Having hurriedly replaced the original troublesome Burman gearboxes with later Albion boxes, they only managed to get Ken

Bills home in 12th place.

At this time I also went about scrounging every piece of information I could about these works bikes, and what was happening generally on development. I heard about the big-port engines which had been prepared for the TT, but mine was a standard-specification bike which was going to be produced for the public.

It was built up with a standard TT10 inch and five-thirty-seconds carburettor. The bike was put together and obviously it was with great optimism that I set off to Brands Hatch for the first race – only for the big end promptly to seize up. Dad had a word with Mr Vincent and Phil Irving about it and they suggested that I test one of their type 4 plain aluminium big ends. This was a plain sleeve of RR77-type material which they counter-sunk into the flywheels, on which the con rod ran directly, held together with a pin through the centre.

I remember watching them put the crankpin in the fridge and the flywheel in the oven at Vincents where we managed to assemble the whole thing successfully, despite people casting doubt as to whether it would all hold together. Well, this was at the end of the 1950 season, and when I unfortunately had to sell the bike at the end of 1952 in order to pay for my first Norton it had run two full seasons without a spot of bother.

My first time out with the new big end fitted was at Aberdare Park in South Wales and I won my first race. This was a wonderful place to race because of the enormous enthusiasm which was displayed. I particularly recall the organisers David and Marion Pryce, and how we were 'billeted' at one of their friends' house; the prizegiving was accompanied by an energetic sing-song of the type one obviously associates with the Welsh!

I had by this time made a number of other changes, fitting an RN carburettor. Again, this came out of Dad's stock, having come off a Norton. This had meant increasing the inlet ports as it was a slightly larger diameter, one and three-sixteenths. The compression ratio had been raised to 9:1 and I had spent time drilling a few more holes and replacing a few nuts and bolts with RR77 items which had been lying around from parts made for the TT Vincents.

Another aspect I spent a lot of time on was the dampers. The original Vincent dampers were susceptible to losing their oil at frequent intervals, something we had experienced quite often at our dealership. As a result, we came up with a different type of sealing for the shaft and this modification was also carried out on my bike.

We replaced the tank with one from Father's Black Lightning which was in fact a standard tank with the bottom cut off halfway up. This gave more room for the carburettor and held less fuel, which was fine for the relatively short races in which I was to compete.

I had all the winter months to think about preparing the machine. It was all taken apart, the paint stripped off to the bare metal, but when we took the components along to the shop which did Dad's stove enamelling they could not match the grey-green paintwork in which the Vincent Grey Flashes were now being turned out. So the Silver Flash was born, as they had some Ford silver paint available.

We added an extra piece to the rear of the fuel tank which flattened off the top. This made it a little more comfortable as I also cut out some knee holes, so that I could tuck myself in a little tighter.

I started my apprenticeship at Vincents earning about £2 10s (£2.50) per week, out of which I had to find some money for my lodgings. These were with a nice couple by the name of Mr and Mrs Wittering. It was a fairly flexible arrangement. If I could get there in time for dinner, then I could have dinner. If not, my standard menu was at a little café opposite the factory. And the menu? It was Welsh rarebit. It was good and it was cheap. Anyway every weekend my mother, who always provided an excellent table, could feed me up for the coming week, and Mrs Wittering did not let me go hungry – the few shillings I paid them couldn't have helped that much, but perhaps they liked the occasional company.

I travelled back the fifty miles or so to home as often as possible, because I kept my bike back in Palace Green, Addington, where we were living, and working on it was a very time-consuming exercise. I normally used to borrow a test machine from Vincents, ride home on it, or perhaps borrow a bike out of Dad's shop.

It was possible to complete this journey in about 45 minutes, something that just would not be feasible today. Father had some customers in London, so there were occasions when I would ride down from Stevenage, drop in and perhaps carry out a service or an inspection of a machine for them, before continuing on home.

I was changing my ideas slightly as far as my racing was concerned. At last I had a machine which was responding to me and which was sending a message back. Apart from the pure challenge of riding, I was really getting pleasure out of extending the machine to the full and reckoning that I could do better than my rivals. It was a great challenge and I was enjoying it.

This was my world, into which I was totally absorbed. It would be rather romantic, in retrospect, to say I had much interest in what was going on in the outside world, that I studied the results of every motor cycle Grand Prix and major international race, because, to be honest, I don't think I did. I was completely involved with the family, my own racing and my apprenticeship with Vincents.

Of my relationship with Vincents, I must say Philip Vincent was enormously understanding and indulgent of my own racing activities. I was allowed to turn up at nine o'clock rather than eight o'clock in the morning, everybody knowing full well that every spare moment of my time was spent either racing or preparing my bike, and there's no doubt that I have a great deal to thank them for. Their heart was in the right place.

As this book is being prepared, 35 years have passed since Vincent ceased the manufacture of motor cycles and I think it is important to put the company's position in the industry into perspective for those readers and enthusiasts who are too young to know very much about it.

The story of Vincent fits in with the story of the British motor cycle industry in general and, to a certain extent, the European industry. You had a situation where a lot of people came together, working very hard, with a lot of good ideas, producing what were basically quite advanced motor cycles for their time.

The thinking behind their operation was perhaps rather too small-scale in a country where everything is controlled by banks, whose only interests are short-term. In fact, to be quite frank about it, some of my thoughts about the state of this country as we go into the 1990s reflect the sort of problems which Vincent found themselves up against.

However much people may talk about the country's hidden earnings from banking and the City, and the amount they contribute to our overall assets, I would also raise the question of how much they contribute to the downfall of certain enterprises. I think it is quite immoral the way the financial institutions require to see short-term profits, especially in the engineering sector – the sort of situation where a company may have produced 20 per cent profit last year, but if it doesn't produce 30 per cent next year its shares get marked down, making it vulnerable to a predator.

However, to return to Vincent . . . The situation there revolved largely round Philip Vincent himself and, when he had an accident testing one of his own machines, the company lost its leader and inspiration. He was left in a badly concussed condition for a long time and the side-effects of the accident were quite damaging and disorientating. To my mind he never regained his previous clarity of thought as far as decision-making was concerned.

In turn, the banks took the opportunity to put in a receiver – a Mr Baillie – who was a very understanding man who, in fairness, attempted to do a very genuine job in making the best of a difficult situation. But the company then tried to cut corners. They didn't do this by employing a few better-quality people and cutting away at the dead wood which had become completely useless now that there was nobody strong and capable to direct their efforts.

Vincent cut back on quality, changing to cheaper materials, allowing bigger manufacturing tolerances to slip through the net. But commercial reality caught up with them. If you were charging between £300 and £400 for a motor cycle in the early 1950s, you really could not expect to keep selling them if the big ends would go in the first 500 miles, or the cams would wear out. Suddenly what was basically a superb design was being compromised by cheap materials and sloppy assembly.

Slowly they got to the point where no serious engineers remained. Phil Irving, Jack Williams, Matt Wright, Denis Minet, George Buck and, of course, the Brown brothers had all left. Only a very stressed and unwell PCV remained. This is what set the seal on the end for Vincents, sad to relate. It was a great tragedy, for the basic concept of the Vincent – with a fully stressed engine/gearbox unit and a bolted-on spine frame with fully cantilevered suspension – was advanced for its period. With modern equipment its manufacture could have been simplified and the machine produced for a more competitive price. For example, it was a far better bike than the Hesketh of the late 1970s, which gives you an indication of what a superb bike the Vincent was in 1950.

Gradually I progressed through my Vincent apprenticeship, starting in the machine shop before eventually moving through to the experimental department, a section run by a Major Honeychurch, a man well versed in dealing with the various ministries and the Civil Service, with whom Vincent did a lot of business. These connections were particularly important as one of the current projects was the Picador engine, being produced for target planes for the forces, in conjunction with a firm called ML Aviation based at White Waltham.

Aside from having fuel injection and a bevel-drive to accommodate the propellor, this engine was virtually the same as the 1000 cc V-twin motor cycle engine. On occasion I would have to go down to White Waltham to try and sort out various problems with the engines, usually connected with their ancillary equipment.

These engines were supposed to have around 65 bhp, which I recall was the minimum acceptable for delivery to the ministry and I remember how, at times, there would be Honeychurch with one foot on the scales trying to coax up the horsepower readings to an acceptable level.

Unfortunately Major Honeychurch was totally lacking in technical knowledge, a fact which rather rankled with the head tester, Cliff Brown, who, with his brother George, had been among the first people to race Vincents in the post-war period.

The Grey Flash was responding all the time to the detailed work we were carrying out in order to try and find a little more performance, as, in turn, I gained experience and confidence. I was particularly competitive on the tighter tracks, especially Brands Hatch, although it was a bit breathless on the faster circuits. But it was on Sunday, 3 June 1951 that I achieved a particularly sweet moment of success when I returned to Brands Hatch and got my own back on Harry Pearce, beating his Triumph-JAP twice with my Vincent. It was one of those days when I just thought the world of motor cycle racing was my idea of paradise, but, thankfully again, my father saw to it that I did not lose my sense of perspective.

At a later meeting, I fell off coming round Clearways and, as I sat dazed by the bank, I saw all 14 stone of my father, leathers flapping in the breeze, running towards me. When he saw I was all right, he lifted me up and gave me a quick clip round the ear. I must say that I am always reminded of that episode by some of the old faces who are still around whenever I go down to Brands Hatch to this day.

After I started winning with my 'Grey Flash' the factory offered me the use of one of their TT machines which had been over to the Isle of Man in 1950, encountered some mechanical trouble and was now just lying around in the factory. They offered to loan this to me as a spare bike, something I gratefully accepted without a second's hesitation.

That first full season with the Vincent was, of course, Festival of Britain Year and the Auto Cycle Union was anxious to make it an appropriately outstanding year for the sport. The big event of the year was intended to be the Festival race meeting at Thruxton on August Bank Holiday Monday, a six-race programme which included a sidecar event – in which I crewed for my father – in addition to a 1000 cc event and an invitation race, both of which I contested with the second Grey Flash, the factory-loaned bike.

Although only a handful of Continental riders appeared, there was quite a gathering of top-flight works British riders on hand, including Bill Lomas, Cecil Sandford, Bill Doran and Geoff Duke. The weather was dank, rainy and depressing, as befits the image of a traditional English Bank Holiday, but a huge and enthusiastic crowd had turned out to watch the action.

I finished second in the 12-lap invitation race behind Geoff Duke and then had the heartening experience of leading him for the first seven laps of the 15-lap 1000 cc Festival race, an achievement which gained me a reputation as 'the rider who made Geoff Duke hurry', even though I eventually had to settle for second place again by the finish. It was very satisfying, because I was ahead of all the other Nortons, the AJSs and the Moto Guzzis.

On reflection, I would have liked to have had the opportunity to race on the international scene at the same time as Duke did, with the Featherbed Norton in 1951. It was a very exciting time in motor cycle racing history with a lot of opportunities. There were many pre-war riders just finishing their careers and Geoff Duke, I suppose, was among the first of the post-war new blood. Our careers overlapped from that Thruxton meeting in 1951 through until 1960, although his peak years were probably 1953-54, so to some extent I took over the mantle from him.

I continued with the Vincent through the 1952 season, winning on the majority of circuits I went to, particularly Brands Hatch, but it was becoming increasingly clear, with Featherbed Nortons now becoming widely available to private customers, that something more competitive was required if I was to have a realistic chance of taking another step up the ladder and progressing my career. What was really required was a Manx Norton, although there was no way my budget could run to that at the end of 1951. Consequently, it was a case of consistently trying to improve the Vincent's performance by tiny increments and make it last through another season of British national racing.

Towards the end of 1951 I was offered a ride on a 350 cc 'Garden gate' Norton, down at Boreham, which I obviously jumped at without a second's hesitation. However, while the Vincent had quite considerable ground clearance with its 21-inch front and 20-inch rear wheels, I failed to appreciate that you could not necessarily lay every machine right over onto the walls of its tyres when cornering hard.

The Norton only had 19-inch wheels and my habit of really putting it onto its footrests resulted in the frame promptly grounding on the road and the bike chucking me off on the slowish corner just before the old pits. I suppose it was a lesson that every machine needs to be analysed carefully in advance and one's riding style adjusted accordingly.

We then had a word with Gilbert Smith, Norton's Managing Director, to see if there was any chance of getting hold of a Manx Norton Featherbed – which, of course, featured a McCandless-developed frame and was given its nickname after Harold Daniell tested one of the early prototypes at Silverstone and made the observation that it 'felt like riding a feather bed'.

Gilbert Smith, however, made it clear that a Manx Norton could only be supplied if I entered a World Championship race. Of course, now I was in a situation where I wanted to prepare for my first visit to the Isle of Man TT races, and the logical event to serve this purpose would have been the Manx Grand Prix, an amateur event held over the TT course itself and for which I had been offered rides on Nortons prepared by the highly respected Francis Beart, who had made his name as a motor cycle racer at Brooklands prior to the war.

Unfortunately I was no longer qualified as an amateur within the terms of this particular event. Earlier that summer, as a Vincent employee, I had been among a group of more than a dozen riders who had gone to the Montlhéry track near Paris to take part in some record runs – everything from 500 km to 12 and 24 hours. I had received confirmation, or so I thought, prior to this event that it would not debar me from competing in the Manx Grand Prix, but – much to my frustration – this subsequently proved not to be the case.

The Montlhéry trip with Vincents had really been quite an experience. There were some Black Shadows, modified for the purpose of endurance running, but there was also a Black Lightning, on which the French rider Lefevre was to attempt shorter distance records. The Black Shadows ran very well, but unfortunately were fitted with the crowded needle roller big ends which were not quite good enough for the constant speeds we could maintain at the bumpy Montlhéry speed bowl and the very high temperatures we would experience.

The record attempt with a Black Lightning involved removing the mudguards and there was no tail to the seat. I remember seeing Lefevre going round the banking and a crack suddenly ringing out. The machine slowed to a halt. A whole section of tyre had peeled off its tread and slapped poor Lefevre straight on the backside. He certainly wasn't going to feel like sitting on a bike again for a while!

I was asked to do some further test runs. Although I was the young boy of the team, I was racing very successfully at the time, and I was also somewhat lighter than Lefevre. But after a few tests the Avon engineers decided that the combination of banking and temperatures was just too much. However, we did come away with some records with the Black Shadows and, as a consequence, I was unable to enter the Manx Grand Prix.

Therefore I had no option but to enter the Ulster Grand Prix on the Clady circuit on my new Manx Norton which, as you can imagine from the foregoing, represented a simply enormous financial commitment. I had to sell my own personal Grey Flash. It was sad to see it go, but the money raised from its sale had to be used as the hire purchase deposit on the Manx Norton.

The new bike at that time cost about £280 – an enormous amount of money when you compare it with what we had been paying for my motor cycles up to that stage of my career. We got about £150 for the Grey Flash, a good price, but, frankly, if I didn't go out and have some success – picking up five pounds here, five pounds there for a win – I just wasn't going to be able to go to the following weekend's race, wherever it might have been. It was that tight and the Manx Norton really had to be made to work for its living!

The Clady circuit was notorious for its seven-mile straight. In fact, it was the last year that the Ulster GP was run on this track. As things turned out I finished sixth, and got a World Championship point. It was a bit of a fluke, for a number of the leading riders, including Les Graham, broke down. The race was won by Cromie McCandless on a Gilera and only five competitors managed the full 15-lap distance. I was lapped by Cromie at the hairpin, a short distance from the finish, and saved the effort of another long lap!

My experience of that seven-mile straight was quite an eye-opener. On my first practice lap I snuggled down tight on the tank and was motoring along as fast as I knew how. Up to that point I suppose the biggest jump I had experienced was lifting my front wheel coming up the Mountain at Cadwell Park. But what I was about to encounter was something in a totally different league . . .

I was building up to about 110 mph – and then I hit that first bump. I was out of the seat, my feet came off the footrests and I was hanging on to the handlebars for dear life. I got quite a wobble on coming down, heartbeat pounding. But, on the following laps, after some experimentation, I gradually got the hang of the technique of getting the front wheel to jump slightly higher than the rear, so that you landed with the rear wheel touching the ground fractionally before the front, and learned to rise up on the footrest slightly to balance the machine.

Towards the end of the race I well remember Les Graham's MV coming past on one side, Cromie McCandless on the Gilera on the other – it seemed as though they were six feet higher in the air than me! In fact it was probably only a foot, but they were travelling some 20 mph or so faster than my Norton. It was quite a telling experience, believe me, and the image of being overtaken by those two front-line competitors made a big impact that still lives in my memory.

I spent the rest of the season riding my new Norton in national-level meetings throughout England. This run of successes continued into 1953, by the end of which I had won thirty races out of the sixty I had entered.

From the start of the second year with the Norton everything went well and, since we were managing to pay off the loan for the first bike quite successfully, we also acquired a second-hand 350 cc Featherbed. This was fitted with a long-stroke engine which had previously been used by Ray Amm and Syd Lawton before their elevation to the works team. This would allow me to compete in more races throughout the season.

The decision was made to go to the TT in 1953 and, when I got there, I had a big compliment paid to me for somebody who had never seen the Island before. I was invited to ride one of the pukka Joe Craig works Nortons but, although I was to do a practice session on the works bike, I would not get to the startline.

In order to gain as much practice as possible on the circuit, I had also agreed some time earlier to ride an EMC for Joe Ehrlich in the 125 cc event, and the Norton offer had come after this. I still reasoned that the more riding experience I could get on this 37-mile track the better, because I really needed to make up for time lost in not having taken part in the Manx Grand Prix.

Joe Craig did not want me to ride the EMC, but I felt I had a moral obligation, having given my word to Ehrlich. My father and I asked Joe whether he would release me, but he replied that it would present too many problems for him, so I had to go ahead.

Unfortunately, as I went over Ballaugh Bridge on the first lap of practice, the EMC's forks broke, I veered off into the kerb and went skating down the road, hitting a kerb and breaking my scaphoid, a little bone deep down in the wrist. So that was the end of my first visit to the Isle of Man, and my chance to ride a works Norton.

The episode upset Joe Craig terribly. There were originally five works Norton entries for Ray Amm, Ken Kavanagh, Rex McCandless, Syd Lawton and myself. Lawton suffered a practice crash which would end his racing career, so it was perhaps hardly surprising that Joe thought I had been extremely foolish in compromising my chances of an outing with the works Norton team by riding the EMC.

He told me himself that, on merit, he would have liked to give me a ride in 1954, but, in a way, felt that I had to be taught a lesson. He didn't really forgive me until 1955.

I remember going home on the ferry from the Isle of Man in a rather dejected mood, listening to the BBC radio reports from the races to keep in touch with what was happening. At that time those broadcasts were extremely detailed and wide-ranging, but I can vividly recall a mounting feeling of unease when there was absolutely no mention of how Les Graham had got on riding the MV Agusta in the 500 cc event. It turned out that my concern was not misplaced. We later learned that Les had crashed fatally on the second lap of the race.

That scaphoid injury kept me out of the reckoning for six weeks, but I returned to racing in July with a win at the Ibsley airfield circuit in Hampshire and was second to Derek Farrant's G45 Matchless at Blandford at the August Bank Holiday meeting.

In the meantime, AJS asked me to ride for them – an invitation which would be repeated for the following year's Ulster Grand Prix – but Joe Craig fired a well-aimed warning shot across my bows. He got in touch and said, in effect, 'If you want to ride one of our works bikes, you don't ride an AJS.' This was sad for me, because I had always wanted to try a Porcupine AJS. I also had to turn down an offer to ride one at Scarborough earlier in 1954, but Norton did loan me two '53 works bikes to contest the final races of the year, at Aintree, Scarborough and Cadwell Park, as an incentive to stay loyal to their products and not switch to AJS.

Joe Craig, of course, was one of the pivotal personalities on the English motor cycle racing scene at that time. He could be difficult to get through to, though – in fact, impossible, some people said. He'd been something of a wheeler dealer in his early days, but a man who had amassed an enormous amount of knowledge through his wide experience. He had been involved in the design of the Porcupine AJS, but then returned to Norton.

I don't think he was technical in the sense that you would refer to Ing. Carcano of Moto Guzzi, or even Remor of Gilera, but while he may not have been responsible for anything radical in the way of new designs he had a well-earned reputation for the steady development of race-winning motor cycles.

Perhaps Joe was too conservative, perhaps he should have pushed to do a deal with Vandervell and produced the four-cylinder Norton which had been on offer or hastened the development of the horizontal machine. He could be pretty dogmatic.

For all that, though, I got on pretty well with Joe on a personal level and learned a great deal from him; not so much from what he said, but from his subtle reactions and the odd throwaway remarks he made. And I'll always remember the tears in his eyes at Silverstone at the end of 1955 when I managed to beat Geoff Duke's Gilera.

Joe retired from Norton at the end of 1955. His first wife had died some years before; he later remarried and went to live in Holland, the home country of his new bride. Very sadly, he was killed in a road accident near Landeck, in Austria, during March 1957.

He may not have been the greatest motor cycle engineer, but he was certainly a splendid character and a very important part of Norton racing history. The fact is he did win a lot of races for Norton, and you can never take that away from him.

Gilbert Smith was much out of the same mould. Although I would have to say that he was one of the people who helped preside over the death of the British motor cycle industry, he was absolutely as straight as a die in his business dealings with us. No question about it.

They were both great characters, but belonging to a past era, in my view. Norton could not face up to the commercial challenges which were destined to appear from both Europe and Japan in the 1950s and '60s. In the aftermath of the war, they failed to re-equip their factories so as to compete at the level which was going to become required from anybody in the motor cycle industry.

There was an overwhelming sense of conservatism and self-satisfaction which pervaded the British motor cycle industry at the time. I encountered another example of it when Joe Craig and I approached Edward Turner, the chief of Triumph, which was then the biggest manufacturer in England, about whether he would consider a fully fledged racing programme.

He was totally negative. He shrugged the whole project aside, saying it was no problem, Triumph could do three-, four-cylinder engines, or whatever, but there was no point in going racing. Triumph could sell all the bikes they made, and more.

People ask me whether the problems which heralded the demise of Norton and Vincent were similar, but I have to say that I honestly believe that Vincent were potentially more advanced than Norton from a technical standpoint. Vincents were more aware of the need to adapt to the future than Norton.

For 1954 I had two brand new, short-stroke Manx Nortons and sold my previous 500 to Alan Trow, who was starting to make something of a name for himself at Brands Hatch. This was the year in which I fully established myself as a potential winner in any circumstances. But in addition to riding these two bikes, I got an enormous amount of

satisfaction from my outings in the 250 cc class with Bob Geeson's self-built REG.

This was quite a remarkable story because Geeson literally manufactured this highly competitive little machine in his garden shed. Bob was a project engineer with the Metal Box Company and, together with a colleague, completely manufactured this twin-cylinder, twin-overhead-camshaft racing engine which put to shame much of the motor cycle industry.

The bike featured a pair of Matchless forks, Norton wheels and an Albion gearbox, but the engine was totally a design of their own. Any race in which I had a trouble-free run with the REG we won. It was a great project which reflected just how much engineering initiative existed in England at the time, underlining just how much hidden potential our motor cycle fraternity had for competing with the best Italy could produce.

We took the REG out for the first time at the Easter meetings at Brands Hatch and Crystal Palace. We won both, but it was particularly satisfying to finish well ahead of Maurice Cann's Moto Guzzi, widely regarded as the fastest 250 in the country, on Easter Monday at the Palace.

At that Crystal Palace meeting I also won the 350 and 1000 cc races on my Nortons, but there was still plenty to learn, as my first experience of racing in the Isle of Man TT taught me. In the Junior race I lost about three minutes when I stopped out on the circuit in an attempt to find out just why the engine kept cutting out. I tried changing the plug, as well as every other possible cure, until I discovered that a rubber clip securing the breather pipe from the fuel tank was causing the pipe to close when it became warm and flexible. Once that had been fixed, I continued to finish 11th.

A great deal of controversy surrounded the conditions in which the Senior TT was held, for heavy rain and swirling mist caused the start to be postponed to midday. The race was stopped after only four laps with Ray Amm's Norton winning by over a minute from Duke's Gilera and, bearing in mind just how treacherous the conditions were over the Snaefell Mountain, I counted myself reasonably satisfied to have finished my first Senior TT in 15th place. I didn't yet know the circuit in good conditions, and in mist and rain I was lost!

Back to the mainland, and I had a tremendous run of wins throughout July, with both the REG and my Nortons, at Cadwell Park, Crystal Palace again, Brands Hatch and Castle Combe. But since my 1951 races against Geoff Duke at Thruxton, I had not come up against the man then regarded as Britain's top rider, so the 1954 Hutchinson 100 meeting at Silverstone during August gave me another great chance to have a crack at him, albeit in conditions of torrential rain and mist.

I started the day by taking a close second place to Bob McIntyre's AJS in the first 350 heat, then in the final, although we were both briefly passed by Cecil Sandford's ART-Velocette, I managed to overtake again and go on to win.

The conditions were absolutely appalling by the time we went out for the 500 cc championship event, so much so that McIntyre and AJS rider Derek Farrant chose to withdraw. I managed to get ahead of Duke's Gilera and pull away, but the bottom bevel gear stripped and robbed me of a win I really ached for. I still have the broken bevel drive in a cabinet in my office to this very day!

The season drew to its close with another satisfying win on the 350 Norton, ahead of Bob McIntyre, at Scarborough and another crack at Duke in the 500 cc event at the same meeting. But, although we had a race-long battle, he stayed ahead to the finish.

People talk about me tending to carve my own furrow as something of a lone wolf in those early days, but, to be honest, while I instinctively tended to be a private person, there really wasn't very much time for anything else. I was still apprenticed to Vincents, earning about £4 a week by this stage. They were busy times, whistling back and forth to Stevenage, preparing my bikes and going round to the races at weekends. My mother did all the form filling connected with my race entries, which took a welcome amount of paperwork off my shoulders.

I never drove a car until I was 18. In fact, it wasn't until I was riding back to Vincents one day in a really dreadful storm that I stopped in Hatfield and saw this little gold Jowett Jupiter in a car showroom on my route. I thought, right, enough is enough, I must get a car. So, having won quite a reasonable amount of prize money which was just balancing the books, I put down a deposit and bought the Jupiter.

This would allow me to shift more bits and pieces backwards and forwards between home and Stevenage. It took a little longer, of course, than with the bikes. The Jupiter gave me super service, but in 1955 I changed it for a Porsche Super which Father managed to get at a favourable price because of his past connections with the AFN company. It was one of the ex-demonstration vehicles and was very much a motor cyclists' car – but very tail-happy!

Vincents then suggested that I might like to compete with an NSU Sportmax in 1955. I discussed the matter with Bob Geeson and, although he had plans for a second-generation REG to follow up the one I had been riding, the decision was made that I would switch to NSU.

So the 1955 season brought about a number of changes. While I would still ride my own machines in all the domestic events, I would also join the Joe Craig-managed Norton team for major races. By this time I believe that results had shown I could compete with anybody who was riding, subject, of course, to having a relatively competitive machine. The results through 1955 would prove that point.

Yet the Norton deal I was offered, along with Jack Brett and John Hartle, was based round Joe Craig-run Manx Norton development production bikes, rather than purpose-built racers, the idea being that what was learned from the race programme could be fed back into the production machines. Castrol paid us a £500 retainer, but that was the sum total of our financial support as so-called works riders.

We three riders had a very happy relationship and I got on particularly well with John Hartle, who hailed from Chapel-en-le-Frith, up in Derbyshire, and had worked as a coal-miner before trying his hand on motor cycles. He was a very stylish, as well as fast, rider.

John was also actually responsible for saving my life at the non-championship Swedish Grand Prix at Hedemora when we went for a swim in one of the nearby lakes. At least they did. I, as a non-swimmer, reckoned there couldn't be that much to it, so I just jumped in off the end of a jetty on the theory that I would learn pretty soon. If it hadn't been for John coming to my assistance, the story might have ended there and then. From then on, I confined myself to paddling!

Jack Brett was a veteran of the Norton team, a really good old stick. He wasn't really a number one, but a super team rider and a really reliable number two. Basically we got on very well, together with Charlie and Arthur Edwards, the mechanics, who had been long-time members of Joe Craig's original team. They were a very knowledgeable and experienced pair.

Norton also made it clear that they were only going to do selected events, not the full World Championship. The plan was that I would still use my own Nortons when I was not riding for the factory, as well as the 250 cc NSU Sportmax. This had first been introduced in 1954, and Vincent, who were in partnership with NSU on the sales of their machine in the UK, volunteered to bring one in for me to ride in the 250 class.

I started the season with a 350 win at Brough, up in Yorkshire, followed up by victories in all three classes at Brands Hatch on Good Friday, Snetterton on Easter Sunday and Crystal Palace on Easter Monday. At Silverstone the following Saturday I once again thought my big chance had arrived to beat Geoff Duke, but I only managed to hold the lead of the 500 race for five laps.

The 1955 season was to prove very satisfying. Highlights which stand out in my memory include a splendid battle at Oulton Park on the NSU to beat Cecil Sandford's Guzzi, and my first outing at Mettet, the Belgian circuit, with Joe Craig, when I chased home Fergus Anderson's streamlined Guzzi in the 500 cc event. There was also the occasion when I had four straight wins at Aberdare Park one Saturday before rushing back to compete at Brands Hatch the following day where I did the same.

On my third visit to the Isle of Man I finished fourth in the Junior TT, behind McIntyre on Joe Potts's streamlined Norton, Sandford's works Moto Guzzi and Maurice Quincey's Norton. In the Senior there was just nothing to touch the Gileras, so Duke and Reg Armstrong raced away to a commanding 1-2 finish.

Carburation was always a big problem on the Island with its frequent changes of temperature and variations in altitude, and during the race I had to contend with an engine running some 300 rpm down compared with practice. But I managed to pull up to seventh before running out of fuel at Creg-ny-Baa on the last lap. I pushed it home to gain my bronze replica with a 29th-place finish!

It was a memorable year, strenuous certainly, but great fun. I won the Lightweight Ulster Grand Prix with my 250 NSU, but threw it up the road at the Nürburgring on the first lap and suffered a seized piston at Monza. At the 'Ring, I was invited to ride the horizontally opposed BMW twin in the 500 cc German Grand Prix, which Norton was not contesting. Although I stopped in the race with a flooding carburettor float chamber, I think it was my performance on this bike which alerted Count Agusta to my potential and indirectly led to the invitation to join MV the following year. In fact, if BMW hadn't dithered around, I might well have ended up riding for them in 1956 rather than for the Italians.

There is actually a directive on file in the BMW museum in which Alex von Falkenhausen said, 'in John Surtees we have the man who can win the races for us.' But the directors dillied and dallied.

Reference:

German Grand Prix at the Nürburgring

Mr Surtees, who was recommended to us by Mr Aldington, started in this race for the first time on an RS machine with 52 horsepower engine and four-speed gearbox. Although Mr Surtees knew neither the Nürburgring nor the BMW engine, he soon settled in and rode the third-fastest time in practice. During the race, after a bad start, he worked his way through the whole field to third place, but then had to stop to change a spark plug. He worked his way back to third position and then had to abandon the race because of continued oiling up of the spark plugs (the reason for this was a flooded flotation chamber).

If we want to take part as a works team in next year's races, it would be necessary for Mr Surtees to commit himself soon.

Sporting Division

(signed) v. Falkenhausen

Riding the twin had certainly been different, but I was doing the same sort of times as regular rider Walter Zeller, despite the fact that I was not using a full works-specification bike like his, and was in third place. I think this is what convinced von Falkenhausen – and certainly convinced me – that I could have won the championship in 1956, and perhaps beyond, if BMW had given full support to a Grand Prix programme.

From the standpoint of personal satisfaction, there was still one stepping-stone to achieve, and that was to beat Geoff Duke in a straight race. I had competed with and, on the whole, beaten everybody else who really counted, on what were basically private machines.

Geoff, of course, had mainly been involved in the World Championship. I had only come across him in Sweden, where I had given him a close run, but he had still finished first.

I was to square up to him in the Aintree Senior, a 20-lap race for 500 cc bikes, and the Aintree 90, a 30-lap solo class handicap where Geoff would again be on the 500 cc Gilera and I would be using the 350 cc Norton. Well, it was a familiar story in the first two races, picking a bit up under braking and cornering, but Geoff just managed to pip me.

For the Aintree 90, I thought 'I wonder . . .' I discussed strategy with Joe Craig, who said it would be very difficult if we were going to try beating Geoff's Gilera in the same capacity class. Why not take the chance of racing the 350 and take the benefit of the handicap?

Well, we did just that. What was very convenient was that I caught up with Bob McIntyre on his 500 Potts Norton. With the bigger engine, he was capable of lapping slightly faster than me; I could get through the corners quicker, but he was quicker on the straight. So I would get ahead of him on the corners, then he would come past me down the straight and I would tuck in behind him and get pulled along in his slipstream. This gained me about 300 rpm which enabled me to lap only a fraction slower than Geoff on the 500 Gilera.

As a result, I was able to keep the advantage of my handicap and come across the line ahead. But you could not say it was really a straight win, although tactics had played their part, which was the main thing. If one is competing and attempting to reach the top, then one obviously has to set one's sights on trying to beat the acknowledged top rider/machine combination of the time. Geoff in fact remarked afterwards that it took 850 cc to beat him.

Geoff was obviously the man to beat. Back in 1951, when I had managed to stay in front of him for a while with the Vincent Grey Flash at Thruxton in the rain, I had set my mind on trying to make it a clear-cut win some day. The disappointment on the rainy, windswept day at Silverstone in 1954, when I was leading only for the bevel to fail, was another example of getting frustratingly close to realising that ambition.

After that 1954 meeting, I gave quite a lot of thought to building a special to do the job. I obtained from Eric Oliver a complete 1952/53 Manx Norton, minus its engine which had been sold off to go into an F3 car. I then thought about installing a big-twin Vincent.

At that time, Father had experienced some problems with his Black Lightning which required a new crankcase. I briefly thought about using this as the basis for a new engine, but eventually spoke to Mr Baillie, the receiver at Vincents, and asked whether there were any components I might have.

He replied: 'If there is anything that hasn't quite passed inspection, we will do our best for you.' Well, a new crankcase, totally perfect apart from a lower cylinder deck height, became available. Mr Baillie said: 'John, it's yours.'

I then had a few words with Major Honeychurch and managed to acquire a pair of the big-port heads which I fitted with 1½ GP Amals and a Black Lightning flywheel assembly. So I built up what amounted to a Grey Flash-specification Black Lightning engine.

With some juggling, I mounted this into the Norton frame and, in fact, completed the bike late in 1954. Then Nortons came along with the offer of a pair of '53 works bikes, so the Norton-Vincent got put to one side and never raced and my chance to pit this machine against the Duke Gilera never came about.

Many years later in 1979, when my interest in motor cycle riding was reawakened after I went to the Isle of Man and had my short demonstration run there on the MV Agusta – a standing-start lap at 97 mph after 18 years out of the saddle – I got the old special out again. After we had put it to one side, it had been loaned, complete with number plates and forward-mounted footrests, to a friend of my father called Mr Greenfield.

He had used it only for the occasional blast from his home in Cockfosters to the café he owned in Dunstable. It was eventually returned to me, hardly used, in the late 1950s. It lay in my garage for over twenty years, in component form, until I decided to reassemble it.

But should we put it back as it was? No, I decided to reassemble it with Grey Flash Vincent frame and modified suspension unit, and it has since given me great pleasure on various demonstration runs I've used it in.

As far as the remaining Norton components were concerned, I found a Norton engine from exactly the same period, which had been taken out of a Cooper, within two engine numbers of the one which had originally been taken out of the frame. So a long-stroke Manx Norton, similar to the one I raced, will eventually be put together. All the parts are there; all we need is the time!

Eventually the Hutchinson 100 meeting at Silverstone came round again and, although I had the disappointment of retiring my NSU in the 250 race when it hit valvegear trouble at Stowe after leading 18 of the 20 laps, I had the chance of squaring up to Duke in the 500 event. This was a very special meeting, of course, because it was the very last in which Joe Craig would be acting as racing manager for Norton and I dearly wanted to give him a goodbye present!

He was to finish a long and illustrious career with this event. John Hartle, Jack Brett and myself were the team as usual and, in practice, we got a feeling that we were in with a chance. Tyre development was proceeding at a faster rate than ever before, mainly because of Avon challenging the previously dominant Dunlop.

Avon had a really good competitions department, and in Tom Joy and the other technicians they had a committed group of people really searching for advances in tyre technology. This was also bringing about a change in riding style. The old way of cornering – up the outside, right to the deepest point in the corner, then straight across to the apex – was to some extent being superseded by the short-circuit style.

When you were running by yourself, the need to go deep in the corner, make full use of the road, and get the power on as early as possible was vital. But, running in company, it was also important to be able to brake right into the apex of the corner and still get the machine over far enough to line it up for the exit and still get the power on. Thus the short-circuit style of riding was being quickly transferred to the Grand Prix tracks, effectively narrowing the gap between long-circuit and short-circuit riders.

Well, Silverstone turned out to be perhaps one of the most important meetings of my life. I was good at starts; I made sure I was, and that I understood my machine intimately, ensuring that it would fire perfectly after a few yards.

I made a good start. Geoff was a little slower getting away and he was fifth at the end of the first lap, but gradually pulled through to second place. We didn't have any sophisticated pit signalling equipment, but the old chalk on a blackboard told me the story. I kept up my maximum effort to the end, and the feeling as I crossed the line, and particularly when I came back to the pits and saw the tears in Joe Craig's eyes, made it a very special event I will always remember. At last I had achieved a straight win over what was considered the world's best combination at the time.

We still had Brands Hatch to come the following day and Geoff was coming. Could we make it a hat-trick? In fairness, Brands was my home track and very much a specialist circuit. The angles you needed to lean the machines over at meant that the narrower Norton had a slight advantage at Paddock Bend and, to a lesser extent, also at Clearways with the adverse cambers.

The Gilera was nowhere near as wide as the MV Agusta which I was later to ride at Brands Hatch, but, just the same, Geoff still had some of the problems that I would later have there when, indeed, I would get beaten by a Norton as well.

The circuit was crowded like never before, with queues backed up all the way to Swanley, and there were in the region of 35,000 spectators crammed around the old short circuit. It had been some time since I had lost a race at Brands Hatch, so to some degree it was not surprising that I won, but full marks to Geoff for trying.

It was even more pleasing that a 500 Norton which I had prepared for Alan Trow finished second. In fact, when I was beaten on the MV at Brands Hatch, it was also Alan Trow's Norton – which I had supplied to him – which beat me. Not bad, really!

In 1955 I had won 68 mainland races out of 75 starts, so it was a very good year. I had gained a good deal of experience in international events with races in Sweden and Belgium, plus Grand Prix outings at the Nürburgring and Monza. I had won my first Grand Prix – in Ulster, with the 250 Sportmax – and competed with the best riders in the world, despite my limited international programme.

I therefore had the confidence to take on the world. But where was I to go?

Chapter 2
The Championship Years

For the 1956 season, my first thoughts were to stay with Norton. I had been happy with the little team under Joe Craig, with Charlie and Arthur Edwards looking after the mechanical side. Yes, we'd had our problems; we had worked at a disadvantage, without streamlining or the backing of a thorough, one hundred per cent works effort, but I had still enjoyed myself enormously.

The TT had been a disappointment due to the carburation of the 500 being set too cautiously, particularly as we had expected so much after the way the machine had been performing in practice, and the 350 had suffered partly from the same problem. But I had led my first TT – at least on lap one.

The encounters at the end of the '55 season with Geoff Duke had stimulated many thoughts as to what I could do. I believed there was an outside chance I could win the championship on a Norton. I considered by then I had the edge on Duke purely in terms of riding, and the circuits were changing. We had new tracks coming onto the calendar which put an even greater emphasis on good handling, and the Norton certainly had that.

In addition, if we took a lesson out of some of our opponents' books and developed efficient streamlining, and had a bit of luck on our side and had the odd wet race, perhaps, then we would be in with a chance. Of course, it would have been very nice to get the stillborn horizontal Norton out on the tracks for the first time. Everything that had been heard about it sounded good. The engine had produced more power than the vertical one on its first test; it was lighter, lower and certainly more suitable for streamlining.

That was immediately ruled out, but in discussions with Gilbert Smith, it was agreed that my suggested racing programme would be put to the Board. In turn, I had been approached by various people with offers of sponsorship, the most interesting of which was from a national newspaper. The idea was to support 'this young Englishman taking on the world on a British-built machine'.

We were hardly talking about a fortune, after all. We were only talking about £10,000, and with the added help from the regular accessory manufacturers it seemed like a viable proposition. Norton, for instance, always used Castrol lubricants. Avon were interested, despite the fact that they also supplied the main opposition. Dickie Davies of Dunlop was certainly keen, being anxious to get their tyres back into the winner's circle, while suppliers like Ferodo, Lodge and KLG all expressed an interest in Nortons going international again.

However, it was not to be. I was duly summoned in front of Gilbert Smith and informed that, despite the fact that, yes, they could give credence to my suggestion that we could achieve the stated level of success, due to company policy it would not be possible.

As an aside, I was later told that certain members of the Board had expressed their doubts as to the correctness of a rider actually earning more than a director of the company, which, had I won the World Championship, I no doubt would have done. Again, this might have taken me into the £10,000 bracket, but I really can't be sure.

I had been approached, as I have said, by BMW, but again there was a lot of indecisiveness. Although von Falkenhausen categorically stated that he believed I could win the championship if they were allowed to give me the necessary backing, the directors prevaricated and nothing more came of it.

I also had tentative offers from Moto Guzzi and Gilera, but these approaches expressed the view that, while they would very much like to do something with me, they had doubts about disturbing the Italian family atmosphere which existed within these teams. It was rather nice to see the way in which these companies acted in those times, the way in which they supported their riders and the manner in which they regarded their whole operation as a family.

Well, at this point I was approached by Bill Webster. He had been a great friend of Les Graham and had been partly involved in suggesting that Ray Amm should go to MV Agusta. Ray, however, was tragically killed over the Easter weekend in 1955 competing in his first race for the team at Imola.

Bill explained that Nello Pagani had been very impressed at seeing me staying in front of the MV Agustas while riding the BMW at the Nürburgring, and had gone back to report favourably on my progress to Domenico Agusta. Then I had won the 250 Ulster GP ahead of the MVs with the NSU, and been lapping Monza faster than the MVs with the NSU before its piston seized.

I thought about it and decided that this was really the only option. There had been an awful lot said about MV Agusta; lots of rumours about the problems which had been encountered. There was also a question mark over what had caused Les Graham's fatal accident in the TT two years earlier.

This was fairly well defined by the time I joined the team, and carried out my own investigation, as having been a mechanical error. A longer than standard bolt had been fitted into one of the front damper retaining positions, and this had latched under the mudguard to keep the suspension fully compressed after it had hit the main bump in the road at the bottom of Bray Hill. This, at least, is the explanation of the disaster that appears to have the most credibility. As for Ray Amm's accident, it was just considered to be one of those unfortunate things.

It was agreed that I should fly out to Italy and test the bike, as I said that I would like to do this before we discussed any terms. I duly travelled to Italy and arrived at Monza to meet Arturo Magni, the ex-Gilera chief mechanic with whom I was to strike up a warm friendship which has stood fast until today, even though we did not always agree concerning the machines. Also there was his brother Andrea, who was very much part of the race team in those days before moving over to the helicopter section, and a Mr Callatroni, who was acting as an interpreter, for although obviously Arturo understood some English, having worked together with Les Graham, they thought they should not have any mistakes through misunderstanding!

Well, nothing happened. The weather was dreadful. There had just been one of those storms that hit the Po Valley in the late summer and this, in turn, had brought down all the leaves on the trees overhanging the Lesmo corners. It was quite simply unsafe.

So the decision was taken to go to Modena, a track with which I was to become very much more familiar during my car racing days with Ferrari. We didn't have any problems with leaves, but the rain wasn't any better. We sat there and waited, but the rain didn't stop.

I told Arturo, well, I had better go out and ride anyway. After all, it might be wet one day for a race so we'll have to go out then. That rather took Arturo aback, but obviously he was somewhat satisfied, because Italian riders as a whole did not like the wet and they took my attitude as a good sign. In any event, I considered myself able to cope with wet conditions pretty well.

I ended up going round and round the Modena track, first of all getting used to that silky-smooth power unit. After the Norton, it was just that, of course, silky-smooth. Its maximum revs were 10,000 with the opportunity, so I was told, to let it run to 10,500 in top.

The gearbox had five speeds, there was a large single leading shoe twin front brake and telescopic forks. They offered me a choice of bikes to try from the outset, and I said I thought it would be best to start off with the model closest to the specification I was used to, so I chose the one fitted with telescopic forks which they had developed in 1955.

The large tank felt a little cumbersome, but by the time the handlebars had been adjusted the riding position wasn't very much different from the Norton's. There was no full fairing; just a little nose cowling round the front and a small screen. It was more than we had had on the Nortons, mind you, but not like the Gileras, Moto Guzzis, or even my own NSU.

My initial impression was that the bike felt a little too soft, demonstrating too much dive under braking and too much reaction to the application of power, although this only began to become apparent as the track surface started to dry.

Nevertheless, I ended up pretty happy because, on a far from dry track, I had been within one second of the lap record. It had been a real experience. The mechanics' faces also demonstrated their satisfaction and a call to the Count resulted in an invitation to 'Come to Monza tomorrow. We are getting the track swept . . .'

Well, we moved back to Monza. It was still rather greasy through the Lesmo corners, something which is fairly standard at that time of the year, but just the same I got down to within four seconds of the fastest lap that had ever been recorded. They were delighted and I was invited back to Casina Costa, the MV Agusta headquarters.

I duly got in the car with Bill Webster and off we set. We drove down to Gallarate and through the arched gates, past the aircraft hangars and on to the office buildings where the Count was based.

Agusta basically described itself as an aeronautical company. It had been involved in various projects, one of which was a Dakota-like aircraft which was wheeled in and out of the hangar each time the Ministry came down to see it and, as far as I know, never flew!

They were also deeply involved in helicopters and this represented their long-term future. When Les Graham had been with the team, and one of the American Bell helicopter family had visited Monza, Les had been the first person he met who could speak English. With Les's Air Force background, they immediately opened a line of communication between the two companies which produced an arrangement by which Agusta would build

Bell helicopters in Italy.

Agusta had also moved into motor cycles after the war and was building a range of small lightweight machines. He decided to take on the might of Moto Guzzi and Gilera and the first thing he had done was to recruit Engineer Pietro Remor from Gilera. In many ways, I always thought this had been to Gilera's advantage. They immediately looked at what they had in terms of equipment and proceeded to redesign it.

Thus, by the time Geoff Duke arrived at Gilera, they had made a very much more compact, smaller and lighter four-cylinder. In contrast, Remor had gone across to MV and reproduced essentially what Gilera had previously had, except that he had incorporated shaft drive and torsion bar suspension, front and rear, on his first model.

It wasn't until Les Graham appeared on the scene that this was changed to an Earles fork-type arrangement at the front and normal units at the rear, but it still meant we were left with a rather large, wide and heavy unit.

The Agusta family was headed by the Countess, Domenico's mother. Domenico himself headed up and seemed to run the entire operation, backed up by his brothers Mario, Vincenzo and, the youngest, Corrado. Mario I recall driving around in a Mercedes 300SL gullwing, having quite a liking for that type of machine. He also had a passion for high-powered boats and in fact sponsored a number of boats fitted with ex-Grand Prix Maserati engines.

The brothers all obviously had their parts to play, but Domenico was the one who slept, breathed and ate the Agusta company. He was the first one there in the morning and the last one there at night. If you wanted a decision – and that could be difficult at times – he was the one who gave it.

So we arrived at the office; Mr Callatroni was to do the interpreting again. Incidentally, Callatroni had an interesting background. He had been a missionary in China at the time of the Chinese revolution and had been obliged to leave the country rather quickly. Just after I had agreed my contract with Count Agusta, Callatroni took me to one side and said, 'Look, I have some priceless items from the Chinese Crown Jewels. Would you be interested? I could do you a good deal.'

I thought to myself, well, this must be the reason he had to get out of China so quickly! Anyway, at this time I needed every penny I had in order to finance my racing for the coming year as I had to prepare for a lot of travelling. I would need to think about transport and a small amount of capital, something I had never had up to that point. I also had to pay back some of the debts I had incurred in funding my own racing. First things first.

Obviously, there had to be a wait to see Count Agusta. There always was; nothing ever happens on time in Italy. I was eventually shown into a rather musty, dimly lit office with lots of trophies around the wall.

Most of these were from minor events or dating back to aeronautical activities because MV had at that stage not won very much on the international scene. They had enjoyed more success in the smaller classes, but relatively little major success, compounded by the two tragic accidents to Graham and Amm in the larger capacities.

Count Agusta came straight to the point when I was finally ushered in to see him. He said, 'We want you to be our rider and tester. Yes, you can have some machines for the early-season events in England. We would like the contract to be for more than one year. This is the amount we will pay you and there will be a bonus for first, second and third places. We are on Mobiloil fuel and oil, but, in response to your request, you can use whichever tyres you think best. Nello Pagani is the day-to-day team manager and co-ordinator, and the head of the racing department for the 500s is Arturo Magni. What do you think?'

I replied, 'Yes, we will go from here, although there are one or two other aspects which I would like clarified as regards machines and development.' I was then told to wait a moment as they had to go through other formalities before the arrangement could be confirmed.

I waited some time, just gazing around while Agusta chatted to Pagani and Callatroni. Then the door opened. In came a lady completely clothed in black and wearing a black veil. She came into the room. I stood up and she came across, looked me over, and went back to the table where she addressed Domenico.

There was a brief exchange of words and she went out. I later asked Callatroni what this was all about. He replied, 'Ah, that was the Countess. She was just there to check as to whether she liked the look of you and whether you were suitable to be allowed into the Agusta family.' This is how it was, so I now became a member of MV Agusta.

I was in a country which I had visited only once before. I didn't have the slightest grasp of their language, apart from understanding 'Benelli, Gilera, Moto Guzzi' and so on, but at the same time I immediately felt that this could be home.

Father had also travelled out, keeping an eye on proceedings, and double-checking lap times while I was out on the circuits. He thought it was a good move and, with Bill Webster's enthusiasm, that sealed the whole thing.

After the first meeting, I sat down with Magni to discuss various points on the bikes and I explained there were certain things I would like to try. I took all the various dimensions relative to suspension units, asked for one or two changes to be made to the riding position, and said that I would return to Italy for more testing when they were ready.

I duly returned to do another short test at Monza, again in fairly poor conditions, but it was agreed that the main testing would take place in England at the beginning of the 1956 season when we would also assess Dunlop and Avon tyres.

Other changes, however, were to come about in 1956. The family was to move from Old Addington to Callendar Road, just up from Catford, and not very far from where Father had his business in Forest Hill. In fact, it was just round the corner from where Henry Cooper, the boxer, lived.

I also left Vincents. It may sound strange, but of course I was still doing my apprenticeship. It had been a little difficult getting away for my racing, but I had tried to make up as much time as possible. I had been working in the experimental department, mainly by that stage involved with the Picador engines, so this meant there was quite a lot of outside work at ML Aviation at White Waltham in connection with the installation of these engines. However, there were question marks on the horizon as to whether this programme would be continued with, and a certain amount of blame passed backwards and forwards for performances which had not really come up to expectations.

Philip Vincent, of course, was now back on the scene after his road accident, but he was not the person he had been, and many things had been left in the hands of people who, in my view, were less than competent and certainly did not have the right motivation. All the main engineers had left and it was just a question of time . . . It was very sad.

Certainly it was a great opportunity lost, because that company undoubtedly had more potential than any other when it came to meeting the demands which would be made of machines in the 1960s.

Father no longer had an involvement, as he had passed over his dealership to Deeprose Brothers, again in Catford. So where could I go to finish off the last year of my apprenticeship?

As I've already said, I have always had a deep affection for the countryside, and a rider in those days could never expect to earn enough in his racing career not to need to work again. In any case, I felt you were likely to die of boredom in such a situation.

After some consultation, the opportunity arose for me to join a Ferguson agricultural engineering distributorship, spending part of my time at base camp near Northampton, part of the time at the Ferguson training establishment and still rushing backwards and forwards trying to win a World Championship. I was not able to settle in Italy immediately, which would have been ideal, so as soon as a race or test was over it was a question of jumping in the car and motoring hard back home.

This was all possible because of an old friend of Father's, Peter Chapman, who later became a sponsor of Chris Vincent during his sidecar racing days. Peter had been with Father at Catterick for some of the time and, when they talked things over together, he suggested that this agricultural engineering project would be an opportunity for me to do something I was interested in and, bearing in mind the enthusiasm I always applied to anything I became involved in, could well help his establishment.

I was sad to have to leave Vincents. They took a sympathetic view of my request for a transfer and said that I must do what I felt was right. In some ways, I would have liked to contribute a lot more to the Vincent effort, but it was a little bit too early in my career for me to be in a position to do that.

At MV, my team-mates in the 500 class would be Umberto Masetti, who had been 500 World Champion riding for Gilera, 'Bouncing' Carlo Bandirola, an Italian Champion and a rider of considerable repute, and another Italian, Tito Forconi, who was going to be reserve. There was also a possibility that Remo Venturi would step in at times.

For the Lightweights, MV had an equally comprehensive team: Carlo Ubbiali, Angelo Copeta, Remo Venturi and Luigi Taveri. Luigi was, in fact, a Swiss rider who was later to become World Champion in his own right with Honda.

Through 1956 MV Agusta was not to undergo any radical change of equipment at all. It was to be basically a question of using the '55 machines as I last tested them. Some work was progressing with streamlining, although not enough, in my view, considering the aeronautical background of the company and what we had seen Moto Guzzi showing themselves capable of. However, MV's main hope was to improve the reliability of the engine as well as improving its spread of power.

Apart from the 500, I was to ride a 350. In fact, this was purely a scaled-down 500; not the ideal way to achieve a really competitive machine, but it was an opportunity for another ride and, hopefully, to achieve some more success.

Early in '56 I received a call asking me out to do some testing in Italy. I duly got permission and set off. Once there, I began communicating with Arturo Magni, with Arturo's pidgin English and my sign language, plus the odd few words, getting us through to start with!

I was staying at a little hotel in Gallarate, not far from the cinema, where there were a lot of 'spaghetti westerns' on the programme – not very deep and quite easy to follow. So this was the method whereby I picked up a little Italian. I used to go along there in the evening, try to link together the actions and the words and improve my Italian in that way.

At least that early-season testing managed to sort out the riding position and got the suspension movement a little more to my liking; we were able to put some mileage in to demonstrate that the various modifications carried out over the winter had been to some effect.

I was to be given a pair of machines to take to England for the early-season races; not a 350 and 500, however, because there was no 350 ready. I had asked to race the 250s occasionally, but they replied that riders had already been signed for that class and they didn't want me competing. I later learned that Ubbiali had in fact specifically requested that I did not have 250 machines – or, at least, the 203 cc machines which were available at that time.

I was duly given a 203 and a 500 four-cylinder for the English races, plus Andrea Magni to look after the bikes for the trip. Mother and Father drove out to Gallarate in their van, picked up Andrea and the bikes and returned home again. That was our works team effort!

My first race on an MV was to be at Crystal Palace on Easter Monday. The four-cylinder bike was non-streamlined, but the little 203 had its full fairing. I already held the lap record at Crystal Palace on a 250 with my NSU, but in my heat with the little MV I managed to beat that, adding about 3 mph to the fastest time.

It was a very pleasing start, and how nice that little machine seemed. The 500 event was next and it nearly proved something of an embarrassment to me. During testing I had not paid too much attention to the technique of racing starts with the MV, so shortly before the event I thought I had better begin thinking about it. After all, I had often won races from the moment the starting flag dropped thanks to the demoralising effect my getting swiftly off the line had had on my opponents.

Moreover, on short circuits getting off the line was all-important. Therefore, on the paths round Crystal Palace I practised nothing but bumping the MV into life and getting the clutch home. By the time I came to the line for the heat, I felt I had everything taped.

However, I was just a little too keen to put up the best possible show. Two steps; bump; let the clutch in. The engine came alive and I fed the power in. A little too quickly, as it turned out!

I had always tended to ride side-saddle for quite a distance until I was ready to snick into second gear. This time I went off the line side-saddle, but with the front wheel pawing the air. It looked spectacular, but it certainly wasn't intended.

I stayed in front, set a new record and finished comfortably ahead of John Clark, a short-circuit star riding a Matchless G45. That wasn't a bad start: two wins on my first racing acquaintance with the machines.

I scored two more wins at Snetterton the following weekend and followed that up at Silverstone a week later at the BMCRC Championship meeting where I was again to ride the 203 and the 500. It was one of those really wet Silverstone days with a chilling, blustery wind blowing across as it only can on airfields, the track surface full of pockets and puddles of water. I was thankful for my wet testing at Modena.

My main opponent was going to be my friend John Hartle, who was still with Norton, plus another old racing colleague and great competitor, Bob Keeler. John won the 350 with Bob a close second, but my first race was to be the Lightweight event.

The little MV, basically a scaled-up 175, handled superbly, no doubt helped by its narrow-section tyres. I never had any problems and it cut through the water with re-assuring confidence.

For the Senior race, I had drawn a position at the back of the grid because they didn't go on lap times in those days. John, meanwhile, was at the front and kept ahead for a while before I managed to come up on him and overtake on the fifth lap. We had enjoyed some good friendly rivalry when we had been Norton team-mates and John, now that he was the opposition, was clearly not going to be any less determined. However, I man-aged to stay a little way ahead until, in fact, later on in the race he slid off at Stowe, allowing Bob McIntyre into second place, about half a minute behind me.

Of course, I will always look upon the TT races in 1956 as my starting-point to the World Championship. Mind you, in those days the TT was rather different, and anybody with grandiose ideas of how MV tackled it had better think again. Certainly, they fielded lots of machines if you consider the 125, 250, 350 and 500 events, but with none of the luxury trimmings which go with racing today.

The bikes were brought over to England by truck and van, and we actually collected two of the 500 machines ourselves with our own van. They were all taken to London, placed on the train and we all travelled up to Liverpool, then wheeled the machines down to the docks, onto the boat and so we arrived in the Isle of Man. Our own van took over the spares and some other equipment.

Having run out of petrol on the last lap of the 1955 Senior TT, I rather thought it was the last time this would happen to me. How wrong can you be! This was to happen to me again this very year, this time in the Junior race.

My position had not looked particularly good at the end of lap three. The MVs were very thirsty and we had to come in for refuelling. The Moto Guzzis were very economical and carried a lot of fuel, so they didn't have the same problem.

Bill Lomas's Guzzi was ahead with his Australian team-mate Ken Kavanagh running second, but it was a long race and, as Joe Craig always insisted, many things could hap-pen between the start and finish. Conditions were wet, something which might possibly have given me a slight edge for, although I cannot positively state that I loved racing in the rain, it never really disconcerted me to the extent that it did many riders.

Gradually, lap by lap, I managed to improve my position and, by the time the last lap was under way, I had actually taken the lead. Then, at the Stonebreakers Hut signalling station, on the Mountain climb, with a quarter of a lap to go, the engine missed a beat and then petered out.

I looked in the tank. No petrol! One of the few onlookers up there produced a milk bottle and we borrowed some petrol from a machine on the roadside, filled the tank, started up and continued to the finish. Of course, I was disqualified. In any case, we were there to try and win . . .

It seemed that too much haste, because of the amount of time we knew we would lose in the pits, had been the problem during my refuelling stop. It was a mistake, something they should have noticed, of course, by the amount of fuel they had left, immediately after I had left the pits.

During my first visit to the Island, in 1953, when I missed my works Norton ride through that tumble on the EMC, Ray Amm had achieved the double, winning at record speed. It would have been very satisfying to have achieved the double in 1956, and matched his achievement, but perhaps it would have made MVs a little too complacent.

As it was, the result was quite a surprise, even to the winner Ken Kavanagh, for, apart from my misfortune, Bill Lomas had also retired. He had been running ahead of me when his engine failed on the Mountain climb.

Mind you, he had tried to hide his machine away behind a bank so I wouldn't see it and be prompted to make a supreme last-lap effort to keep ahead of Kavanagh. In fact, I had spotted Bill's bike and had put in that little extra spurt. Not that it served any purpose!

When it came to the Senior TT, I really paid the price, because when I came in to top up with fuel at the end of the third lap, they took a full forty seconds to do the job, even though the machine had a nine-gallon fuel tank.

While the Norton, if tuned to its optimum with its plug just about glowing, could do approximately one 37-mile lap of the TT course to every gallon, the MV Agusta had a much heavier thirst, something in the order of 23 miles to the gallon.

To win the '56 Senior, I was obliged to use my hack machine; in fact, I believe the majority of it was based round the bike I had used in England. And why? Because in practice, I had hit a cow!

In the Isle of Man they take a lot of precautions to ensure that animals are kept off the road and that the course is relatively clear and safe, particularly during those early-morning practice sessions. But, of course, it is rather difficult when you are dealing with a lap of that length.

I had taken out the race machine for that final morning's practice, to settle it in for the big event, and was pulling away up the steep climb from Glen Helen, and round the right-hander at the top. I was just about ready to snick from second to third gear when a cow jumped over a bank in front of me.

I hit the cow full amidships. It, however, actually got up, lumbered away and, I am told, made a full recovery. It certainly suffered a lot less damage than the bike, which sustained a bent fairing and twisted frame and, as it skated down the road, picked up a helping of gravel in its outside carburettors.

At this meeting, I found how very different the MV was from the Norton, particularly at high speed. The centre of gravity on the MV was that much higher. The crankshaft, for instance, was positioned much higher in the frame. This was necessary because of the overall width of the package and the consequent requirement for ground clearance on cornering as well as the need for space for the exhaust pipes.

This, of course, was the reason why Gilera had made such efforts to reduce the width of their engines. Whereas on the Norton at high speed only on rare occasions did you need to manhandle it – you could more or less aim it and give it a slight tweak through the corners – with the MV you had to get up on the footrests and wrestle it from side to side. It called for a much more physical style of riding than the Norton, particularly on sudden changes of direction.

At least I now knew fairly well where I was going round the TT course. I had lost out considerably by not competing in the Manx Grand Prix during those early years, instead coming straight in for my first race in 1954. But in 1955 things had gone pretty well, while in '56 things went somewhat better again and I was able to bring the MV home for the team's first Senior TT victory.

With the trip to the Island over we were off to the Dutch TT at Assen, surely even today one of the very special places when one talks about motor cycle racing. People from far and wide come and line the circuit, the whole place gets taken over; it's the nearest thing to the Isle of Man, I suppose, and just becomes a motor cycling city.

The circuit offered a nice balance. There were slow corners, fast swerves, medium-speed corners, and that quick ess-bend just after the start/finish line was a real teaser which tended to sort out the men from the boys. The weekend started well for MV with Ubbiali and Taveri finishing first and second in the 125 and 250 events. In the 350 my main opposition came from Bill Lomas and Ken Kavanagh on their works Moto Guzzis, and Cecil Sandford on the DKW, along with August Hobl, who could never be underestimated.

There were over thirty riders at the startline and Bill had one of his best rides, charging through after a somewhat indifferent start. I had been battling away with Sandford and Hobl for quite a while, but I tucked in behind Lomas and finished second. The 500, mind you, was the victory I really wanted.

Gilera were not there, Geoff Duke and Reg Armstrong still being under suspension. It was disappointing in some ways, but it gave me a little more chance to become acclimatised to the Grand Prix scene and, particularly, to the MV.

Walter Zeller had the latest in terms of BMW equipment, a fuel-injected twin, the German team having finally decided that they would give total support to one rider. Well, Walter was good at any time, but he certainly tried his utmost that day and the BMW showed the sort of performance it was capable of.

For a while, he breathed down my neck, but once I settled into my full rhythm I was able to pull away consistently until I had a lead of about half a minute. It was obviously pleasing, but I got particular satisfaction from trimming Geoff Duke's records, both for distance and lap speeds, which had been established the previous year.

The Belgian Grand Prix was to come next, on the famous Spa-Francorchamps circuit. I had never seen it before, but I had certainly heard all about its quite spectacular 8.7-mile lap, very fast with one tight hairpin before the high-speed dive down past the start. All this was laid out in a very picturesque setting, and partly created in an effort to establish the fastest race circuit in Europe. It was going to be some challenge and, certainly, would represent a test of mechanical reliability.

The weather in this part of southern Belgium can be very stormy, particularly in July when it can be very hot and humid, perhaps raining at one end of the circuit, but not at the other. The other problem was melting tar. Mind you, if you rode in the Isle of Man in those days, you quickly became accustomed to this, although I must say it was one thing I did particularly dislike.

One aspect which would make this race especially interesting was the return of the Gilera team, with Geoff Duke riding for them in the 500 race. Practice times showed it was going to be difficult to hold the Gileras. Frankly, they had their act together as far as streamlining was concerned, whereas MV had not.

As I've said, this was disappointing because of MV's aeronautical background, and the amount of advantage we produced from the full fairings was not what it should have been. What we gained in aerodynamic improvement, we seemed to lose through impaired efficiency of engine breathing. This was, in fact, something which plagued us right through to the point where streamlining was banned for 1958.

At the start of the Spa race, I led for four laps, then Duke came past and I found it was particularly difficult to hold him on the long climb away from Stavelot. This was partly due to the Gilera's lighter weight, partly aerodynamics, but, more significantly, as we later learned on the bush telegraph, Gilera had built a special gearbox which gave them a ratio particularly suitable for that long climb.

It all just served to demonstrate how serious Gilera were and they were certainly one of the finest racing companies I raced against and, unfortunately in many ways, never raced for. Frankly it didn't look as though I would be able to challenge the Duke/Gilera combination, but fate played its hand and Geoff rolled to a stop, with valve spring failure.

Of course, this is a failure that could easily happen at Francorchamps. It was so fast that at times it could be quite frightening, and was very hard on the machines with the engines running at peak revs for the longest periods that I can recall on any circuit except Hockenheim.

The engine and transmission were certainly fully tested at Spa and, once I got the signal that Geoff was finally out, I took special care to make certain I stressed my machine the minimum amount in order to get it home. In the 350 race I had a terrific dice with Lomas and Hobl on my way to victory, so it was a nice double.

Next on the schedule was the Hedemora Grand Prix, but this was not a World Championship event, so it was decided that MV would go straight to the German Grand Prix at Solitude, a race which would be vital to my World Championship hopes. In the 500 battle, my score stood at 24 points from three wins so, with the contest decided from the best four results out of six races, I needed one more victory to put me in an unbeatable position. My closest rival, Walter Zeller, had 14 points at this time.

In the Junior class I was also in the lead with 15 points, with Hobl second on ten points and Lomas, the previous year's champion, third on eight points. So a win for me here in the 350 race could make my position almost unassailable.

The Solitude circuit was situated just outside Stuttgart, home of Mercedes-Benz, Bosch and Porsche. It was a wonderful road circuit, running through the pine trees, with a variety of slow and fast corners, in addition to a series of sweeps which ran alongside the lake back to the startline.

DKW's three-cylinder two-stroke, ridden by Hobl, could produce lightning acceleration and was clearly one of my biggest rivals in the 350 race, but there were also Lomas, Sandford and Kavanagh to consider, with Bill probably being the one most likely to emerge as the main challenger. I made a good start, just behind Hobl who had beaten me into the first corner. I got ahead of him, but Bill Lomas quickly came up behind; he pulled past and I tucked into his slipstream. Bill's team-mate Kavanagh slid off his works Guzzi, Bill set a record lap and pulled away slightly, but I replied and closed right up on him.

Solitude had recently been resurfaced and was in good condition, but there was quite a lot of sand around the edges of the road. As we became more and more involved in our dice, I was using that much more road all the time. You really had to ride the 350 MV at 110 per cent if you were going to stay with a combination like Lomas and the Moto Guzzi.

Just as I was clipping one of these kerbs that much closer, I lost the front end. It slid away, put me down and I slithered across the road and came to a standstill against a rocky bank. For a moment I was very dazed, but when I came to my senses I looked up into the face of a rather pretty young German Red Cross attendant. I had crashed just below a medical point.

I was taken off to hospital where they told me I had broken my humerus – although I certainly didn't find it very funny at the time! I worried about that accident as I didn't know what had really happened. Another slight reason for it did materialise afterwards, in that I began to question why the 350 had felt somewhat different at this meeting.

The bike had been checked over relative to spring rates, damping and so on, and it was all to regular specification. I later found out that they had changed the yokes on the forks in a way that was hardly discernible, but did change the geometry. They told me they had done this to improve the ground clearance under cornering, as previously I had been complaining about the way in which the exhaust pipes and fairing were scuffing on the road and restricting my cornering performance.

This at least explained why the bike had felt different. Whether or not I would have had a better message from the machine in its normal form, I really can't say. They certainly knew after that accident that they were not to change a thing without prior discussion.

As Bill Lomas went on to win the 350, that meeting at Solitude meant I was not going to take the Junior title. The 500 class had somewhat gone my way, however, for Bill went surprisingly quickly on the V8 Moto Guzzi and diced with Geoff until they both retired, leaving Reg Armstrong to win on the second Gilera. Walter Zeller had retired with gearbox trouble, so the second man to finish was my team-mate Umberto Masetti, while the third man home, Pierre Monneret on a Gilera, was not really involved in the World Championship struggle, although he still had his interest in the French national title. Thus, the position was now that only Walter Zeller could challenge me for my first World Championship, the outcome all depending on the Ulster and Italian Grand Prix meetings, which were still to be held.

One day the doctors came to me in hospital and said, 'Now the swelling has gone down, we are going to nail you.' Nail me? Of course, what they meant was that they were about to put a pin in my damaged arm, but the term used in the Stuttgart hospital was 'nail'. Strangely enough, putting that pin into my arm was to have quite an effect later in the year.

The German doctors and nurses were superb and I felt they were very understanding as I waited to hear what the result would be from the Ulster Grand Prix, particularly as, after all, Walter was one of their fellow-countrymen. They were fantastic!

I don't believe that I am particularly superstitious, although I had little habits as to what I would wear, or not wear, when I was competing in a race meeting. For instance, in later years, I never used anything new in a race for the first time. It always had to be 'run in' during practice. A set of overalls, for example, would always go through the wash once before I actually used them in a race.

This all stemmed from a series of coincidences in my very early years when I first started motor cycling. It seemed to me that, each time I wore something new, I tended to fall off. Mind you, I tended to fall off at each meeting at the very start!

The night before the Solitude event, I was sleeping quite normally and suddenly I had a dream which virtually caused me to throw myself out of bed. I picked myself up from the floor of the room, fully believing that I had been thrown from a motor cycle. It was rather frightening to think that the following day a very similar throwing action took place, but this time on the part of the MV.

The Solitude accident had definitely been the worst of my motor cycle racing career – the only times I injured myself on two wheels were on this occasion and when I sustained that broken scaphoid in 1953. From about 1954 through to the end of my motor cycle career in September 1960, I fell off only four times. So perhaps all those early tumbles had served their purpose!

Finally, the news came through that my old team-mate John Hartle had won the Ulster 500 Grand Prix on the Norton. Geoff had suffered a slide on the Leathemstown Bridge bends and Walter had not been able to do anything. However, there was still no prospect of my making Monza as my injuries were certainly not responding as quickly as I would have hoped. The fracture was too serious and the general swelling had not helped matters.

It would be 1957 before my comeback took place, but the Ulster Grand Prix result meant that I had clinched my first World Championship. The 1956 season had been a crucial stepping-stone.

After those early-season British races, I had taken part in two more non-championship events. The first of those was at Mettet in Belgium, where I had first raced the Norton the previous year. Fergus Anderson actually made his debut here with the BMW, having tired of the political situation which had developed at Moto Guzzi. He had upped and left.

Taking rather the same view as I had done, he had opted for the BMW. He went surprisingly well at Mettet and I had to set up a record lap to win by a small margin from the Moto Guzzi of Bill Lomas who, in turn, was only four seconds ahead of Fergus at the finish.

The next weekend we moved on to the race around the roads of Floreffe. I didn't have a 350, just a 500. Bill Lomas won the 350 race with Dickie Dale second and John Hartle third, but the 500 turned out to be a very sad event.

I won it and Bill Lomas came second with Jack Brett third on a Norton. Fergus, who had made a bad start, really had a big go. He'd got himself really together with the BMW and, in fact, raised the lap record. Then, going down through Floreffe village, where the tar was melting, that little extra effort perhaps proved too much. Fergus lost it, was unfortunate enough to hit a stone kerb at just the wrong place and died at the age of 47. It was a real tragedy.

Meanwhile, back to the hospital in Stuttgart. In due course I was collected by Mother in our Ford Zephyr, neither the Porsche nor the Aston Martin DB2 I owned after it having the interior room required to transport all the necessary kit around.

I was taken off to King's College Hospital to see the same team that had looked after me when I suffered the scaphoid problem. They told me that I must not let the muscles waste; I had to keep at it. The best thing they recommended was . . . woodwork! So from then on I attended their carpentry shop where I made myself some toolboxes which I still have to this day.

Meanwhile, I had come to the end of my apprenticeship, so the time had come for me to address the subject of National Service. I duly received my papers. It was a worry, of course. Here I was, World Champion, and having to consider doing my National Service.

There was a possibility that I might get a special dispensation to take part in at least some events, but that was not certain. The papers were returned, I went for my medical at the centre in Blackheath . . . and I was turned down. They did not want people with damaged limbs; in my case an arm with limited extension and containing a metal pin.

It's strange, if one cares to think about it, how fate tends to take a hand.

What with the carpentry, general exercise and regular use of the spring grips, I worked hard to get fit again. My thought was that as soon as I felt my arm to be reasonably strong, I would attempt a little trials riding.

For this purpose, I managed to get hold of a works-specification Triumph Tiger Cub of the type fitted with the forks used on the 3T model. At the end of January 1957, I went down to Brands Hatch with Father and Frank Lilley, his old passenger, and took out my Norton and NSU. It was my first ride since my German Grand Prix accident.

I went along with George Wilson to take part in the Pressmans Trial, and one or two other local events, to build up my strength again. Mid-March brought with it the sad news of Joe Craig's death.

I had been asked by MV, in the meantime, to recommend another rider as the team did not want to be left in this position again, and they wanted someone for the TT. First of all I suggested John Hartle, with whom I had a good friendship as well as having considerable respect for his riding ability.

Next on the list I put Bob McIntyre. John wasn't able to accept, as he had previous commitments and he was an honourable man. So, together with Bill Webster, I travelled down to Aberdare Park and spoke to Bob Mac. I thought we had persuaded him to join the team. Bob was, in my opinion, somebody who you would always have to rate very highly, particularly so when it came to the Isle of Man. He had an awful lot of experience there and his basic style of riding, and the rhythm he would get into, suited the Island well. So, if I was going to have to take him on, I would rather have him on a similar machine than on one with a performance edge, something that I kept telling MV I believed the Gilera to have.

My first race back in action was to be the Spanish Grand Prix at Barcelona which, in many ways, turned out to be quite amusing. Ken Kavanagh had gone along and talked to Domenico, and somehow persuaded him to make him a team member. Quite what the deal was, I didn't know and, frankly, didn't care.

I had heard a lot about what had gone on in the Moto Guzzi team, in connection with Fergus Anderson's departure and other changes. As I didn't have first-hand information, I could not honestly pass an opinion. But, nevertheless, I thought I had better be a little wary. I believe Ken was getting acquainted with an MV-4 when news came through during March that McIntyre was joining Gilera. That was a bit of a blow, and he was out at Monza getting the feel of the machine.

Back to Barcelona. This wasn't a World Championship event, but Agusta for some reason decided it would be a good warm-up. The Montjuich Park circuit was a testing venue, I suppose a bit like Brands Hatch, but with a few more twists and turns thrown in. It was quite bumpy, on public roads, so it involved all the usual changes in surface, painted lines and drain holes. But, just the same, it was a fascinating circuit and one which deserved a lot of respect.

It was certainly going to be a test of my arm. The right arm, after all, is the one which controls all the braking, and on this circuit there was a sequence of corners immediately past the start which involved accelerating and braking, repeatedly, in quick succession. It was only on the return climb, away from the lower end of the circuit, round a long uphill curve back to the startline when this pattern was not followed.

In practice I had experienced a little trouble, in that once I had done three laps I was having some difficulty with my right hand under braking. It was tiring rather quickly. We had a further worry in that there had been some sports car races as well and the track's tarmac had been rather polished as a result, and it looked as if it might rain. Mind you, that would have perhaps had the advantage of giving my arm an easier time.

However, it turned out to be fine, and there was a little bit of a carnival at the start of the 125 event when the official dropped the flag while Carlo Ubbiali was still surrounded by mechanics. The only one who seemed to get away quickly was the rider of the local Montessa team!

Well, it all turned out all right as Carlo carved his way through the field and finally won the race. But we were a bit apprehensive about the starting tactics when it came to the 500 event, although before then the offical was changed!

I thought, 'Right, 'I'm going to have to play tactics here a bit.' Before the race Nello Pagani suggested I take it very easily and play myself in. 'Don't worry,' he said. 'Bandirola is very popular here. We will quite understand.'

Yes, I thought, understand at this moment perhaps, but back in Italy it would be a case of 'Surtees not what he was!' and any chance I might have had of introducing improvements to the bikes would be ruled out as they would immediately conclude that I was pressing for changes just to make up for my own problems.

As a result, I made one of my usual rapid starts and whistled away, but within three laps my arm was starting to fade. I had pulled out a bit of a lead over Bandirola so, coming onto the bottom straight halfway through the fourth lap, I looked over my shoulder, saw he was a fair distance behind and eased back.

While I was using the climb as a period to rest my arm a little, he closed up, but didn't come past. There he was, sitting on my tail. He obviously thought, 'Ah, John is playing games with me. I won't have this.' Little did he know that if he had kept hard at it, there would have been precious little I could have done about it.

So the race unfolded. I did a slowish lap and he went by, but then eased up. I speeded up again, did my three quick laps, pulled out a bit of a lead, then eased slightly so he closed up on me. So it went on: three laps quick, two laps easing. As we approached the end of the race, instead of doing two laps easily, I turned on the pressure again after completing only half a lap of, shall we say, touring.

At the end of the lap I looked back to see whether I had caught him unawares. There was no sign of Bandirola! The next time I come round, there on the uphill section is one MV Agusta sorting itself out from against a tree!

Bandirola had been totally confused by the point at which I had suddenly accelerated, as it had not followed previous form. He had obviously taken a very large handful and, in turn, had lost it. That was the only race I could recall in my life that I had had to employ those sort of tactics in order to win!

Then I went back to England to take part in the Brands Hatch Good Friday meeting. I won the 250 race on the 203 MV, but got beaten into second place in the 1000 cc event by Alan Trow (as I've previously mentioned riding the Norton I had supplied to him), with Peter Murphy third on a Matchless.

On the Sunday I went off to Oulton Park with the usual pair of bikes. I didn't finish the 250 and was leading the 500 until the gearbox packed up. So that was that.

The following weekend we were off to Mettet, where I was due to try out one of the new streamlined fairings on the 500. MVs had finally decided they needed to make something a little new, so I had spent some time down in a local wind tunnel owned by an associate company in Italy. The unfortunate thing was, of course, that the engine was not running in the wind tunnel, so one could not get any knowledge of how the fairings affected the engine performance.

However, in the tunnel, it seemed as though this fairing would be a considerable improvement. The Mettet circuit was like a big 'X' meeting in the middle. From the start, we dropped down through the village, along the bottom, back up and swept round a left-hander onto a tree-lined straight. Once I got up to speed in fifth gear during practice I remember losing all steering as the thing began to take off.

I just about kept it on the road, but that was an experience which did not make me too enthusiastic about the wind tunnel results. We obviously didn't use it for the race, but that didn't do us any good either. Despite starting well, I retired with mechanical trouble after a few laps.

So it was off to Hockenheim for the German Grand Prix, and another very damp day. We felt that perhaps this could give us a slight edge, for we knew we were in trouble with both reliability and a shortage of outright speed against the Gileras.

Bob McIntyre led most of the 350 race until he fell off, and I had retired very early. Engine trouble! Libero Liberati won on the Gilera with John Hartle's Norton second and Masetti the best-placed MV-4 back in fourth place.

In the 500 race, well, it was again a sorry tale. I was leading from Dickie Dale's V8 Guzzi, McIntyre and Masetti until the 13th lap when the engine stopped again. Afterwards, Masetti slowed up, so this ended as another win for Liberati with McIntyre second and Walter Zeller's BMW third. It was not a very encouraging start to our defence of the World Championship.

Next it was back to the Isle of Man for the Golden Jubilee TT. The Junior event did not go well. I had to stop twice for plug changes, but at least I eventually came in fourth behind McIntyre, Keith Campbell's Moto Guzzi and Bob Brown's Gilera.

For the Senior event, we wondered whether we should use the full fairing. After the rather exciting 'test' at Mettet, we had gone back to Italy and virtually copied the fairings used by Gilera and Moto Guzzi. The only thing was that, although it worked better, it was still not helping the performance of the engine. The old fairing had reduced the power, perhaps due to restricted breathing, but the new one badly affected the cooling. Perhaps it was just accentuating the problems we were already encountering with pistons and valves generally at this time.

After some thought, and a weather forecast which suggested it was quite likely to be rather blustery, it was decided to run without the fairing for safety's sake. This meant that we would be losing out by at least 10 mph on the faster section of the circuit, but that could easily be made up if it really did turn out to be a blustery day.

At the same time if you don't finish, you can't win anything, and we were aware of that piston problem which was the reason for the plug changes in the 350 race. Bob rode a faultless race on a faultless day, weather-wise, and we had to play second fiddle. Frankly, we didn't deserve to be any better placed. We were not as well prepared, or organised, as Gileras, and I certainly do not begrudge Bob his success in that event. It was a pity we hadn't got him on an MV!

Getting a bit tired of this, I returned to England, dusted off my Nortons and pulled out the NSU for a visit to Oulton Park. I shared the honours with Bob Mac, with him winning the 500 and me the 350, and I also won the 250 with the NSU. Then it was off to Assen again for the Dutch TT.

The 125 and 250 didn't go MV's way, with Provini winning on the Mondial in both classes. The 350 race saw us going quite well, but the rear suspension unit broke while I was in the leading group. In the 500 it was the turn of McIntyre to be the chaser, and he kept on after me until he slightly overdid things and crashed. I came in first at a record speed of 82.51 mph with Liberati second and Zeller in third place.

The Belgian Grand Prix which followed produced something of a disaster for the MV team. Roberto Colombo crashed fatally during practice and all the Italian MV team riders were withdrawn from the race. John Hartle was given an MV twin for the 250 event and, although Provini went ahead from the start, John picked him off and went on to win with the Mondials of Sammy Miller and Cecil Sandford second and third.

I kept up what was becoming my fairly familiar 1957 performance by retiring on the fourth lap of the 350 event with engine trouble. This was won by Keith Campbell's Guzzi with Liberati's Gilera second and Keith Bryen, now in the Guzzi team, third. I also retired from the 500 race.

By this stage I was finding it increasingly difficult to get through and speak to the Count. He was so heavily involved with his helicopter business, and also I don't think he really wanted to be reminded of the problems we were encountering. I would wait outside his office only to be told that something unexpected had cropped up and would I come back tomorrow?

After the Belgian race I thought there was only one way of catching him. I left my car and booked onto the overnight train on which he was returning to Italy, ensuring I got the sleeping compartment next to his.

We got together and I raised all the problems with him, particularly the question of pushing through the development of some new front forks which I had been very keen to test and which I was sure would improve the handling of the bike. Not only would they be more rigid, but the changes in geometry were what I wanted for the fast corners.

Well, he said OK, and he also agreed that Arturo and I could make a new frame. All these things were his ideas, of course – he just gave the all-clear for us to proceed! That was the way things had to be done. In addition, an intense investigation was to be made of the engine component failures.

August came and, would you believe it, the new forks were ready! I had the opportunity to test them at Oulton Park on the August Bank Holiday Saturday and then in the British Championship race at Thruxton on the Monday. I was to ride my Norton in the 350 and the MV fitted with the revised front forks in the 500, ending up with two wins at both meetings.

Then it was off to the Ulster GP where, wouldn't you just guess, it was dull and drizzly. Bill Lomas was a non-starter, recovering from a broken shoulder sustained in Dutch TT practice, and I was the lone MV runner. In the 350 race I retired on lap 14 while challenging Keith Campbell's Guzzi for the lead. There were three Gileras in the race but McIntyre and Duke both retired later, resulting in a Guzzi 1-2 with Keith Bryen following Keith home and Liberati on the sole surviving Gilera third.

In the 500 I got away well and built up an ever-increasing lead over Liberati, with McIntyre running third ahead of Duke. I seemed to have the race well in hand, but on lap five I suffered another retirement. The order finally became another win for Liberati, second McIntyre and third Duke. That's the way things were going.

The following Saturday it was back to Crystal Palace and out with the NSU and the two Nortons. It was an enjoyable day, and I ended up with wins in the 250, 350 and 500 events, all at record speeds and with record laps. Mind you, Agusta wasn't too happy because the Italian papers were saying, 'Surtees doesn't need an MV to win,' and the team was generally getting rather a lot of stick in the press because of their constant retirements with engine failures.

By now the World Championship, which had remained a reality up until the Belgian Grand Prix, was out of reach for me. In the 350 race at Monza I got away into an early lead only to suffer another retirement. Montanari and Keith Bryen also retired, as well as Duke, which let McIntyre come home the winner from Colnago's Guzzi with Liberati third.

So to the 500. It was always going to be a hard race. We were down on maximum speed mainly because we took longer achieving it, largely as a result of the extra weight and bulk of the MV compared with the Gileras. There were no V8s running as Moto Guzzi had withdrawn after Campbell had a spill in practice.

The three Gileras were handled by Duke, Liberati and Alfredo Milani, the latter taking over from McIntyre who was suffering from a bad headache following the 350 race. MVs fielded, apart from myself, Bandirola, Masetti and Terry Shepherd.

Well, the race started off rather as I had imagined. The Gileras had a bit more steam, but I would get through the Curva Grande and the Lesmos a bit quicker, the new forks really tightening up the bike's handling and allowing me to be much more precise on these fast corners.

I went into the lead, Liberati passed me, then I overtook him again and we both pulled away from Milani and Duke. Then the engine went flat and suddenly died on the last lap, but I just managed to scrape home fourth. At least it was a finish, although not where we would have liked to have been and, of course, it meant that Liberati was World Champion.

It was a well deserved success, for he had been the fastest rider in the Gilera team, taking the overall European Grand Prix scene into account. He hadn't competed in the TT, which was understandable, but he had done an excellent job in the rest of the races and, to some extent, we had handed the title to him.

At the Scarborough international I was to face Geoff Duke, but we were both on Nortons. I won the 500 and led the 350 until it just stopped – magneto. Geoff actually rode the Norton with which Alan Rutherford was fourth in the Manx Grand Prix. In the 500, John Hartle was second and Jack Brett third.

And so to Silverstone, for the BMCRC Championships and Silver Jubilee 100 Hutchinson meeting. The track was damp and covered with rubber, as there had been a car race meeting the previous weekend. After all the problems with fairings on the MV, I had produced a Gilera-style fairing for the 350 Norton and it worked quite well. I just steamed away from the opposition, winning pretty easily, with John Hartle coming through to pip Peter Murphy's AJS for second place.

I had the MV out for the 500 race, comfortably winning with Alan Trow coming second on his Norton and John Clark's Guzzi single third. Geoff was again without a Gilera and rode a Norton once more, retiring at half-distance while lying tenth.

After Silverstone came Aintree; again, it was very wet. For this event I had both the 203 and 500 MVs, winning both races with Sandford second on the Mondial in the 250 while Derek Minter's Norton followed me home in the 500.

In early October, we returned to Oulton Park in ideal weather conditions and I was happy to shatter my race and lap records. In the 350 I led from the start on my Norton and in the 500, riding the MV, I also led all the way. Interestingly, Duke arrived with a new Norton equipped with a frame designed by Reynolds Tube, but he made a fairly bad start and was not in contention.

Back to Brands Hatch. This meeting produced a bit of a disappointment in the 350 race. I was having quite a close battle with Derek Minter, who had taken over as the Brands Hatch specialist since I had left to join MVs, but I thought I had him well in hand until the rear suspension of my bike started to misbehave. A rear damper rod had broken, something which was not too uncommon in those days, so I had to give best in that event. I had my revenge, however, as I managed to win the 500 and 1000 races, both at record speeds.

However, something very important had taken place before this. I had managed to sneak away to the BMW factory in Munich where I collected my 507 coupé. This was a 3.2-litre V8 sports car, a two-seater. A bit cramped for room, I suppose, but after having tried the Mercedes 300SL, but not deemed it suitable for my type of Continental driving between events, day in and day out, I had met up with BMW Chief Engineer Alex von Falkenhausen during the German Grand Prix at Hockenheim. He had with him this beautiful car.

I looked it over and thought how nice it was. He said, 'Take it for a drive,' so I took it for a run round the roads around Hockenheim and thought, 'This is for me.' I then thought, well, how can I set about getting one?

Agusta had wanted to give me a present after I had won the 1956 World Championship, but I had rather hesitated. Well, after that I broached the subject and told him that I would like a car. Then it was his turn to hesitate, because we were talking about almost £3000 at the exchange rate of around 11 Deutschmarks to the pound which then existed. Who says we haven't had a steadily devaluing pound when you think of today's exchange rate of 2.95!

Agusta didn't immediately respond, so we reached a deal where we put 50/50 in and I ordered the car. Now it was ready, and I was not only to use it right through to when I joined Ferrari in 1963, but I also have it to this very day. It is something of which I have very fond memories and, to my mind, the 507 coupé was one of the most underrated cars in the world.

Mind you, I did get the job of carrying out some test driving for BMW, so my model at least got an additional 40 bhp from the engine, plus disc brakes and an undershield, so it was a little different from standard. In this car, John Hartle and I were to whistle all round Europe to the various motor cycle races.

At the end of 1957, I was approached by Stan Hailwood who asked me whether I would loan him my NSU for Mike to ride. Well, to be honest, I didn't like to see it go, but eventually I thought, 'Why not?' So I loaned the bike to him, just for the South African events, and the next thing I heard was a request for a spare engine. I was reluctant to let this go, but thought, 'Oh well, as long as it is all going to be returned in as-new condition, that's fine.' Little did I know that I was never to see that bike again. However, that's another story.

Immediately after Monza there had been a bit of a shock when Gilera, Mondial and Moto Guzzi announced they were going to retire from racing. Despite the few improvements we had made towards the end of the season, I was pretty disillusioned with what had happened during 1957 with the MV team. We had thrown the World Championship away. There was no sound reason for the continuous unreliability that we had sustained, although outside suppliers and lack of quality control were, I thought, a prime cause.

Apart from the reliability problem with what was basically an aged design, we were not really making progress. The only improvements were achieved at the expense of continuously pushing, shoving and trying to demand. We needed a smaller, more compact engine and a more modern frame, but it was all taking far too long to come about. It could all have taken place so much quicker.

For this reason, when I was approached by Moto Guzzi's Engineer Carcano and asked to try their V8, I was obviously tempted. I had frankly been very impressed by this machine. There were things that I didn't like about it, but I thought it had enormous potential. So I jumped at the suggestion and said, 'Yes, I would love to try it.'

I was due to test the bike after the Italian Grand Prix and the announcement of their withdrawal came on the very day the test was scheduled to take place. Consequently, it was not until the early 1980s that I was in fact to have the opportunity to ride the Guzzi V8 and that brief trial told me that I would have been making the correct decision had I been able to join them in 1958. Clearly, it had fantastic potential and could hardly have been any less reliable than my 1957 MV.

In some ways, people might turn round and say how fortunate I was that I stayed with MVs. The team, in fact, asked me to sign a three-year contract. I thought long and hard about this, but there were assurances that, yes, we could go ahead and build another frame. They also agreed to build a smaller, more compact 350, and said that there would be further developments in the 250 class and perhaps the opportunity of some rides in that category. This latter development never materialised, which was a matter of some sadness for me, as I would have loved to have ridden one of the full-size 250 singles, or the later twins, particularly in the Isle of Man.

Arturo Magni and I gave a lot of thought to putting a better frame round the MV engine. There was no way we were going to install an engine without having a removable tube somewhere, so we put the engine up on one of the benches and placed the tubes round it much in the fashion of a Norton-type frame, but with the two bottom tubes beneath the engine being removable.

This frame actually had a relatively large hump over the top of the inlet camshaft and, as a consequence, became known as 'the camel'. During testing it immediately showed that we had found a bit more speed. The engines, meanwhile, had undergone more development and, although they were not producing more power, they were running more reliably both on the test beds and when installed in the bikes during these tests.

This was in part due to new component suppliers and a little more careful thought as regards internal clearances, while – a very important factor – full streamlining was no longer permitted under the new regulations. As a result, engine cooling was significantly improved and the troubles of the previous year disappeared. It was not that the engines were not having to be pushed so hard, because all our lap speeds in 1958 were faster than those set during the previous year. The bike was simply more ridable and the power that was available from the engine could be utilised to a far greater extent.

The year started with Gilbert Smith, who had played such a part in the story of Nortons, resigning as their Managing Director. Some people might say he had a negative role, but I would credit him with having achieved more than that. Perhaps he was not the man of greatest vision, but he had a very difficult position to deal with. He was followed by Bert Hopwood and, despite what you may read in his book, we all know what he did – or, shall I say, what he didn't do.

This would have been the ideal opportunity for British companies to have again renewed their attack on the World Championship. Norton developments had not stopped and the latest machines were, at times, going extremely quickly. With very little money it would have been possible to have mounted a serious onslaught on the World Championship scene. After all, look what Stan Hailwood's money, together with Mike and the brilliant preparation of Bill Lacey managed to achieve with some of the Norton machines.

Next, I was off to Monza to test the six-cylinder MV. I frankly had not been too much in favour of the machine. It had a very nice frame, which was later virtually to be copied for the 350 development of 'the camel', but there did not appear to be much point. What we still needed was a smaller, more compact engine, taking Gilera's progress a stage further, not a more cumbersome machine, and the six was just that.

If, for instance, it had been able to run at something like 14,000 rpm with a four-valve head, and power to match, then perhaps, even with its bulk, there would have been something to be said for it. But for safety reasons, that's to say because of valve springs, it still only revved to around 11,000 whereas the four-cylinder could be run up to 10,800 in top gear.

It did have a six-speed gearbox which later, after 1960, was transferred into the four-cylinder, and this was used by Mike Hailwood when he joined MVs. Fortunato Libanori, who did a bit of test riding for the family Agusta, and also a little Italian Championship racing, was also present at the Monza test trying out the experimental 125 twin. Libanori also took the opportunity to try the 350 and 500 fours and I had a run to test out the new frames which we had made.

I was not in England for Easter as MV had decided that I should race at the Imola Gold Cup. There were no 350s fielded – I don't know why – but only a couple of 500s for Remo Venturi and myself. We finished first and second and Jack Ahearn on his Norton was third. I must say that I really enjoyed the Imola circuit and it was rather nice to score my final car racing win there, in the Surtees TS10 F2 car, and end up on the winner's rostrum some 14 years later.

Geoff Duke was to ride one of the works BMWs of the type that had been used by Walter Zeller and, of course, had gone so quickly in the hands of Fergus Anderson before he was so tragically killed at Floreffe. Dickie Dale was also to get a BMW ride, although initially his was to be a private entry.

Then it was off to Barcelona again to stir memories of that dice with Bandirola and that rather weak arm after my accident. By now all those problems were behind me. One of the MVs was loaned to a local chap, Francisco Gonzalez, but I am afraid he tried to go a little bit too quickly, fell off and ended up breaking a finger.

I had a good ride and came home without any problems in first place at the end of the 500 event. There was no 350 race and I had no entry in the 250. By now it was becoming clear that there was considerable opposition to me riding my private machines. A pair of MVs were given to me for Mettet and this time John Hartle had a chance in the 500. I won both classes and John followed me home in the 500 event.

Then it was back to West Wickham, in Kent, where we had started our motor cycle business late in 1957. The original idea was that Father would take a bit of an interest, which he did, and that my brother Norman would spend virtually all his time there as manager. That didn't quite work out, as Norman tended to get his interests, shall we say, rather confused at times. But just the same, it was a nice business, and I had to think about what I might do when I was a retired rider. In those days you had to plan for the future because you were certainly not going to be able to earn enough to set yourself up for an easy, non-active retirement.

As I have said before, how fortunate I was as a sportsman to actually be paid for doing what I loved. But I would have liked to be doing a bit more of it. I was getting a little frustrated by the lack of races available to me and, particularly, by not being able to use my own machines in domestic British races.

Back in the Isle of Man for the Junior TT, at the end of the opening lap I found myself having to come into the pits. I had suddenly run into a swarm of flies; one moment I could see, the next moment my goggles were totally covered. We also didn't take any chances with pit stops and had two more to top up with fuel. After setting fastest lap, I won comfortably with Dave Chadwick's Norton finally finishing in second place. Poor John Hartle rather inherited my mantle from 1957 and retired on the opening lap.

In the Senior TT, Jack Ahearn had one of the new-style Matchless G50s, Duke the works BMW, Dale his Rennsport BMW and, of course, there were a host of Nortons, including the works development bikes. After a standing-start first lap at just under 99 mph I had a good lead over Bob McIntyre on the Joe Potts 90-bore Norton and John Hartle with the second MV, who again had a dreadful time when his machine actually caught fire. For me, it was rather nice to score a TT double.

Before we reappeared at Assen for the Dutch TT we were sadly to hear that John Clark from Portsmouth, who had been going particularly well on the short circuits, had been killed in an accident at Moulins, in France. Again I scored a 350/500 double, but on this occasion John Hartle had a better day and finished second to me in both events. It was good for me to see, as I had been instrumental in getting him to join us.

The Belgian Grand Prix produced another double, but what was most encouraging was that, with virtually no more power, I put 5 mph onto the lap record established by Keith Campbell on the Guzzi V8. Just a little bit of development, and sorting out the frame, had been the answer here. Oh, if only they had acted a little earlier, we could have kept that championship in 1957. John again followed me home in the 350, but Keith Campbell's Norton split us in second place at the end of the 500 event, with Geoff Duke fourth on the BMW.

Then came the German Grand Prix at the Nürburgring, as it was then a fabulous circuit, although it was raining. This meeting confirmed me as 350 and 500 double World Champion. I was able to win the 350 with John Hartle second and Campbell third, as well as the 500 with John again second and, this time, Gary Hocking's Norton third.

Clinching the title that early actually worked against me, because MVs decided not to send the large machines to Hedemora, where I had last competed in 1955 for the Norton works team, so I did not get a ride. I was not to be in the saddle again until the Ulster Grand Prix, where rain and low-level cloud made things difficult. Well, it was the Ulster! It was also my fifth double win. Here in the 350 John Hartle followed me home with Terry Shepherd's Norton third, while in the 500 McIntyre's Norton split us and John finished in third place.

Back on the home circuits, it was nice to see that my little NSU – over which I finally had to do a deal with Stan Hailwood because I couldn't get it back! – was still enjoying success; Mike won the BMCRC Hutchinson 100 event as well as a string of other successes at Brands Hatch, Mallory Park and elsewhere.

For me, the next event was to be the Italian Grand Prix. In the 350 race, John and I really got the small fours going and we lapped the entire field. In the 500, John was to use the six-cylinder MV. He made a poor start, hauled back to fourth and retired at around half-distance. It was the last time, to my knowledge, that the six would be seen in competition, although a revised version was later produced. I won the race with Venturi second.

I then decided that I was tired of spending too much time sitting on the sidelines. I prepared my two Nortons for Scarborough, but MVs said 'no', although they agreed that I should have a couple of bikes for the end-of-season races.

Well, I didn't get to Scarborough, but I did go to Aintree late in September where I won the 350 and 500 races as well as the handicap, in which I had to put over 3 mph onto the lap record in order to catch Dave Chadwick, a lap record which had been set by Geoff Duke on the Gilera when he had been attempting to catch me during that memorable race in 1955.

Then we headed south for the special Mallory Park 40-lap challenge in which I rode the 500, coming in first ahead of Bob Anderson, who rode a super race on his Norton. At the next Oulton Park meeting, both 350 and 500 wins came my way, and then it was back down to Brands Hatch for what was going to be a real challenge since the MV fours had never quite coped with the circuit.

I won the 350 event; surprisingly, really, because I still thought the Norton would have the edge on me there. I just got pipped by Derek Minter in the 500 race and even had to hurry to finish second, because John Holder with his Norton was really on form and pushing me all the way. But it was a good ride which I enjoyed.

So into 1959. I was still pushing hard for the MV team to improve and, in particular, to make a smaller and more compact engine/gearbox unit. But I didn't seem to be getting anywhere. We could make detail improvements and I kept well in touch with all the developments going on among the accessory manufacturers, particularly as regards tyre development. I had an especially good relationship with both Dunlop and Avon: I would test both and then use what proved to be the best.

This normally turned out to be the Avons. I would go along sometimes and test a new Dunlop and find that, in fact, it did have an edge. But then it would only be a week or so before I received a call from Avon and, sure enough, they would have made another step forward.

On another front, I was going to build up another Manx Norton and a 350, but also a special powered by an AJS engine. I bought from AJS one of their works 7Rs. This was basically standard, although it did feature a slightly different cylinder head and 7R3 flywheels of the type they were using in their own works machines.

I had tried the standard bike in testing and was surprised how quick it was, although I felt we could build something lighter and certainly a little tighter in terms of its chassis. I approached Anthony Reynolds of Reynolds Tube and they agreed to build me some modified Norton frames and, using some sketches that I had done for the special AJS frame, they prepared me some drawings.

I duly received these and we showed them as offering either a short- or long-circuit type, the main difference being a slightly different configuration relative to how the tubes ran up to the steering head. That bike was built up during the winter, as was the Norton.

For the Norton, I went to Harry Weslake and carried out with him a fair amount of work in connection with the cylinder head gas flow to see if any improvements could be made. In the event, we improved the gas flow significantly, but the engine certainly never performed any better than a nicely prepared standard Norton head.

MV, meanwhile, had tested experimental desmodromic 125 and 250 twins, mainly because of the success which Ducati had previously achieved, but again I was a little perturbed that all the work seemed to be going into these categories while they simply expected me to produce a little more from myself on the 350s and 500s.

During the Easter meeting at Modena which opened the 1959 season, Libero Liberati had given rather a fright to the MV team. First of all, he had been leading the 250 race on a double-overhead-camshaft Morini until he retired with some sort of ignition problem, and then on a special Gilera Saturno he had been in front of the MV fours of Venturi and Ernesto Brambilla until a pit stop meant that he had to settle for third.

My first ride of the year was to be at Imola in April. I had a good run in the 500 to win with John Hartle second and Gary Hocking's Norton third. The meeting was marred by tragedy when Harry Hinton Jnr actually got up to third and then crashed fatally at just about the same spot as Ray Amm had in 1955. I was so alarmed that I stopped momentarily at the pits to report the accident before continuing on my way. The 250 race was won by Dickie Dale's Benelli single.

Back to England for Silverstone and an icy-cold, wet and windy start to the day. Mike Hailwood won the 250 and I won the 350 with a record lap on the MV four. Prior to this meeting, however, I had been testing the little AJS special and had lapped faster with it than I was subsequently to manage on the MV while establishing the lap record.

The rain started to come down again for the 500 event and I suppose I must have had one of those lapses; I don't quite know. Perhaps it was some oil on the track but, after getting away comfortably, going into Club Corner on the first lap I lost it completely. It was something of a rarity for me to fall off at that stage in my career, but it was quite a big accident which was to have further repercussions relative to my getting permission from MV to race in non-championship events.

So, I didn't get to Mettet. I didn't get to Austria, where a Grand Prix was held on part of the autobahn near Salzburg. John was given an MV four and won the 500 event, but I didn't get my next ride until the French Grand Prix at Clermont-Ferrand. I won the 350 with the MV, ahead of Hocking's Norton and John Hartle's MV, but for the 500 Domenico had decided to replace John with Venturi who, in turn, finished second behind me.

Then it was round to the Junior TT again on the Isle of Man. I was unchallenged, but McIntyre had a dice with John Hartle for some distance before his nose fairing came loose, so John followed me home in second with the Nortons of Alistair King, Geoff Duke and Bob Anderson following up.

The Senior TT promised to be something else. This was one of the worst events that I ever rode in. It rained, there were gale-force winds and there was hail so strong that it was capable of stripping the paint from the fairings on the MV!

It was necessary to dodge between puddles and judge your position on the road with regard to where the machine might go when you went past an opening and the crosswind caught it, taking it from one side to another.

I had to adopt a totally new strategy, and it was something which I said at the time I never wanted to experience again. In fact, at the end of the race I virtually had to be lifted off the bike as my hands were so frozen. John Hartle unfortunately had an accident which broke his wrist while I finished first, with Alistair King following me home.

Thankfully, the German Grand Prix at Hockenheim took place in somewhat better weather and I had good races in both the 350 and 500 events, winning them both. The Jawa twins of Frantisek Stastny and Gustav Havel showed their paces at this event. They were always quick, but they tended to be let down by little things. One often wondered what they might achieve if they managed to get real top-class riders and got their organisation a little more in tune. Well, on this occasion they did not get things together, but Stastny did come sixth.

On again to the Dutch TT at Assen where I was able to clinch the 500 world title, winning the race from Bob Brown's Norton, Venturi's MV and Dickie Dale on the works BMW, which had previously been handled by Duke. There was no 350 race held on this occasion.

The Belgian Grand Prix again did not feature a 350 race for the works machines, but I smashed my own 500 race and lap records, averaging over 119 mph in very hot conditions. After that it was up to Scandinavia where the Swedish Grand Prix was due to be held at Kristianstad; on this occasion there was no 500 race for us, only a 350.

John Hartle was back in the MV squad, the two of us streaking away and having quite a dice, with Bob Brown following along behind us, pulling away from Mike Hailwood, Dickie Dale and Ken Kavanagh, who were all enjoying their own battle some way further back. Without being disloyal to my own team, it was nice to see the East German MZ team having some success at this meeting, with Gary Hocking surprisingly winning the 250 race from Ubbiali on the MV twin.

With no permission forthcoming to use my own bikes in the British Championship, my next outing was the Ulster GP, where we enjoyed good weather for once with every race and lap record being broken. The 125 MVs were not sent over, but John Hartle was to partner me in the 350s and 500s. In the smaller-capacity race I got away first, but John set up a record lap on the second tour. He didn't get by and, on lap seven, he unfortunately went wide, hit the bank and damaged his foot. McIntyre and Hailwood both retired their AJSs with broken valve springs, leaving Bob Brown to come home second with Duke in third place.

The 250 race, again with MV absent, saw Hocking win again on the MZ with Hailwood following up on the ex-works Mondial. The 500 turned out to be a good event for me.

All went well and I won, this time from Bob Mac, who came in second.

After those good rides in both Sweden and Hockenheim, we had a word with Gary Hocking and he was invited to join the MV team to ride in the 125 and 250 classes, but to come in on the big ones when he was required. I thought for a moment that I might be able to use this as a lever – that as Gary might have a ride on the 350s and 500s, I might have a ride on the 250s, but this was not to be!

I then went on to the Italian Grand Prix where I won both classes and set up new lap records. As I wasn't to be allowed any machines for the end-of-season British events, the only other race I had on my schedule was a special event put on in honour of General Franco in Madrid.

This was to be held through the city's central park and I duly arrived early to view the circuit on which I was to ride only in the 500 event. It was a typical park-style circuit. Polished by continuous traffic, it was largely made up of wet tar in the really hot weather. This was going to be extremely slippery and there was one particular long left-hander which seemed extremely treacherous.

So what did I see being built on the outside of this corner, just at the point one might expect a bike to end up if you got it all wrong, but a grandstand! When I enquired, I found out that this was to be the special stand for General Franco himself. After I had explained some of the problems to the organisers, they did in fact move it slightly further round the corner.

Race day dawned and we lined up on the startline, joined on this occasion by Bandirola. I made a good start, and came round on the opening lap only to see a bunch of people who then moved back to let me through. This is virtually how it continued to the end of the race, with the people crowding in and then just moving back at the last moment to let you go screaming through on a 500 MV on full chat. Whether it was frightening for them or not, I'm not sure. It was certainly terrifying for me!

Thankfully, the event went off without any major hiccups. I won from Bandirola and that brought to an end my 1959 season. Yes, it had been a successful one where, apart from the Silverstone events, we had done most things right. I had tried to keep the team on the boil as regards little technical developments – we certainly were not getting any big ones – but it was a year in which I had been frankly disappointed not to be able to ride more often, and particularly to ride my own machines.

I had a long talk with Count Agusta at the end of that year, but he seemed set: 'No, you will do World Championship events only.' The story of my meeting up with Tony Vandervell and Mike Hawthorn is told elsewhere within these pages, so you can see what happened in that connection.

So I sold my little AJS special to Rex Butcher, who used it for a while before it ended up in the hands of Tom Arter where its potential was seen and, of course, it then became the Arter-AJS and the Arter-Matchless, becoming the fastest single-cylinder round the Isle of Man. It certainly fulfilled the promise that I had anticipated when I first built the machine and tested it at Silverstone.

As for my 500 Nortons, well, the lightweight model, fitted with an MV front wheel, went to Stan Hailwood. So in 1960 I was due to start the motor cycle racing season for the first time without some of my own privately prepared machines there at the ready.

Yes, I still had the majority of one of my Manx Nortons. I had parts of the NSU, but not

the original bike, and I had a lot of Vincent parts, both for the works Grey Flashes and my big-twin special, and components for a second AJS-Matchless special. But I was not to have the back-up, for Agusta had made it clear that I was under contract and that that had to be adhered to.

The main reason for his stance was not so much the accident at Silverstone, it was the Italian press, who took the attitude: 'Yes, you can say Surtees wins because of the MV, but the fact remains that he beats all the same people if he rides his Nortons. So he doesn't need an MV to win.'

If I coldly analyse the situation, this was absolutely correct, but it certainly stopped Domenico from giving me necessary support. I don't believe it was really in his interest, though, because some of the development I carried out on my own machines was very useful in helping the development of the MVs as well. As subsequent years proved, many of the ways in which MV developments progressed were in line with suggestions that I had pressed for in earlier years.

For 1960, then, I faced a new challenge. I was to involve myself in racing a car. There was nothing in my contract to prevent that and this transitional phase is well covered in the following chapter, so I will now touch on what else happened in the bike world.

Desmos? Yes. Ducati had built some 250s and, in fact, two 350s. These were twin-cylinders and again, it was Stan Hailwood, with the backing of Kings of Oxford, who had gone to Ducati and commissioned their manufacture. If the performance of their smaller-capacity bikes was anything to go by, they could well pose a challenge. Ken Kavanagh was to get one of the 350s.

Norton and AJS were still carrying on their development programmes and there was the Jawa programme, which deserved more success. My first race of the year was in the Cooper Formula Junior car at Goodwood but, somewhat to my surprise, suddenly I found myself entered by MV for one of the Italian Championship events at Cesenatico.

I was to ride just the 500, with Hocking competing in the 125 and 250 events. I duly won the 500 and Hocking came second in the 250 behind Ubbiali, and won the 125. These events were always fascinating because of the tremendous enthusiasm of the Italian public, although these little streets round the seaside town along the Adriatic were, in fact, extremely dangerous.

The circuit was highly polished and you found yourself steering round drain covers and various other obstacles in the road, not to mention trees, lampposts and people running across the track. It was rather like being back in Madrid, not quite as bad perhaps, but, just the same, you never quite knew how wide the circuit would be the next time you came round.

We didn't have John Hartle with us that year. Agusta decided not to renew his contract, so John was back on Nortons. This was a shame, as it frankly hadn't been his fault. He had suffered a series of mishaps with the MVs and it would have been nice to have given him a little longer to come good.

I rode at Imola next, only in the 500. John was challenging Venturi before he slipped off, so Remo followed me home in second place. I wasn't allowed to go to the non-championship Austrian race; I missed Mettet and all the other non-championship events that were taking place, right up until the French Grand Prix at Clermont-Ferrand which I describe in detail in Chapter 3.

For the Isle of Man TT, John Hartle was drafted back into the MV team, which was nice to see, but, shades of 1957, things were going to start going wrong for me. I went off at the start of the Junior race and led for five laps, raising the lap record to just under 100 mph. Then I lost first gear, then I lost third, and so it became a question of nursing the bike home, keeping it in one gear for as much of the circuit as possible.

John came home the winner and I was able to scrape home second with Bob McIntyre coming up behind on the AJS. In the Senior, I made no mistake and the bike didn't let me down. I set a new record lap from a standing start and quickly opened a good lead over John who, in turn, finished quite well up on Mike Hailwood's Norton.

As usual, the Dutch TT came next, only a week later; Ubbiali won the 250, but the 350 was saddened by the death of Peter Ferbrache, a rider whom I could recall from the beginning of the Fifties when I had started racing. The race went well for me, however, and I stayed ahead of Hocking and Stastny on the Jawa.

The 500 race, on the other hand, did not go well for me. I had three pit stops trying to rectify a misfire, setting me back something in the order of six minutes. Frankly, I then just went too quickly and overdid it; I broke the lap record and then, on one of the fast corners, just used a little too much road and lost it.

For the 500 race in Belgium, my bike was sorted out again and I lapped in practice at over 120 mph. In the race itself, my average speed was faster than the previous year's lap record and Venturi followed me home, some way behind. Next came the first meeting to be held on the lengthened 2.65-mile Brands Hatch circuit and, in showery weather, Mike Hailwood had something of a field day. It wasn't going too badly for me either, as I took second place in the British Grand Prix – using four wheels on a Lotus!

The German Grand Prix this year switched back to the splendid Solitude circuit, where it would be particularly interesting for me as I was to compete with both cars and bikes at the same meeting. I drove the Rob Walker Porsche in the Formula 2 event and the MV in the 500. Again, the meeting was saddened by the death of a friend and a really fine competitor, Bob Brown from Australia. He was killed in practice riding one of the new Honda fours; a very sad event indeed.

I clinched the 500 world title with another win, but wasn't quite so successful on four wheels, putting the car in a ditch after messing up a gearchange!

Back over to Ireland and it was time for my last Ulster Grand Prix, where my main opposition in the 350 event was to be Stastny on the Jawa, but I managed to lead all the way and won at a record 93.39 mph. I had quite a dice in the early stages with Alan Shepherd who was riding superbly; his AJS was really flying, but he retired on the fifth lap.

I was deeply disappointed that MV chose to challenge the size of the AJS engine with a protest. I had been telling them time and again, and had shown them timing sheets to indicate that I had actually lapped faster than the MV with my own AJS special. I am sure that, some of the time, the ease with which I was able to win races was partly a result of the psychological effect of my previous successes on the short circuits and my rivals being mesmerised by the fact I was on a four-cylinder. There were opportunities in a number of those races for some people to have given me a much tougher time than they did, and I believe this is partly because they were beaten before the flag had dropped for the start!

I streaked away from the start of the 500 race, but what happened? The gear lever broke off and I lost three minutes in the pits for repairs, going back out in 42nd place. I did not make the mistake I had made in Holland. I repeatedly broke my own lap record as I gobbled up my lost advantage. On lap 16 I managed a record of 99.32 mph and finished only 20 seconds behind race winner John Hartle.

Mind you, if anybody was going to win apart from myself, I would have liked it to be John. At Oulton Park, meanwhile, brother Norman had a win on the AJS, thus keeping up the Surtees tradition.

Finally, off to Monza for the last professional motor cycle race of my life. I was not to sit on a race bike again, apart from a little testing with the desmo Ducatis I was to obtain from Stan Hailwood when I decided to close my motor cycle business in West Wickham in order to concentrate on my car racing, for something like 18 years.

We did quite a lot of work on these 250 and 350 desmos and I even thought about doing one or two races. One of the reasons that I ended up with them was that I had been quite impressed when following Mike at speed on the 350 during the 1960 Italian Grand Prix meeting. It had been just as quick as the 350 MV and I thought it had a lot of potential. In turn, Stan had other things in mind and was about to do a series of deals which would eventually take Mike through to join Gary Hocking in the MV team after I retired.

So, we come to the 1960 Italian Grand Prix at Monza. I had wetted my feet in car racing and I wasn't getting anywhere in relation to what I wanted to do in bike racing. I wanted to race more; if I couldn't ride my private machines, then I needed works machines on more occasions or to be allowed to do another class as well. But none of this was forthcoming, so it was better to call it a day as I still had a further year of my contract to run.

For Monza, Gary Hocking was to join me on a 350 MV four with the usual back-up from Masetti, and Venturi was to be in the 500 class. The 350 started quite well with Hocking behind and I watched carefully, taking a peep over my shoulder, coming out of the second Lesmo and found that I could pull out a nice distance through those two corners, which was quite important for the speed one could attain along the back straight.

Suddenly, I lost revs and the engine went flat. It didn't feel as though it was a mechanical fault, but it had definitely lost its edge. Hocking pulled alongside, pointing downwards. I look down and what is dangling from the stays but a pair of megaphones. I come into the pits and retire; not a very nice start to the day.

The 500 went very well, but disaster nearly struck there as well. Another machine blew up just before Parabolica, the flags didn't come out and I arrived and saw the oil too late. I almost lost it, got up on the footrests and had to go straight on onto the outfield, and only just turned the bike in time to no more than glance the bank.

As I did so, it caught my left foot rather badly and tore off my boot, but luckily I stayed on. I motored back onto the circuit and continued on to win. It was nice to finish like that in what was to be my last race.

After that, I told Domenico Agusta that was the end of the line. I had succeeded in racing because I raced the way I believed I should race. I wasn't doing sufficient racing and I believed that my skills were still developing and I was certainly not necessarily at my peak.

There were now new horizons which offered new challenges and so I was turning my back on motor cycles. I said I was not concerned about leaving the company as they had the prospect of good riders: Gary Hocking was very competent and I felt he could do a good job for them, and they could still call on John Hartle whom, again, I could recommend.

So I had no doubts that I was doing the correct thing. Initially, there was some anger. It was looked upon as an affront that I should decide to tell them that I was not going to be part of the Agusta family any more.

Later on this animosity showed itself to be only skin deep. In many ways it was quite an honour that, as I recount later in this book, of all the riders who rode MVs, I was the only one who, during his lifetime, was given one of his own racing machines.

Chapter 3
On Two Wheels and Four

At the end of 1958 I was invited to the Sportsman of the Year gathering and found myself on the same table as Tony Vandervell, Mike Hawthorn and Reg Parnell. Tony's Vanwalls had just won the Formula 1 Constructors' World Championship through the efforts of Stirling Moss, Tony Brooks and Stuart Lewis-Evans, but Mike had taken the drivers' title in the Ferrari. Reg, of course, was the highly respected team manager for the Aston Martin sports car team which would go on to win Le Mans in 1959 with the DBR1, having in the past been an accomplished driver in his own right.

Tony Vandervell had, in effect, a foot in both the two-wheel and four-wheel camps. He was a great motor cycling enthusiast and the family had been directors of Norton back in the 1930s. It was only after Norton's refusal to go along with the development of multi-cylinder engines that Tony decided to remove himself from the Board and go off to do his own thing.

He was also inspired in this by his involvement with the BRM Trust. He found that he couldn't get on with the other partners and instead decided that he would build his own Grand Prix car, the Vanwall. He still had, as a gift from Norton, one of Harold Daniell's TT-winning 'Garden Gate' bikes converted for road use. He had also encouraged Leo Kuzmicki, the very talented Polish engineer who had come to Nortons and been respon-sible for developing the squish-type cylinder head that was employed on the short-stroke Manx Norton engines, to apply his efforts to a Vanwall racing car engine. In effect, the first Vanwall engine was four big Norton engines linked together, developed with a few tweaks which were still to be incorporated on the works Norton bikes which were still being operated by Joe Craig.

Anyway, we all fell into conversation, with Mike and I discussing motor cycle trials, in which we both enjoyed competing. We were chatting about the forthcoming Pressmans Trial, which was scheduled to take place in the Bagshot area later that winter, and agreed to go together. We chatted loosely about the difference in the technique required by two- and four-wheeled racing machines, and were due to meet again in London when Mike was killed in a road accident on the Guildford Bypass in his Jaguar 3.4 saloon in January 1959.

Before his death, Mike had remarked to me, 'Four wheels do stand up better than two, you know. Give it up. Have a go at four!' I just shrugged it aside, saying something like, 'No, no, no . . . that's not for me . . . I'm a motor cyclist,' and never really thought any more about it, except that Tony Vandervell had remarked that I ought to have a try at the wheel of one of his cars and Reg Parnell also made a similar invitation.

To be honest, I didn't think a great deal more about all this until one day in October 1959 when I received a telephone call from Reg Parnell asking me whether I would like to come down to Goodwood and have a run in the Aston Martin DBR1 which Stirling had used to win the Nürburgring 1000 Km. Out of interest I asked whether my team-mate John Hartle could tag along for the day, and Reg said this would be fine, so we both hopped into my BMW 507 and went off to Goodwood, a circuit which I had never seen before, one morning a few weeks later.

It's worth mentioning at this stage that, apart from seeing the odd race car at the docks, where I recall chatting to George Abecassis as he was off to do a Mille Miglia reconnaissance in the HWM, and being at Monza when the Grand Prix cars were practising prior to the 1958 Italian Grand Prix, I had never seen a racing car, even less sat in one. The first car race I ever actually saw was the first I took part in!

We were told that this car had been specially fitted with a Maserati gearbox, something which wasn't to be mentioned at the time because, of course, David Brown, who owned Aston Martin, were transmission people and this was virtual sacrilege!

The weather was cold, but conditions were pretty good apart from a few damp patches on a couple of corners. I completed about 30 laps with a fastest time of 1m 33s. Almost before I had climbed out of the car, Reg Parnell was at my elbow saying, 'Right, we would like you to sign a contract to drive next year.' But still my reaction was 'No, no . . . I'm a motor cyclist. I'm not really thinking of making the switch . . .'

I must admit, though, that the Aston felt good. It was a fabulously forgiving car, which was a big benefit to somebody as inexperienced as I was, having never driven a racing car before. Its engine was very flexible and I have very fond memories of the test. The Aston DBR1 is certainly one car I would like to have in my own personal collection. It would be very nice to own one, but the sort of money they command today will probably rule that out!

Since that day I had decided I wasn't going to be at the mercy of the English weather any longer on my trips back and forward from home in Addington to the Vincent factory in Stevenage, and I purchased my first car, the Jowett Jupiter, I had enjoyed a succession of high-performance cars. Subsequent to the Jowett, I had a Porsche 356 Super, which was a fabulous little machine in which I had my first experience of spinning a car when I put it into a ditch near the boundary fence of Hatfield House late one night when a couple of curves caught me out in wintry conditions.

Later, because of the need for a bit more space when I was travelling round Britain, I thought that an Aston Martin would be the answer. I part-exchanged the Porsche for a DB2/4 with a lift-up tailgate which was ideal for all my kit, spare parts, odd engine bits and so on. Then, in 1956, I very nearly became the owner of a Mercedes 300SL. In fact, I think I did actually own it for about a week . . .

The car looked fabulous. I had seen it in the showrooms of Rose and Young, the Mercedes dealers in Streatham. My father had known John Young, so I spoke to him and arranged to go along and see it. He said, 'Try it, John; take it away and drive it.' So that's what I did.

In those days, of course, such expenditure would obviously require a degree of financing. I talked with my father about it and even contacted one of his finance companies to see what we could do. I think we spoke to North West Securities on this matter.

It so happened that, while I was testing the car, my mother, who unfortunately suffered rather badly from rheumatic fever, had a visit from the doctor. He saw this 300SL and raved about it. He said, 'I would love a ride,' so off we went.

At that time we were living in Catford, so we went up onto the Sidcup Bypass. This was one of my first experiences with the car. One of the things which had made me think about buying it was that Count Agusta had said, 'If you can win the championship, we will do something for you rather special.' This was a short time before my accident at Solitude.

So off we went; into second, third, into top. We touched about 100 mph. And we ran into rain. I must say, I had a rather frightening moment and just about lost it. The 300SL was certainly a car you needed to know well, particularly the standard version on cross-ply tyres and without the stiffened suspension or any other tricks. It could be rather sudden in its characteristics.

It slid one way. I caught it. Then it fishtailed the other way. I caught that too. And so we went up the road in a series of zig-zags, sorting it all out between one kerb and the other. Eventually it came back under control, as much through luck as skill. The doctor went very quiet and remained so until we got home!

He went straight in to see my mother and said, 'He can't have that car, Mrs Surtees, don't let him buy it. He'll kill himself . . .' This carried on and on and, while Mother never brought any pressure on me, she did urge me to think twice about it all.

Well, I was thinking twice about it. It wasn't that I was worried about its handling, but, in fact, the £3000-odd that the car would cost was going to put a real strain on our finances. In addition, if John Hartle and I were going to jump into it and head off to race meetings all over Europe, there was hardly any room. All things considered, I went back to John Young and told him that it wasn't really for me. So that was my touch with the SL.

Then it was on to the 507, the story of which continues through to the present time as I still own that car. I'm still very fond of it and it holds many special memories.

So, back to Goodwood. All in all, it was a very different experience, which was very pleasing because they all said, 'You're going as quickly as anybody has gone round here in this car,' but I still shied away from making a commitment. So they asked me down for a couple more test sessions, and I eventually got the hang of the DBR1 to the point where I lapped at 1m 35s on a totally wet circuit.

One of the mechanics looking after the car was Jimmy Potton, who comes into the story again, as he worked on a number of my Grand Prix cars, including the English end of the Honda operation, and was also in at the start of Team Surtees. Later, he would become responsible for maintaining Trojan boss Peter Agg's collection of cars, and these days he concentrates on the restoration of classic cars.

I remember seeing a DBR1 in recent years at Silverstone and mentioning to some so-called experts that I had once driven one fitted with a Maserati gearbox. They pooh-poohed the notion and told me that this just wasn't the case. But the facts remain firm: when I drove it, it was equipped with a Maserati gearbox!

According to my diary, on 5 January 1960 the third of these tests took place and they also brought along the Aston Martin DBR4 front-engined F1 car for me to try. I managed a 1m 32s best with that, but couldn't really understand why it felt a lot more nervous and unpredictable. Roy Salvadori, one of the team's regular drivers, was also present and he hopped in for a few laps before reporting that something was really quite badly wrong with the car. On closer examination, the team found that the chassis had broken, so that was that. It was loaded up and taken away!

Reg was still pressing me to sign for Astons, but I kept fending him off, saying that my lack of track experience on four wheels, not to mention my continuing motor cycle commitments with MV, really made it impossible to reach a deal. Anyway, no sooner had word got out about my tests for Aston Martin than Tony Vandervell was on the phone saying, 'What the hell are you driving that so-and-so for?'

I won't describe the exact words he used because Tony wasn't really a big Aston Martin fan. For some reason, he didn't consider the likes of David Brown to be the sort of people who should be running racing teams. Anyway, he remarked rather gruffly, 'You're only supposed to be driving a Vanwall. We will bring one down to Goodwood for you to test.' So David Yorke, their team manager, duly appeared at the track the very next day with one of the 1958 cars and, according to my diary again, I managed to lap in 1m 26.4s.

The Vanwall was a big car and I particularly recall how I had to climb up onto a rear wheel in order to drop into the large cockpit. I was very impressed with the whole Vanwall organisation and, I like to think, they with me. But inexperience was almost my undoing on this particular occasion.

David Yorke said to me, 'You're getting round here quicker than anybody else apart from Stirling.' In fact, Stirling was a fraction quicker and we later fell into conversation at a press conference, during which he happened to mention that he managed to get through the very fast Fordwater right-hander – which was always a bit of a teaser – without lifting off.

So I thought . . . well, if he can do it, maybe I'll go through without lifting. By that time I had already been round Goodwood as fast as the Vanwall had ever gone. So I tried to follow Stirling's advice, but ended having the most almighty spin which took me a long way off the track into the winter oats which had been planted on the infield. But before this off, I had the satisfaction of pipping Stirling's fastest time.

I came back the following day for another run about which the notes in my diary read: 'track not as good as the previous day.' I did 60 laps on fresh Dunlops and this time got down to 1m 27.4s, using maximum revs of 7400.

Vandervell was very excited and enthusiastic about my performance, although, of course, the team by this stage had been withdrawn from racing for more than a year. Frankly, Tony Vandervell hadn't been all that well and his staff were very anxious that he shouldn't get too excited or worked up.

All this experience of four wheels rather encouraged me to tell Count Agusta that, since he didn't seem to want me to race other bikes outside the World Championship series, I would start driving cars. There wasn't anything in my contract with MVs to prevent that, so on 14 January 1960 I had a meeting with Tony Vandervell at which we reached a verbal agreement that, if he should build a car, I would do a number of races for him, and that he would act as my manager to ensure that I wouldn't lose out in any way by making the switch to cars.

The following day I saw Reg Parnell and told him that I was going to work along with Vandervell. I thought that course of action would probably enable me to learn more, but I realised that I would need to get some car racing experience pretty quickly, so I went out and bought my own car!

During this period, I went through some personal turmoil as to what might be the best route into motor racing and what sort of car would really suit me. During a visit to the Campagnolo wheels headquarters in Bologna, I took the opportunity to visit the adjacent Osca factory which, of course, had been established by the surviving Maserati brothers after they had left the company carrying their own name, which was now owned by the Orsi family.

Strangely enough, some years later, they were all bought up by Count Agusta when he was considering car racing and, to complete the circle, he actually bought one of the Lola F1 cars which I had driven with a view to building his own F1 car and engine.

It occurred to me that, if I planned only to do the occasional club event, one of the Osca sports cars would fit the bill, but once I decided that I would try and make a professional go of it, I knew I had to get into single-seaters. After talking it over with Dad, we decided to go it alone with our own set-up. We would be independent, make our own mistakes and learn from them on our own.

Four days after that meeting with Tony Vandervell – on 19 January – I went over to John Cooper's factory at Surbiton and ordered a Formula 2 Cooper-Climax for £2437. He was pleased to see us, because word of my testing time at Goodwood had obviously got around. The car was painted a dark blue, we had a spare set of ratios, a Don Parker trailer and we were ready to go off racing.

The next thing I had to do was qualify for my RAC competitions licence for which I needed to take part in at least one club race. I tried to hire a sports car, without success, and then AFN Ltd, who imported Porsches into the United Kingdom, and from whom I'd bought my 356 some years earlier, offered to lend me a sports car for the club meeting organised by the British Automobile Racing Club which opened the Goodwood season on Saturday, 19 March.

Unfortunately the car was out of the country at the time and they could only promise this subject to it returning in time, but their offer was rendered unnecessary when Ken Tyrrell very kindly loaned me a Formula Junior Cooper-Austin for that meeting, and I agreed that I would drive it during the coming season whenever my prior MV Agusta commitments permitted. Ken just happened to be there when I made that visit to Cooper and, much later, he told me that it hadn't been a coincidence at all. John had telephoned him and told him to be there. It was also Ken who contacted the RAC to confirm what was needed for me to qualify for a licence.

I earned a place on the front row alongside Jimmy Clark's works Lotus 18 and managed to lead through Madgwick on the opening lap. On the second lap Jim came past me, but then I made a small mistake and tried to go back through a gap which was a bit too narrow on the fast right-hander after the pits. That dropped me back a little and, although I briefly slipped through into the lead again on the fifth lap, I then dropped back to third; however, I managed to pip Trevor Taylor, in the other works Lotus, to take second place on the last lap.

That season with Ken produced a lot of good placings, but the Lotus-Fords of Jim Clark and Trevor Taylor always had a slight edge and we never managed a single race win. Their chassis was better and the Ford engine had a better spread of power and more revs available than our BMC unit. The Lotus chassis also put its power down better and could be driven more precisely through the corners, not scrubbing off speed as it did so, whereas the Cooper was a little tail-happy.

Nevertheless, towards the end of that year we were in a position where there was a possibility of snatching the overall championship, so Ken decided to buy his own Lotus which we used in a couple of races at Snetterton and Oulton Park.

Unfortunately, on both occasions, our chances were thwarted by poor assembly of the Renault-based gearbox. It was no consolation to be told, rather casually, by Lotus that on their works cars they modified those particular components!

Ken only had two full-time mechanics at that time, Neil Davis and Alain Stait, both of whom, at the time of writing, are still working for the Tyrrell Grand Prix team some thirty years on. Neil is Ken's factory works manager while Alain is a highly skilled machinist employed in the machine shop. We also had the services of Geoff Read, who worked for KLG on spark plug development, on a part-time basis at most of the UK races contested by the team.

My first race at the wheel of my own F2 Cooper-Climax came at the BARC's Oulton Park meeting on 2 April where I was entered under Ken Tyrrell's wing and managed to qualify second to Innes Ireland's works Lotus 18. Mike McKee's Lotus was third on the grid with Harry Schell's Cooper-Climax making up the front row and it was McKee who led the first few laps before Innes and I overtook him. I finished second again to the Lotus. Our F2 team consisted of myself and my father, rather a small outfit even by the standards of the day, but we had an extremely enjoyable time nevertheless.

The only other F2 race I managed to take part in with the Cooper, due to the fact that my MV commitments clashed with most of the races on the calendar catering for this category, was the Aintree 200 on 30 April. Stirling won at the wheel of Rob Walker's Porsche, heading a 1-2-3 for the German cars, with Jo Bonnier and Graham Hill next up and me going hell-for-leather in an attempt to catch up, setting the fastest lap in the process. It was another extremely satisfying day out, particularly as I had run ahead of the works Lotus and Cooper entries and established a new F2 lap record.

Meanwhile, Tony Vandervell came on to me and said that he was going to buy a Lotus 18 and install a Vanwall engine in it, just to get an idea of what was involved in building one of the new breed of rear-engined cars, and the next thing I knew Colin Chapman was on the phone saying, 'Come and try one of our F1 cars.'

Despite protesting that I really hadn't had sufficient experience to tackle F1, I accepted and went up to a test session at Silverstone. Innes Ireland first drove the car, being team leader at the time, then Colin, and finally I had a go. Unfortunately I made a bit of a mistake at Becketts and popped it into the bank, damaging the nose cone.

That started Innes raving on about the danger of giving cars to inexperienced novices – I can hear him now! – but Colin just shrugged it aside and asked me whether I would drive the car when I was free. Before that minor shunt I'd been doing lap times which were virtually the same as Innes and Colin Chapman, who at that time was not only the father of the team but also a very competent driver himself. This is an important fact that many people tend to forget. Incidentally, my mechanic at Team Lotus was Dick Scammell, who is today manager of the F1 racing department at Cosworth Engineering.

Colin simply said, 'Right, you've got a place in the works team. Drive when you can; when you're not free, Alan Stacey or Jimmy Clark will drive it.' I remember starting to think, well, this is all right, but now we're talking about Jimmy, now Stacey . . . how many drivers has he got under contract?

My first F1 outing turned out to be the Silverstone International Trophy on 14 March where I was paired with Innes. Although he won handsomely he managed to shunt his car in practice, picking out the marker drums at Woodcote after only a handful of laps. In fairness, he apologised handsomely when he saw the irony of his earlier criticisms, and from then on we got on pretty well. Unfortunately I was sidelined from this race with a leaking oil filter and only Innes, Jack Brabham's Cooper and Graham Hill's BRM managed to complete the full distance.

On 29 May, I had my first World Championship Grand Prix outing at Monaco, quite an experience because I had only taken part in the occasional bike race on proper street circuits, and had never encountered anything like the challenge of the Mediterranean principality.

In practice, I qualified well back due to gearbox problems. At the time, the F1 Lotus 18s were using a Chapman-designed box using a motor cycle-type gearchange where you didn't have a conventional gate but a lever which you just moved forward and back in a straight line to select the ratios.

Although in concept it was probably a very good idea, it was certainly one of the weaker points in the car, and it was because of this unreliability that Alf Francis, who looked after Stirling's Rob Walker car, got involved with Valerio Colotti in the development of an alternative gearbox. Anyway, we had constant problems at Monaco with our box, as well as some engine trouble, so I qualified well back and only lasted 19 laps before the final drive broke.

It's important to remember, of course, that while today's Grand Prix drivers enjoy the opportunity to test here, there and everywhere between races, in those days such testing didn't take place. Anyway, during the summer of 1960 I was still very actively engaged in my motor cycle racing programme and the F1 teams didn't really have the budgets for testing, nor the back-up in terms of spare engines and equipment. Most of the time, Lotus just had one engine in each of the three cars plus perhaps a single spare to share between them all.

My next outing for Chapman came in the British Grand Prix at Silverstone on 16 July, by which time poor Alan Stacey had sadly been killed driving for Lotus in the Belgian Grand Prix at Spa after losing control when a bird apparently hit him in the face on the Masta Straight. I qualified only 11th, suffering from a persistent misfire which was eventually traced to plug leads chafing against a bulkhead, but managed to finish second to Brabham's Cooper-Climax, and ahead of Innes in the other Lotus.

A week later, with Stirling still sidelined recovering from injuries sustained in a practice crash at Spa, Rob Walker invited me to have a try in his Formula 2 Porsche in the Solitude Grand Prix, held on that splendid road circuit near Stuttgart where I'd come a cropper on my MV Agusta four years earlier. This particular meeting was for both bikes and cars. I won the bike event and had a very busy weekend switching from overalls to leathers and back again.

Of course, I had fond memories of my own road Porsche, but much of this particular weekend was spent trying to select fourth gear – and engaging second! Rob's mechanic Alf Francis assured me that he had made alterations to the gearbox in an effort to cure this problem, but the jinx persisted in the race when I inadvertently stuck it into a much lower gear than intended and just spun into a ditch!

My intermittent F1 career then continued on 14 August in the Portuguese Grand Prix at Oporto where I really began to feel I was getting the hang of this F1 business and qualified in pole position ahead of Dan Gurney in the rear-engined BRM, Brabham and Stirling in the Rob Walker Lotus.

The Oporto track was a real road circuit, running along the seafront for part of its distance, with tramlines and cobbles all mixed in as part of the challenge. Again, it was a circuit I had never previously seen, although road circuits were quite regular features on the motor cycle racing calendar. Somehow, in Oporto, I got into the necessary rhythm and it was quite a nice experience, because this was a situation where I was more equally pitted against my rivals, very few of them having had much experience of the track. We started on a much more even level.

One of the aspects which helped me, I suppose, was the number of really quick corners at Oporto. One of the problems I had encountered in my switch to cars was dealing with slow corners. The difference in technique on slow corners between a motor cycle and a car is enormous, whereas the lines and need for sensitivity through the really fast ones are not that much different. In any event, I think the F1 Lotus 18 was much more of a motor cyclists' type of car: less forgiving than the Cooper, perhaps, but extremely efficient at high limits.

Naturally, Ferrari were present, but their front-engined Dino 246 could no longer really compete against the best of the rear-engined cars, which were the Cooper and the Lotus. Some of the curves were very quick indeed, but I remember one in particular which was quite close to a sardine-canning factory; even driving at speed, you couldn't help but get a pretty pungent whiff up your nostrils on every lap!

I think I performed pretty well that day, bearing in mind that Innes, Jimmy and Stirling were all ranged against me in identical cars. From the start I built up a good sound lead, but then Stirling, who was returning to F1 after recovering from his Spa accident, came out of the pits in front of me after losing time with a pit stop in his Rob Walker Lotus and, for a few laps, I just followed him round.

What you've got to remember, of course, is that, coming into F1 as a new boy, I sparked off some quite prickly feelings among some members of the Grand Prix fraternity. Not from people like Stirling, on the whole, but from the likes of Jo Bonnier who did not seem particularly receptive to a young man coming straight into F1 and going faster than them after only a handful of races. So there was quite a lot of niggling behind the scenes, and I suppose I rather rose to the bait more than perhaps I should have done.

After a few laps behind Stirling there was still a nagging doubt in my mind as to precisely where he was in the race order. The pit signals were a little difficult to read, as the pits were over on the far right as we came along the seafront before turning right up the main boulevard where the tramlines ran up the middle. You weren't necessarily able to get the best of information, so, as I say, there was still this slight doubt as to exactly where he was. I also found that following a car slightly tended to spoil my rhythm and fluidity. Even with cars not being so aerodynamically effective as they are today, there was obviously still a certain degree of uncomfortable turbulence.

In any event, I thought, 'Well, I was faster than him in practice, so there's nothing he's doing that I can't do.' I tucked in behind Stirling and pulled out, but my foot came off the pedal momentarily. Unfortunately, although I had noticed some time earlier that my Lotus had developed a slight leak in its front fuel tank, I failed to allow for the effect the 120-octane fuel would have on the sole of my shoe and it slipped off the brake pedal at a point where the old tramlines ran virtually parallel to the direction of the circuit.

I locked up the front wheels and made the mistake of turning into the corner. That was my main mistake. I should have followed the tramlines, gone up the slip road and turned round. I was almost half a minute in the lead, so I had plenty of time to do so. I bumped the kerb very lightly, but it was just hard enough to split open the water radiator, so I lost the chance of winning a championship Grand Prix at only my third attempt.

I rounded off my first season of motor racing with an outing in the United States Grand Prix at Riverside, and I'm unhappy to recall that it turned out to be a rather demoralising and I suppose very embarrassing situation. I had never seen the Riverside circuit, which was renowned for being extremely slippery off the racing line due to the amount of desert sand that was always being blown over it, and, of course, I learned that, very early in the race, you go off line at your peril. Perhaps I didn't pay sufficient heed to the prevailing conditions in a way that a more experienced driver might have done in a similar situation.

We hadn't got it together particularly well in practice, but I was determined to make up for this once the race started. Having made a lousy start, I was a bit over-eager to compensate. I tried to come rushing through the pack, driving off line to pass people, and just as I'd overtaken Jimmy I ran wide, lost it and he ploughed into me. It was extremely frustrating, because we had both been in with a good chance, but I had been a bit too eager to get to the front too quickly.

There was another, rather amusing, aspect to the race in that it had a big-money prize fund which Innes, Jimmy and I were all obviously keen to have a share of. Before the event, it was agreed that whatever money was due to the drivers would be evenly split three ways. As things turned out, Innes was the only one of us to finish and, of course, had to split his winnings with Jimmy and myself. I think it's certainly something that stuck firmly in Innes's mind because he was still quick to mention it on occasions that we met up more than thirty years later!

Despite this, Colin Chapman was extremely supportive over the whole business; he was just happy that somebody was having a big go at the wheel of one of his cars. He didn't lose his cool and get annoyed. I liked Colin and respected him, and it fascinates me to think how my Grand Prix career might have turned out if I had stayed with the team, partnered by Jimmy in 1961.

Basically, I believe that the Lotus 18, even allowing for its unreliability, was the most competitive car on the track that year. Reflecting on my car racing career as a whole, the silly thing is, and it's my own fault to a large degree, that I possibly had the most competitive car of my entire career, relative to the opposition, during the 1960 season. That was, I suppose, a reflection of some of the mistakes I made and some of the let-downs I suffered from people who never produced what they said they were going to produce.

On the other hand, the history of Lotus, and what happened to some of their drivers, is something that you can't really dwell on. Whether I would be writing this book now had I made the decision to stay with Lotus is another story. There is no doubt that, at that time, the person who knew most about what was needed to make a fast, modern Grand Prix car was Colin Chapman.

Colin, above everything else, wanted to win races. His budget in those early years would have meant cutting many corners, part of the reason for the cars at times being referred to as 'frail'. If the Lotus 18 had been built to the engineering standards produced by people like Tony Vandervell, Mercedes, Franco Rocchi at Ferrari, or the modern-day teams like McLaren, then none of the opposition would ever have had a look-in. And for a while this was proved by the performance of Chapman and Clark, who made a fabulous team together.

Meanwhile, of course, I had been busy winning the 350 and 500 World Championships on the MV Agusta, but I don't think I really quite realised that circumstances would lead to this being my last season on two wheels. There was still a mood of aggravation between the Count and myself over his decision not to let me ride my own bikes, but he obviously made an effort to soft-soap me by dropping the odd hint that MVs might consider making a car engine, or even their own racing car.

Eventually, towards the end of 1960, I went to see him and asked him if he could be more specific about what was going to happen in the future, particularly as I was concerned that more effort and intensity should be applied to the development work, and, anyway, I wanted to take part in more races. This need for development was particularly the case with the 350, where I had proved to myself that there were other machines that could more than compete with it in terms of performance.

Secondly, the Japanese were waiting in the wings, steadily progressing, and sure to appear on the scene soon in the larger-capacity classes, nor was there any overlooking the Czechoslovakian Jawa. Count Agusta replied that they were not totally sure what they had in mind for their programme, so I have to admit I got the feeling that they were being rather complacent and not suitably aggressive as far as the future was concerned.

At the time, Agusta was getting very heavily involved in the helicopter business and the future was quite clearly moving along those lines, so I didn't really like the thought of tying my career to a team whose long-term plans seemed less than totally clear. I admit it was a time of considerable uncertainty for me, because on the F1 scene there was the new 1½-litre formula being introduced at the start of 1961. In addition, Tony Vandervell was still talking in terms of my driving his new car in the domestic Intercontinental series which was being touted by British organisers as an alternative to the 1½-litre F1, to which the British constructors were very strongly opposed.

Meanwhile, Colin Chapman had asked me to go off to do the Tasman series, in Australia and New Zealand, for the Lotus team, but I didn't want to leave MVs in the lurch because I'd had a very good time there, although I hadn't agreed totally with their racing policy. So I suggested to them that they promote Gary Hocking, who had been going very well as my new team-mate throughout the 1960 season, and told them that I would retire from bike racing.

Gary had made his debut for the team in the French Grand Prix at Clermont-Ferrand in May. The silly part of it was that, whereas Agusta had not authorised the 350 and 500 section of his racing programme to develop a new, lighter and smaller machine, he had allowed the 250 twin to be increased in size. In my view this is always a good way to go. Upgrading the capacity of a small bike is always better than downgrading a big bike; this has been proved time and again over the years. The penalties of size and weight of the larger machine cannot be easily overcome.

Of course, my first outings for MV had been riding a 203 cc bike which I had been loaned for those first few races on the British scene at the start of 1956. Perhaps because I had won all my races with that, and previously beaten Carlo Ubbiali when I rode the NSU Sportmax, they didn't like the idea of me riding the smaller machines. I would have loved to have ridden the 250 in events like the TT, which would have allowed me at least to have a go at the triple, but Ubbiali had a tight rein on that category and, after all, he was very successful, so I suppose I can't complain about that.

Nor did I get the chance to use the experimental 280 cc twin-cylinder MV, which was much lighter than the four-cylinder bike, in the 350 race at Clermont. At least the four-cylinder I was riding was noted for a reasonable degree of reliability. The race started in conditions of steady drizzle and Gary streaked ahead so commandingly that it took a full two laps of this twisting track before I could get anywhere near him.

Coming into one of the tight hairpins before the pits, I was right behind him when he got into a slide and came off. I just managed to brake to a near-standstill, breaking the windscreen on his fallen bike as I weaved round him to take the lead. He recovered in second place, but I managed to lengthen my advantage as the track dried out, only to have the MV lapse onto three cylinders, which forced me into the pits for a plug change.

I resumed in about tenth place, but while I carved my way through to third at the finish Gary and Frantisek Stastny, on the new twin-cylinder Jawa, were still ahead at the chequered flag. It was Gary's first 350 cc race win for MV Agusta and the end of my unbeaten run in World Championship races which stretched back to the start of 1958.

Mention of the twin-cylinder Jawa also brings back a lot of mixed memories. It was always a great sadness to see Jawa and MZ people coming out from behind the Iron Curtain, seeing the sort of restrictions they were subjected to. For instance, Frantisek Stastny couldn't travel with his wife; one of them had to stay at home. It was also depressing to see the brilliant man behind the development of the MZ, Engineer Kaaden, who developed the technology on which all the Japanese two-strokes were based, bartering products such as cameras in exchange for suitable quality steel, simply because the materials were not readily available at home. I developed a tremendous appreciation of the little Jawa and I believe they could have achieved so much more had they not been subjected to such restrictions and had a faster rider to back up Stastny.

I won the 500 cc race at Clermont-Ferrand and John Hartle was back in the team with us in time for the Isle of Man TT, where my efforts to win a hat-trick of doubles in the Junior and Senior events were not successful. While I managed to beat John in the Senior, I lost first and third gears – a rare occurrence – in the Junior and had to be content with second place to him, ahead of Mike Hailwood's Norton.

After that I enjoyed a pretty successful run through the summer, rounding off my year by winning the 500 Italian Grand Prix at Monza, despite sliding off on an oil patch at Parabolica during the course of the race, ripping most of my left-hand riding boot off as I grazed an earth bank. Although I didn't really know it at the time, my motor cycle racing career was over.

Initially I'm afraid Count Agusta and the MV team regarded my decision to quit bikes as something of a slight, and my decision wasn't very well received. Thanks to the Italian press stirring up various stories which were not anywhere near the truth, the whole situation was badly misrepresented for some time and a fair amount of personal unpleasantness arose as a result.

Eventually, feelings were calmed down and it is nice to recall that, in fact, they promised to give me one of their machines, perhaps because Count Agusta had felt a little bit embarrassed when it was discovered that Ubbiali had been paid rather more than me during the 1956 season!

It took 18 years before I finally received it, though, and it eventually arrived in 1978, but the fact remains that I was the only rider ever actually to be given one of the works MV Agustas, which served as a happy memory of the good times I'd enjoyed with them!

Even then, it arrived in the most unexpected way. I received a phone call from London airport advising me that a crate had arrived for me. I wasn't expecting anything, so I asked what was in it. They replied that it was a motor cycle. Where from? Italy. Sure enough, it was the MV Agusta promised to me by Count Domenico Agusta all those years before, but which had subsequently been sent to me, seven years after his death, by Corrado, his last surviving brother. I had always sustained a cordial and friendly relationship with the family after I had retired from the team, sharing a chuckle with Corrado over some of our exploits together.

Anyway, off I went to Australia and New Zealand for Lotus, where I'm afraid we had a fairly disastrous time. The tracks were pretty rough, and various components such as steering arms, suspension uprights and steering boxes kept breaking, most of these parts being modified Triumph Herald components. I suffered steering failure on three occasions during this winter tour and ended up feeling quite jaundiced about the whole programme.

One episode particularly sticks in my mind in connection with this trip. It was a long haul out to Australia in a BOAC Comet and the journey included several stop-overs, so we had to check pretty carefully which vaccination and medical certificates we would require for the various countries involved. Having checked everything out beforehand, the Grand Prix fraternity arrived in Karachi to be told that we all required certificates to say that we had been injected against yellow fever.

Jack Brabham had one such document which had expired – I vividly remember him quickly altering the date on it – but Innes, Graham Hill and myself hadn't got one. Immediately on our arrival they announced that we would have to go into quarantine, despite the protestations and apologies of the BOAC station staff.

Consequently the three of us were taken off to a little isolated building in the middle of the airport and suddenly treated as if we were lepers. We were ushered in, sprayed with what looked like insecticide from little spray guns, and left with a few bottles of whisky which had been supplied by BOAC.

Well, the hours went by and we all turned our attentions to the Scotch – led, of course, by Innes – and then the whole affair degenerated into something of a sing-song. The lyrics of then popular songs were suitably adapted to be aimed specifically at our Pakistani hosts!

It came round to the early hours of the morning and we rightly expected the officials to return with their wretched spray cans again, but this time we vowed to be ready for them. We'd kept our overnight bags containing all our shaving equipment, so we got our canisters of foam shaving cream at the ready and gave those officials as good as we got, covering them from head to toe with foam in retaliation!

Suddenly the whole episode was over as abruptly as it had started. They told us, 'The plane has arrived; you can go now.' But instead of escorting us to the aircraft steps, they bundled us into a minibus and just deposited us in the crowded departure lounge as if nothing had happened. So much for the potential health risk!

I don't think I'm a particularly superstitious person, but I must admit that I did have a slight thing about the colour green, so that was nagging slightly in my mind when Colin Chapman sat me down and said, 'Look, we want you to drive for us full-time, as number one, for the 1961 season. Who would you like as your team-mate?'

Well, I had hit it off pretty well with Jimmy Clark, for although he was rather more experienced than me in terms of car racing I think I had actually had more track experience, taking into account my motor cycle career. He had a relaxed personality and I thought we would work well together, so I replied, 'I'd take Jimmy, but what about Innes? He has been your team leader and you remember the row we had when I first joined the team?'

Colin rather brushed this aside, saying, 'No, no, Innes is all organised. It's all fixed,' and so on. Then I said, 'Look, I've got a little bit superstitious about green because of all the problems we seemed to have in the Tasman series. Could we paint the cars a different colour?' Colin replied that this would be no problem and, in the end, we eventually decided that the cars would be turned out in a black livery, and it was agreed that Jimmy would be my team-mate.

I was going to have one of those lovely little Climax-engined Lotus Elites as my road car and everything seemed organised. The next moment, of course, I got this phone call from Innes in Paris saying, 'What's going on here? What are you doing? You're taking my place in the team?'

Understandably, I was a little taken aback by all this. I replied, 'As far as I understand, everything between you and Colin is all fixed.' So he replied, 'No it's not. You're coming in and taking my place in the team. I've got a contract with Colin that says I'm the team leader.' So I went back to Colin and asked what on earth this was all about, but he just reiterated his assurance, 'No, no. Innes is all fixed up . . .'

Eventually Innes came on the phone again and I said, 'Look, if we're going to sort this matter out we'd better go and see Colin together.' So that's what we did. Colin hummed and hahed for a bit before explaining that he was setting up a second works team with the British Racing Partnership, and 'we're passing his contract over to them'.

So I asked Colin about his previous assurances and, with a twinkle in his eye, he said, 'Oh yes, I may well have a contract with Innes, but it's all fixed up. I want you and Jimmy as you agreed.' But I didn't like the sound of all this and said, 'I'm sorry, you know, enough is enough. I don't understand all this. You'd better count me out.'

The irony is, of course, that a year later, Innes was booted out anyway. But at the time I didn't really know where I stood and didn't really know anybody in motor sport whom I could go and talk to for advice. I hadn't grown up with the car racing fraternity and for every person who would give one opinion, there always seemed to be another saying, 'No, don't listen to him; he's only suggesting that because he wants you to do this . . .' sort of thing.

Admittedly I talked the whole business over with my father, but he didn't really know enough about the complexities of motor racing, and Vandervell wasn't very complimentary about Lotus after his experiences with the Vanwall test chassis. 'They're all rubbish,' he told me, 'they always fall apart. We're having to build our own chassis in order to be sure that the car is safe . . .'

In retrospect, although I obviously couldn't see it at the time, I was about to take a massive step backwards for 1961. I often wonder what would have happened had I stayed with Lotus, because up to that stage I had had a really good rapport with Colin and, to this day, I tend to make comparisons between him and Enzo Ferrari. In their own ways, they clawed a place for themselves in motor racing history, and I use the word 'clawed' in its literal sense.

The difference, of course, was that Colin was a brilliant engineer when it came to creating the concept of a racing car. Having said that, though, his budget, and consequently the number of experienced personnel, and the quantity and quality of the parts that were available left something to be desired in the early Sixties. What happened after I left, of course, was that the partnership that I had started to create with him was picked up by Jimmy Clark.

Colin and Jimmy made a wonderful team. Somehow Jimmy had that ability to distance himself from the motor racing circuits and click back into his farming environment. From my own point of view, if it hadn't been for that call to test the Aston Martin and Vanwall, bearing in mind the problems I was experiencing with MVs, I think there is a very good chance I would have retired from motor sport at the end of 1959 or 1960. I would probably have gone on and established myself in other fields, because, during 1958, I had put in an offer to buy a garage site that I had seen at Edenbridge, in order to set up an agricultural engineering company.

By a strange twist of fate, in 1978/79, at the time we were winding up Team Surtees's activities, part of the salvage operation that we tried to get under way involved us taking over the very garage I attempted to buy in 1958. And, in fact, the F1 Surtees TS20 which we loaned to Peter Briggs to run in the Aurora British championship was operated from the back of those premises.

I think it is quite possible that I could have concentrated on that for a couple of years and, perhaps, if the Japanese, say Honda, had invited me to ride for them, I might have come out of retirement and returned to bikes in around 1962.

Trying to pin-point whether I derived more satisfaction from car racing or bike racing is difficult. The relationship between a rider and a motor cycle is, to a large extent, more personal than that between a driver and his car. On balance, I think, I would say that I derived more pleasure from my bike racing career than from my time with cars. But a lot of that probably stems from the fact that I grew up in the bike world with a generation of people who were contemporaries. When I was pitchforked into car racing, I was suddenly on my own with few people to turn to for advice and guidance.

Of course, it is very important to remember that, while I was earning good money during my motor cycle years, I didn't really have any ongoing money in terms of real investments. Father was still dabbling in car and motor cycle sales at this time, so, as I mentioned previously, I took the opportunity to establish a motor cycle business under the name of John Surtees Developments late in 1957 to provide for the future.

My brother Norman was involved with this from the start and the idea was that he could be involved in running the shop on a continuous basis, but by the time we got to 1960 I was faced with this question of racing cars and bikes and was, frankly, away too much to give it sufficient of my attention. Norman was also paying too much attention to his own racing.

Eventually we were faced with the prospect of losing our service department, which was in other premises immediately adjacent to the showroom, so when I finally decided that I would continue racing professionally we sold the majority of the stock to Stan Hailwood, Mike's father, who owned Kings of Oxford, one of the largest motor cycle dealers in the country.

Part of our payment for that stock was the 250 and 350 twin-cylinder desmo Ducatis which had been built for Stan Hailwood and Kings, to be ridden by Mike Hailwood and Ken Kavanagh. I carried out a bit of a development programme on them and Norman actually raced the 250 Ducati in 1961.

Interestingly, at around that same time – when I was at Monza for the motor cycle Grand Prix – Kavanagh approached me to see if I might be keen on purchasing a trio of ex-works Maserati 250Fs, one of which was Fangio's lightweight special from 1957. Two of them were in a crashed state, but although I felt I could decline this offer he was trying to raise around £20,000 for the whole package. I was told that, in the end, it went for £12,000!

Chapter 4

With Bowmaker, Cooper and Lola

In 1960 I had driven for Colin Chapman without entering into a formal written contract. We simply had a gentlemen's agreement sealed with a handshake. It was the same with Ken Tyrrell in Formula Junior and with Tony Vandervell. After that enlightening experience involving Colin Chapman's commitment to Innes Ireland, I suppose I could look back on my first F1 season as an educational and salutary experience.

I had liked being with Lotus, and Colin always expressed total faith in me, but our relationship had been soured by the episode over Innes. From the viewpoint of a competitive car, I now made the wrong decision for 1961, but it was really a question of heading for any port in a storm. And, in this case, the port was Reg Parnell.

Reg was an old smoothie! He actually thought that, together with the Samengo-Turner brothers, who were the guiding forces behind the Yeoman Credit organisation, he was going to get what amounted to a parallel works Cooper team for the first year of the 1½-litre regulations, running alongside the factory cars of Jack Brabham and Bruce McLaren. As it turned out, of course, Yeoman Credit got off-the-shelf T53 production cars which were based on the previous year's chassis. But Reg remained optimistic and said, 'Don't worry, we'll do our own streamlined bodywork and we'll have our own engine development programme,' – which was going to be carried out, partly on my recommendation, by Bill Lacey, the former Brooklands man who had more recently been responsible for preparing Mike Hailwood's motor cycles.

In fact, we did our own slimline body, but it wasn't really the answer and neither were the engine developments. My experiences in 1961 convinced me that F1 wasn't really feasible on a competitive basis unless one was involved with a works effort.

The Yeoman Credit team was based just off the Bath Road at Hounslow and staffed with a lot of former Aston Martin men who had made the switch to stay with Reg Parnell. It wasn't very far from the Yeoman Credit headquarters near Kew Bridge, so it was convenient for them to bring out their clients to see the set-up from time to time. It was handy being pretty close to Heathrow airport, as well.

I was partnered by Roy Salvadori and we started out quite optimistically with me scoring a win and fastest lap in the Glover Trophy race at Goodwood at the beginning of April. But basically, although I was quick, my early progress wasn't sustained when we came to the World Championship events. Ferrari, of course, had the upper hand with their 1½-litre V6 machines and I suppose my most satisfying performance must have been fifth, behind four Ferraris, in the Belgian Grand Prix at Spa. This season was one of the rare occasions when Ferrari really did have the edge on the opposition in terms of power, something they would subsequently often be rumoured to have in the press but which, as I would find out, was not always the case.

There was another memorable episode at Spa that year, of course, which occurred while I was staying at the Hotel Val d'Amblève, a regular haunt of the Grand Prix set. Wrestling to get to sleep one night, I eventually lost my temper with all the guests who seemed to be making merry and dancing on the terrace below the window of my room. I went out and loudly berated a group of them who included Jimmy Clark, who was dancing with a dark-haired young lady. This turned out to be Pat Burke, who would become my first wife less than a year later, and over whose father's head that same evening I tipped a jug of water in my efforts to get everybody to keep quiet!

There were other less successful hiccups, of course. I collided with Bonnier's Porsche in the Brussels Grand Prix at Heysel, finished fourth in the Aintree 200, 11th at Monaco and seventh at Zandvoort in the Dutch Grand Prix. Roy won at Crystal Palace, but then I had an accident in the French Grand Prix at Reims and failed to finish the British Grand Prix at Aintree. All sorts of silly mechanical failures intervened to make the whole affair extremely frustrating.

One notable bright spot occurred a couple of days after I returned home from Zandvoort. I had one of the greatest honours bestowed on me when I was awarded the MBE for my services to motor cycle racing in the Queen's Birthday Honours list. It was certainly an extremely proud moment and one which seemed to put a perfect final touch to my career on two wheels. Reflecting on this award, I must say that I find it a great shame that such honours have become rather devalued in recent years by increasingly being used as political tools rather than straightforward acknowledgements of genuine endeavour.

Meanwhile, I also felt a continuing obligation to Tony Vandervell, although by this time the Vanwall racing effort had been scaled down quite dramatically as he himself was then in a very poor state of health. In 1959 and '60 he had continued toying with a revised version of the front-engined car, then, as I mentioned previously, purchased a rear-engined Lotus 18 into which he fitted one of the 2.5-litre engines as something of a mobile test bed.

Tony had not been very impressed with the engineering standards of Chapman's machines, so they effectively cast this aside and built their own rear-engined car, the VW14, for the short-lived Intercontinental formula. Now powered by an enlarged version of the Vanwall four-cylinder engine, extended to 2.6 litres, which was the maximum the cylinder spacing would allow it to go to, I drove it in the non-title '61 International Trophy race at Silverstone. It was dubbed 'the Beast' by some observers, more for its rather rotund profile than anything else, and, after dicing for second, I managed to coax it home in fifth place after a lurid spin on the rain-drenched track.

Truth be told, I was pretty unfamiliar with the car because, since Vanwall didn't have a fully fledged racing programme in operation by then, there was precious little opportunity for pre-race testing and we had considerable problems matching the Bosch fuel injection system – which had originally been developed for Mercedes – to the engine's requirements.

This had been a major problem with the Vanwall engines since the change from alcohol fuels to pump petrol in 1958 and it was a hitch we would later encounter with the 1½-litre F1 Ferrari V6. Extremely good power could be obtained on the test bench, but considerable holes in the power curve would exist and, in fact, be quite inconsistent, so making it extremely difficult to rely on the engine's power delivery to steer the car on the throttle.

One moment you would have power, the next, nothing – or a sudden surge up the back just when you didn't want it. However, I'm sure the car had the potential to do well.

Many years later, I was very disappointed not to have been given a sympathetic hearing by either the GKN Board, or the management of Christie's, the auctioneers who had been asked by GKN to invite specific individuals to bid for all the cars and parts. Tony Vandervell had promised the rear-engined car to me and there were many people at Vandervells, then part of GKN, who remembered the Old Man's pledge.

In commissioning Christie's to sell the cars, GKN had also reserved the right to accept any offer; in other words, to do what they liked. So I contacted Mr Robert Brooks, then in charge at Christie's, and, with some apparent reluctance, he gave me a quote.

I put in my bid at a level above this quote, but also qualified it by writing a letter to the GKN Board, via Christie's, outlining my connection with the car, and with Tony Vandervell, asking that, should my offer not be sufficient, I be given the opportunity to match any quote which was received.

They did not respond and the whole Vanwall *équipe* – one front-engined car, the VW14 and the Thinwall Special – all went for about £400,000, which was a pittance for GKN as well as a depressing short-term expedient.

Of all the single-seaters I was involved with during my career, this Vanwall was the one I felt the most affection for, linked as it was to the start of my car racing career, as well as reminding me of my tremendous respect for what Tony had done and, certainly, how he had been one of the few genuine enthusiasts I could rely upon as a friend in those early transitional days.

The following winter, early in 1962, we took the Coopers down under to the Tasman series for my second crack at this championship. After the Australian Grand Prix at Lakeside I flew home to get married to Pat, after which we had a brief honeymoon at Acapulco on the way back to the race at Longford in Tasmania, which I won. But by then it was very clear we needed something better than a customer Cooper chassis for 1962.

We returned to stay with my parents in Purley. The plan was that we should live in that house, while my parents would move down to a new bungalow near Biggin Hill, which is in fact what they did. But Pat wasn't happy living in that house; I feel she wanted something which didn't have previous connections.

Well, I chanced to be driving through Kent – with my mother, as it happened – when my eye was attracted to a house for sale near Limpsfield. It was a colonial-style house with a wash-brick lower section and all-Canadian cedar top. And it had a lovely view from its back garden over Forestry Commission land. This was Grey Timbers and I fell in love with it almost at first sight. But it was way over my budget.

I reckoned we could probably go to £11,000 and, when it came to it, the vendor, Sir Paul Bentall, was talking about £21,000. He was only selling the property because the National Trust was offering him his family seat back. I gathered he would accept, for a clear deal, about £19,000. So I went through every little thing I could dispose of.

However, the first snag was that Pat didn't initially seem very enthusiastic. It took some time to convince her because she was rather put out that, by chance, my mother had been with me when I first saw it.

Anyway, we surmounted that hurdle. Then I tried to sell a few bike bits I had left, and got on to Reg Parnell to see if it was possible to obtain an advance. But in fact it was Yeoman Credit who told me to speak to their bankers, a Martins branch near Whitehall, and they arranged the necessary overdraft facilities. Finally, I got Sir Paul Bentall out of his bath at two o'clock in the morning, ringing from the other side of the world, and did the deal.

Pat and I lived there very happily until the early 1970s when things started to fall apart as regards our marriage. Under the rockery I piled a lot of old junk, including NSU frames, an engine that had come from a special scrambles bike, a 7R 350 mock-up engine that I had used to build up my special AJS, and numerous other bits and pieces. Some of this I was subsequently able to dig up in 1979, when I once again got the two-wheel bug and started to build up some of my past machines. Strangely, it was all remarkably well preserved.

Returning to the racing scene, Bowmaker had taken over Yeoman Credit by this stage, but the Samengo-Turners continued in charge and Bowmaker agreed to continue the backing into 1962. So together we decided that they would support, in effect, a works effort and I put Reg in touch with Eric Broadley who had been building his little Lola sports cars in Bromley, only a couple of roads away from where I was living with my parents. I'd seen the cars they were making and his little Mk 1 Climax-engined sports racer was pretty successful at around that time, not to mention their Formula Junior cars. He was, to a large extent, out of the Chapman innovative mould with similar thinking, ably backed up by Rob Rusbrook on the manufacturing side.

Again, things didn't quite work out as they should have done as regards the supply of the latest 1½-litre Coventry Climax V8 engines, but from the outset they were very quick. One of our early races was the '62 Glover Trophy at Goodwood where Stirling, in the UDT Laystall Lotus 18/21, and myself in the new Lola were trading times for the fastest lap. Both of us had been delayed early in the race with pit stops, losing any chance of victory to Graham Hill's BRM. But we were both going quicker than him and it was when Stirling came up to pass Graham that he had the accident that brought his career to a premature end.

As I saw the situation, although Graham was under no pressure, he was certainly out to hang on to his lead. But he hadn't expected Stirling to come up on him so quickly. Going down to St Mary's, you would normally not use the extreme left-hand side of the road except if you were scratching hard. I think Graham was taking the traditional line, nearer the middle of the road, and just didn't see him. Stirling, being a racer as always, saw a gap on the left, but it disappeared as Graham edged across to take the correct line into the next right-hander. I suspect that Stirling then got his left-hand wheels on the grass and that was it. That's what I think happened.

As it turned out, I retired after 35 laps with engine trouble, a lap before Stirling had his accident, but we both shared the fastest race lap of 1m 22s exactly, an average speed of 105.37 mph.

From then onwards, our team was beset by teething problems as we got into the

World Championship programme. The series opened at Zandvoort with the Dutch Grand Prix, where Jimmy Clark debuted the new monocoque Lotus 25. I managed to qualify the Lola in pole position, with Graham's BRM and Jimmy alongside, and while Jim sped away in the opening stages I dropped to fourth on the opening lap behind Graham and Dan Gurney in the flat-8 air-cooled Porsche.

The Lola Mk 4 hadn't really impressed me as having very predictable handling in the first few races of the season, but I certainly wasn't prepared for what it had in store for me at Zandvoort. On the ninth lap I was coming over the brow into the fast right-hander which led out onto the pit straight – a fourth-gear, 125 mph affair – when a left-front suspension link broke and sent me hurtling off the track at high speed.

I suppose that I must thank circuit designer John Hugenholtz for his catch fencing – and the Dutch love of bicycles – for my escape. Just behind the catch fencing was a bicycle park for spectators and, between the two of them, they brought the Lola to rest without my suffering any serious harm. I was able to walk away unhurt and hurried back to the pits where I told Reg what had happened. Immediately he took the decision to call in Salvadori before the same problem befell our second car!

In this connection, I always held the view that catch fencing was a far better method of restraining a wayward car than the guard rails so firmly espoused by Jackie Stewart, even though it later came into a certain amount of disrepute due to flying posts causing a number of injuries. Together with sand traps, it worked much more effectively than any other solution, in my opinion.

For the Monaco Grand Prix my car was rebuilt with redesigned tubular top front suspension arms and, not being 'seeded works runners' with guaranteed places on the grid, Salvadori and I had to qualify. The cars were still not handling too well, particularly relative to putting their power down, and I had to be content with a lowly place on the inside of the fifth row, 2.5 seconds slower than Jimmy's pole-position Lotus. Under the circumstances, it was quite satisfying to finish up with fourth place in the race, one lap behind Bruce McLaren's winning Cooper and the Ferraris of Phil Hill and Lorenzo Bandini.

The week prior to the Belgian Grand Prix at Spa I took part in the Whit Monday non-championship International 2000 Guineas race at Mallory Park, qualifying in pole position and leading all the way to score my first F1 success. It was quite a satisfying experience, but I still realised that the Lola chassis really wasn't quite up to the mark and, when we got to Spa the following weekend, I made a discovery that set us along the path to improving its handling.

The Lola really didn't seem to like Spa, having been more at home on smoother tracks like Goodwood. It was nervous at high speed, sensitive to the bumps and rather prone to an unnerving weaving motion which meant that I was having to leave an extra couple of feet to spare coming out of the corners. We were garaged just off the main street in Francorchamps where we maintained the cars. Eric Broadley had cause to jack up one corner of the Mk 4 and I suddenly noticed that the remaining three wheels stayed firmly planted on the ground.

'Surely that can't be right, Eric?' I remarked. 'The thing's twisting in every direction.' Clearly, it didn't say much for the chassis's torsional stiffness so I suppose it wasn't really surprising that I was again well off the pace and started from the inside of the fifth row alongside Jimmy, whose Lotus 25 had also experienced a lot of practice problems.

However, while Jimmy cleared off and won the race, I could only struggle round to take fifth place, one lap behind. Clearly we had to do something pretty dramatic and, by the time we turned out for the non-title Reims Grand Prix on 1 July, the chassis frame had received additional bracing tubes around the cockpit area which significantly enhanced the car's handling.

It started to handle more progressively, we got the power down onto the road much more effectively and began to get the message. Now it was a very different proposition and, although a broken valve spring sidelined me in the race, I gained considerable satisfaction from having qualified third to gain a place on the front row of the grid, my time bettered only by Jimmy's Lotus and Graham in the BRM.

That year's French Grand Prix was held a week later at the demanding Rouen-les-Essarts road circuit where, again, the revised Lola didn't perform too badly. Jimmy, Graham and Bruce McLaren's Cooper took the front row with me alongside Jack Brabham's private Lotus 24 on the second rank. I ran a comfortable second to Graham in the early stages, but this time my efforts were thwarted by two pit stops, the first to tend to a misfire, the second caused by selection difficulties with the Colotti gearbox.

I was only 12 laps from the end of the race when the gears started playing up, so the mechanics helped jam it in third and off I plodded, determined to make it to the finish. I was intending to pull into the pits immediately, and both Maurice Trintignant, in Rob Walker's Lotus 24, and Trevor Taylor, in his works 24, thought likewise. But I was prevented from doing so by a cordon of gendarmes which meant that there was not space for three cars.

Trintignant had to swerve to the left to avoid me, which in turn left Taylor nowhere to go. He collided with Trintignant and both cars were badly damaged, although thankfully neither driver was hurt. It was a very close call indeed which underlined the dangers of employing a police force which is unfamiliar with the business of motor racing to officiate in such a dangerous position.

The British Grand Prix at Aintree followed, where I qualified second to Jimmy's Lotus and then held that position throughout the 75-lap race, but I was to come closest to scoring my first Grand Prix victory a couple of weeks later at the Nürburgring. The front row of the four-three-four grid was composed of Gurney's flat-8 Porsche, which had been the winner at Rouen, Graham Hill's BRM, Jimmy's Lotus and my Lola.

With Jimmy being delayed at the start, this soaking race developed into a three-way battle between Dan, Graham and me. The conditions were terrible, but eventually we settled down with Graham running first, me second and Dan third. The BRM had a bit more steam on the straight, so I worked out that my only real chance of getting past would be to come through the fast right-hander onto the final straight quickly enough to haul up onto his tail and sling-shot past before the finishing line.

This wasn't as easy as it seemed, bearing in mind how much spray was flying around. It had to be a last-lap, do-or-die situation. While I was right up Graham's exhaust pipe, I had Dan scrambling all over me on the tight sections of the track, so, although I needed to drop back slightly in order to take a run at Graham through that right-hander, I couldn't slacken the pace too much because Dan was looking for any opportunity to push me down to third.

So I was nicely placed for a big effort, came flying over the brow into that right-hander

– and who was cruising along in the middle of the road? Heini Walter in a slow four-cylinder Porsche! So that was it. Again, it was a scramble to the line and another frustrating second place.

During the course of '62 I was also able to sample a racing Ferrari for the first time, for Bowmaker hired a Ferrari GTO from Maranello Concessionaires, the English importers. Possibly the most promising outing in this machine was in the Goodwood Tourist Trophy, shortly after the German Grand Prix. I took an early lead and was feeling pretty confident when I came up to lap Jimmy in the Essex Racing Team Aston Martin DB4 Zagato, only for him to spin across my bows at Madgwick, taking us both into the bank fairly hard!

There were four Grands Prix remaining in 1962 – at Monza, Watkins Glen, Mexico City and East London – and, to my acute disappointment, the Lola failed to finish in any of them. To be frank, Coventry Climax were only able to make a very limited effort with their new V8. They did wonderful things, and made some super engines, but they didn't really have the resources. And, rather like when the Cosworth DFV programme started, they channelled their efforts into certain areas and a new team like ours didn't come high on their list of priorities. Let's be clear, we were not treated badly, but we were not at the top of the list.

I suppose the '61 and '62 seasons served as a reminder to me of the career possibilities which might have beckoned had I taken a deep breath and kept quiet during the difficulties between Innes Ireland and Chapman back in 1960. Had I driven for Lotus during those two years, it could certainly have changed the course of F1 history slightly!

During the course of the season I received an approach from Ferrari through Keith Ballisat of Shell. I had originally been asked out to Maranello at the end of 1961 when I met all the key staff members. I wasn't very happy with the scene there, particularly with all the drivers they seemed to have on their books, and I realised that I didn't know enough about car racing. By that stage I had only done a handful of car races and decided, on the basis of past experience, not to enter a hornet's nest like that at the time without some sort of foreknowledge. I didn't accept their offer.

I suppose, in that respect, I must be among a very small minority of drivers who have been offered a contract by Enzo Ferrari and turned it down. I think subsequent events proved that I made the correct decision on that initial occasion.

The first indication I had that Ferrari might be interested in my services came through a phone call from an accessory manufacturer with whom I was doing business. Naturally, I was intrigued, and decided to fly out to Milan to see what it was all about. I was met at the airport by Dr Fabietti of the Italian Shell company, who had been a close associate of mine during my motor cycle days, even though I had not been using his company's products.

As we drove from Milan to Modena I was glad to hear that he too had an appointment the following morning with Mr Ferrari, and that we would also be joined by Mr Vecchi, Dunlop's man in Italy. The thought of meeting Enzo Ferrari 'solo' was just a bit too daunting. Consequently, as I went to bed that night at Modena's Palace Hotel, I was comforted by the thought that there would be a couple of familiar faces around for the all-important meeting in the morning.

Although the main Ferrari factory is at Maranello, some 12 miles out of Modena, our appointment was at Ferrari's Modena office where, curiously, I never subsequently saw him. Prior to the war this had been the headquarters of the Scuderia Ferrari when they were operating a number of semi-works Alfa Romeos. By the time I finally joined Ferrari in 1963, its only remaining link with racing was the continued presence of roly-poly bodybuilder Medardo Fantuzzi, who was still responsible for the bodywork of nearly every F1 Ferrari, and who still occupied one corner of the Modena premises.

It was a curious feeling as I walked through the door of Ferrari's office that morning, as if I was stepping into another world. It might have been my imagination, but it seemed as though everybody was going about their jobs with a reverential earnestness which was almost unnatural. I was experiencing for the first time the unique magnetism of Ferrari, under whose influence many a famous name has been made to feel curiously humble.

The actual meeting with the man himself came almost as an anti-climax. We were led into a room, about thirty feet by twenty feet, with a sort of old-world atmosphere which immediately reminded me of Count Agusta's office at Gallarate. To describe it as musty would be unkind; that suggests it was dirty, which it most certainly was not. Perhaps 'mellow' would be a better word.

It was also full of history. Trophies of past successes lined the walls and there were photographs of some of the great drivers from the past – Farina, Gonzalez and Hawthorn among them – to remind me that Enzo Ferrari had been breeding World Champions long before I'd climbed into my first racing car.

As I was soon to discover, Enzo Ferrari could be a man of many or few words, depending on his mood. That morning, evidently, he thought that economy of words suited the occasion. He spoke no English, and would normally be accompanied by his secretary, Valerio, or the press officer, Franco Gozzi. Forgoing the usual pleasantries, he came straight to the point: 'I would like you to drive for us next year: Formula 1, sports cars and anything else we might decide to race. Here's the contract.'

It was as simple as that. Or was it? Was I really ready to drive for Ferrari? Had I the necessary experience? In addition, I already had a number of racing and business commitments arranged for 1962 which I might not be able to honour if I was to race for a foreign team which would, necessarily, mean me living abroad for much of the year.

Perhaps sensing my hesitation, Ferrari introduced me to Carlo Chiti, his portly and jovial chief engineer, and he was told to take me to the Maranello factory, show me around, and then report back with me to the boardroom.

That day, I was shown quite a lot of the Maranello works in a rather rapid tour from which my overwhelming impression was one of neatness and cleanliness. Even with a lot of constructional work being carried out, everything seemed to be spotless.

I had quite a revealing talk with Chiti about Formula 1 as we walked around. This tended to confirm my one reservation about the whole set-up: namely, there was an air of confidence, bordering on complacency, regarding their prospects for 1962 which I didn't really feel was justified. Certainly they had won the Drivers' and Constructors' World Championships in 1961, but only because Britain could offer no effective opposition due to our lack of preparedness for the 1½-litre regulations.

In 1962 BRM and Coventry Climax would have their V8 engines available at full strength. Given reasonable reliability, these could be expected to be faster than the V6 units which Ferrari was continuing to use. Had I been Ferrari, I should have been showing rather more concern over my ability to fight off the British F1 challenge than in fact he was. Of course, this almost lackadaisical attitude could have been a try-on, just to test me out. But I didn't think so.

By the time Chiti and I arrived in the boardroom I was resolved not to make up my mind either way until I had had time to think it over. There was so much at stake, so I wanted to get away from the rarefied atmosphere at Maranello so as to look at the thing objectively. Having established that Ferrari was not interested in having me just for F1, I explained that, although I was very interested, I could not commit myself until I had returned home and attended one or two critical business meetings. Only then would I know whether I would be free to spend the necessary time abroad.

I was able to write to Mr Ferrari within a day or two of returning home, declining his offer. I arrived at this decision for several reasons. Firstly, I felt that I would prefer to go to Ferrari feeling completely sure of myself. My previous experiences with Italians had taught me the value of knowing exactly what I was talking about.

Ideas you put forward must be based on firm experience and, as far as car racing was concerned, that was one element that I still lacked. There was also the Lola project in the pipeline which I had put in operation the previous summer as a private venture between Eric Broadley and myself, but for which we had now received the offer of sponsorship by Bowmaker. Not only was there a strong moral commitment to see the Lola project through, but it was obviously just the sort of experience I needed in my motor racing apprenticeship.

I was still very conscious of my lack of knowledge in certain directions, including the finer points of racing car design and development, and this was one of the reasons behind originally approaching Eric. Now the Ferrari offer had put things right in perspective for me. It was clear that the opportunity to help take a car through from the design stage to the point where it might be able to win a Grand Prix was exactly what I needed before I could be of maximum value to Ferrari.

My final reason for declining the Ferrari offer at this stage was the conflicting demands of my business commitments away from the race track. But in writing to Ferrari, I tried to keep the door open by expressing the hope that it might be possible for us to get together at some time in the future, to our mutual benefit.

As I had anticipated, by remaining with Reg Parnell, the man who had given me my first drive in a racing car, the 1962 season developed into a most educational experience. It was also a year which started with great promise, but gradually developed into one of frustration, disappointment and near-heartbreak as we struggled with the virtually impossible task of designing – and simultaneously developing and racing – a team of F1 cars over the space of a few months.

It was also a tantalising year, because several times we came close to success, only to see the chance of victory slip away. At first we seemed to have the power but lacked roadholding. Then, when we finally fixed the handling, we found we were down on power. I can also recall some pretty hair-raising moments as I learned the hard way about the problems of inconsistent handling. But, for all that, I think it was a year in which Eric Broadley's achievement, without any previous F1 experience, of producing a car which was basically competitive did not receive the recognition it deserved.

By the end of 1962 it was clear that the door at Maranello had been left ajar. Ferrari contacted the late Ralph Martin, Shell's competitions manager in Britain, asking if I might still be interested. The quick answer to that was definitely in the affirmative. Few people had known about my earlier negotiations with Ferrari and there was a certain amount of eyebrow-raising when the news leaked out that I was about to 'go foreign'.

There was even the suggestion that I was somehow letting Reg Parnell down, but, as a close friend and colleague, he had been fully apprised of my visits to Italy and was the first person to be told once I had come to my decision. It is also necessary to bear in mind that we received information towards the end of 1962 that Coventry Climax could not guarantee to supply us – or anybody else – with F1 engines for the '63 season. This in itself was pretty shattering news, and when Bowmaker announced that they would not be continuing their support, there seemed little prospect but to disband the team.

As it turned out, Coventry Climax decided to stay in F1 and Reg took over the Bowmaker team to run on an independent basis, but they proved unable to score a single championship point in any of the following season's races. Before I finished my association with the team, we contested the Tasman series with 2.7-litre four-cylinder Climax engines installed in the F1 chassis.

Fitted with this engine, the Lola became a much better balanced and nicer car to drive. The mounting of the four-cylinder added a little more rigidity to the rear end, and of course you had a power curve when you needed to steer on the throttle.

This was quite a successful outing and I opened the series on 5 January 1963 with victory in the New Zealand Grand Prix at Pukekohe, then suffered gearbox troubles at Levin and Christchurch and failed to finish at Invercargill. We then moved on to Australia, where I took second place in the Grand Prix at Warwick Farm behind Jack Brabham's Brabham-Climax (on a scorching day when I was forced to slow while leading when I burnt the sole of my throttle foot) and won the Lakeside International at Brisbane in pouring rain ahead of Graham Hill in the four-wheel drive Ferguson P99.

My second talk with Enzo Ferrari was very different from the first. This time it took place in his office at Maranello, smaller than the one in Modena and a lot lighter. It was simply and neatly furnished, the focal point of the room being a permanently illuminated photograph of his late son Dino.

The venue was not the only thing to have changed. A few weeks after my earlier visit, there had been a mass revolt of key personnel over a number of grievances. As a result, many heads had toppled, including those of Chiti and the team manager, Romolo Tavoni. New men had taken their place and the '62 season had certainly not been an easy one. Indeed the team's fortunes had plunged as low as they had ridden high in 1961. They fully appreciated that they had been beaten, fair and square. Now there was no sign of the complacency which had pervaded the place a year before. They had their backs to the wall and, as I was to learn, at Ferrari that's when things got done.

I made my second journey to Maranello with Ralph Martin, a most lovable character to whom Modenese pasta and Lambrusco, the local vino, acted as a magnet. He never missed any such opportunity to entertain his palate. When he died early in 1964, motor racing lost perhaps the most colourful of all its personalities from the trade and industry side.

We found Ferrari in a talkative mood. Above all, he wanted to know my views about motor racing generally, and we had a long talk about Formula 1. He asked me my thoughts on the running of a works team, and whether I had any strong views on any particular aspects of the subject.

Straight away I made it clear that, in my opinion, a racing programme should be supported by a thorough schedule of testing, and that if a car is to have a chance of winning races, it should be fitted with the best available equipment, regardless of what arrangements with component suppliers might have been made in the past.

We also talked about driver relationships, and whether I thought a team should have a number one and a number two, driving to order. I made it clear that I had never taken team orders and didn't wish to start doing so now. I had always been against the whole idea of a number one and a number two; it can be extremely demoralising to a driver who is obliged to follow another when he thinks that he can beat him. I always adopted the attitude that a driver's place in a team is determined by the results he can bring.

I think Ferrari enjoyed our talk together, and I must say that the sense of purpose I felt in the team on this occasion was more my kind of music than the 'we've got it made' attitude I had sensed 12 months before. It seemed to me that everybody in the team was out to bury the recent past as quickly as possible, and to stage a fighting comeback.

But I have to say that I liked many things that I saw. I love the Italians and many of the things they do: their creations, their attitude. At the end of the season with the Bowmaker Lola I figured that I had sufficient F1 experience to make the correct judgement, so when the opportunity arose again, I decided to make the change and go to Maranello.

Racing was controlled to a large extent by the fuel sponsors. Lotus were Esso. Stirling and Rob Walker were totally involved with BP, as were the Cooper team. I was made an offer to go to BRM, but there were complications with Graham Hill and, while they were superb engineers – and their cars very rarely broke – it just didn't seem the right thing. Likewise with Bowmaker and the Lola project: I couldn't be sure where the long-term future lay.

After that promising start to the 1½-litre formula in 1961, Ferrari had been through a pretty dismal time in 1962 when the British V8s from Coventry Climax and BRM outclassed their V6 engines. Our Lolas had been far more competitive than the Italian cars. But Ferrari did control their own exclusive engine supply and I'd had a frustrating time with customer engines with Yeoman Credit and Bowmaker over the previous two seasons. It seemed like a good opportunity to join what was effectively a brand new team, also offering a chance to drive in sports car events.

It had to be the finest time to go to them. They were on the floor, but they also wanted to pick themselves up and have a bit of a go. Mauro Forghieri had been brought on as a junior engineer and I got on with him fine. He was a new boy like me, and I think I was able to inject a little of my recent experience into the whole project, offering them a fresh approach.

In many ways we started with a bit of a hotch-potch really, because we had to choose from this great pile of bits and pieces in order to put something workable together. This effort was underpinned by the more seasoned Walter Salvarani and Franco Rocchi, who were mainly responsible for all the projects which had come out of Ferrari since the Chiti period, and who would continue when I was there. So it was a nice balance of youthful enthusiasm and experience.

If I joined the team, I would be doing so as a new boy among many other new boys, each of us anxious to prove that we could succeed in our respective jobs. All in all, it seemed to me like a pretty good set-up. A brief test session was laid on at the nearby Modena autodrome where I tried a 156 prototype F1 car which Willy Mairesse had used the previous season at the Nürburgring and Monza. It had been built up around the little Belgian driver, and I found the only way I could drive it was to take the seat out and place some sorbo rubber on the fuel tank – and then cut off the toes of my shoes!

After only a few laps I was satisfied that the machine had the makings of a proper racing car. The handling needed sorting out, but basically it felt good and strong. That seemed a pretty good formula to start with. I also had some testing with the shark-nosed, 3-litre V12, single-overhead-camshaft sports car which had been powered by a V6 the previous year. This was the first sports car I had driven since the Aston Martin DBR1 and would form the basis of the very successful 250P sports prototype which we used in 1963.

I went back to Maranello, and this time when Enzo Ferrari handed me the contract – a simple document, signifying my agreement to drive any of his cars for one year – I signed immediately. I'm not the sort of person to show my emotions, but I knew as I wrote my name on that piece of paper that I was making one of the most important decisions of my life.

Maybe the year ahead would not be an easy one but, ever since I had exchanged my motor cycle leathers for a driving suit, which year had been?

Chapter 5

Settling in at Ferrari

I like to think that I had a good understanding with the people who worked with me in the Ferrari team. They had immediately given me virtually the main responsibility for test-driving the sports and F1 machines and the odd production car. However, I have to confess that my association started out on a tricky note with an episode at my first race which made me so livid that I almost walked out on the spot. The event in question occurred on the eve of the 1963 Sebring 12-hour endurance race which was scheduled to be my maiden outing for the Prancing Horse.

The whole affair started at Monza soon after I joined the team. We were there to try out the new 3-litre V12-engined 250P sports prototype which had been built for that year's series of endurance races, of which Sebring would be our first event. This was a development of the car I had driven on my first visit to the factory at the time I agreed the contract.

I've always believed, whether it be a bike or a car, that time spent tailoring it to your personal requirements is time well spent. It is only common sense that, especially in long-distance races, a driver can produce a better performance if he is completely comfortable behind the wheel, has all controls within convenient reach and, of course, has the car's handling suited to his driving technique. This question of tailoring the cockpit is very important if a driver is to have full control of the car, but also introduces the problem, for long-distance races, of a compromise in terms of balancing the requirements of drivers of varying size.

The team's cars were all built and given a short test at Modena. Having been told which car I was to share with Lodovico Scarfiotti, I also put in quite a lot of time tailoring the cockpit just as we wanted it. By the time the car was shipped to America, it felt very different from when it had first left the factory and I was very happy with the transformation.

However, I was not so happy when I arrived at Sebring and found that my competition numbers had been put on the wrong car. At first I assumed that there had been a genuine error, but when I pointed it out to Eugenio Dragoni, the team manager, I quickly realised that it ran a bit deeper than that.

It seemed that Willy Mairesse, who was driving the other entry with Nino Vaccarella, had already tried both cars and found mine very much more comfortable, hence the change of numbers. I protested strongly, but Dragoni made out he couldn't understand what all the fuss was about and he simply didn't seem disposed towards having the numbers on the cars changed back again. He just shrugged his shoulders and turned away,

Above: *On the startline at Brands Hatch with the little Triumph Tiger 70 (number 23).*

My father enjoyed considerable success in sidecar events and I began my racing career as his passenger.

*My father pours me a glass of
Lucozade as Alan Trow looks
on just prior to the start of the
1957 Isle of Man Junior TT.*

Left: *With one of th[e]
Manx Nortons wit[h]
which I became a
regular race winn[er]
in 1954.*

Above: *I chased Bob McIntyre hard to finish second in the 1957 Senior TT without the aerodynamic benefits of full streamlining.*

A new boy at MV Agusta in 1956, with, on my right, Arturo Magni and, on my left, Count Agusta, Umberto Masetti and Carlo Bandirola.

Totally wet through and frozen after victory in the worst possible conditions in the 1959 Senior TT.

Opposite: *My MV Agusta – wearing its full fairing – making a pit stop during the 1957 500 Belgian Grand Prix.*

Below: *Heading for victory in the 1958 Isle of Man Senior TT, the MV Agusta now wearing the maximum fairings permitted by the new regulations.*

Waiting to start the 1960 Portuguese Grand Prix from pole position in my Lotus 18 (right) alongside Dan Gurney's BRM and Jack Brabham's Cooper, with Stirling Moss's Lotus 18 and Graham Hill's BRM on the second row.

With the Yeoman Credit Cooper-Climax at Monaco in 1961.

I learned a lot in 1962 as we worked to make the Bowmaker Lola competitive. I was fastest in practice for the Dutch Grand Prix at Zandvoort but my race ended in dramatic fashion when a front suspension link broke.

My first Grand Prix win on four wheels, with the Ferrari, at the Nürburgring in 1963.

At the wheel of a Ferrari GTO in the 1962 Tourist Trophy, where Jim Clark's Aston Martin spun in front of me and put me out of the race while I was in the lead.

With the Ferrari 156 (below right) in the 1963 British Grand Prix at Silverstone. Staying up half the previous night fitting an auxiliary fuel tank certainly paid off as I managed to finish second ahead of Graham Hill's BRM.

JOHN SURTEES

Easing through the Esses with the Ferrari 250P during the 1964 Le Mans 24-hour race which Bandini and I came close to winning.

Although I became World Champion in 1964 with the Ferrari 158, in many ways it was an extremely frustrating year.

Hustling the V8 Ferrari through the streets of Monte Carlo in 1965. My efforts proved in vain when I ran short of fuel on the penultimate lap.

In earnest discussion with (left to right) *Trevor Taylor, Ronnie Bucknum and my former Lotus team-mate, Innes Ireland, in 1964.*

I derived a great deal of enjoyment racing and developing the Lola T70 sports car in conjunction with Eric Broadley.

Opposite: *Leading Jackie Stewart's BRM at Monaco, 1966, with the 3-litre Ferrari V12. I retired, Stewart was first and Bandini finished second in the little Tasman Dino 246 with which I had told Dragoni I would win him the race.*

Below: *I rounded off the 1966 season on a high note with victory in the Mexican Grand Prix with the Cooper-Maserati V12.*

The United States Grand Prix produced BRM's best performance of the 1969 season when I came home third in the P139.

In the Honda RA301 I chase Jacky Ickx's Ferrari down the hill at Rouen during the tragic 1968 French Grand Prix which cost the life of Jo Schlesser in the Honda RA302.

Opposite: *In discussion with Honda's Yoshio Nakamura (right) at the Nürburgring in 1967, where I finished fourth in the old RA273 chassis.*

Left: *Leading the South African Grand Prix at Kyalami in 1971 with my Surtees TS9, a race I almost won.*

whereupon I became really mad, stormed out of the circuit and went back to my hotel.

I was packing my things, intent on catching the next plane home, when there was a knock on my bedroom door. It was Lodovico. Gradually he eased me out of my temper by explaining that my action, however justified it might be, had put him in a very awkward situation. Eventually I cooled down and, in the end, we decided that the best thing to do was to beat them at their own game. I didn't really believe this business of Mairesse not being comfortable in the other car, and felt it was just a bit of calculated needling of the new boy, just to prove who was boss. So I said, 'All right, Lodovico, we'll take the uncomfortable car and, what's more, we'll beat them with it.'

And that's exactly what happened. It would have been a very clear-cut victory indeed had we not run into electrical trouble near the end, as a result of which we finished only one lap ahead of the other team car. But that was sufficient – at least we thought so, but it seemed that not everybody shared our view.

After making a reasonable sort of start I found myself in about seventh place, moving up to third midway round the opening lap, with Phil Hill's AC Cobra having taken the initial advantage. I had been used to braking at the end of the main straight at about the 300-yard board but, as I moved up to challenge for the lead, I decided it would be more prudent to start slowing at the 400-yard board as the 250P was heavy with full fuel tanks.

Unfortunately, although I had bedded in a number of sets of pads during practice, nobody advised me that the car had been fitted with fresh brake pads, and I shot past Hill about 70 mph faster than the Cobra was travelling and went straight up the escape road! It was an immediate lesson that I had to create a clear understanding with the mechanics on my cars as I could not rely on the team manager. That was the first of several incidents which were to make that race such a tough grind for Scarfiotti and myself.

In fact, the car we drove was significantly unsorted compared with the one we did the testing on. Before the race was very old, Lodovico and I started to be affected by exhaust fumes seeping into the cockpit. This was really a legacy of the car's newness. The rear engine cover was secured at two points behind the cockpit, one on each side of the car, and we soon discovered that the cover was not a good fit. At high speed, air pressure beneath it was causing it to lift.

The cockpit of the Ferrari was, of course, a low-pressure area, which meant that the air was liable to be sucked in, so there was a steady flow of exhaust fumes drawn forward through the engine compartment and into the cockpit. Apart from that, we had some plug trouble after I had worked our way back up to about fourth place, and after a pit stop I had to go through the whole routine again before I could hand the car over to Scarfiotti in second place.

By then we were still behind the front-engined 4-litre Ferrari of Graham Hill and Pedro Rodriguez which we saw as our main threat. Fortunately for us, they were delayed by lighting troubles (as we had been), without which we would not have been able to notch up a victory for the new Ferrari prototype. However, it was the exhaust problem which had really made life so unpleasant for much of the race, and nearly every time we changed places the out-going driver ran straight out behind the pits and brought his heart up.

I must say that I couldn't have seemed very gallant when the two Florida beauty queens cuddled up to us both on the winners' rostrum. 'Mine' started to get really amorous, cooing into my ear, 'This is nice,' to which my reaction was to turn my back hurriedly and be sick for about ten minutes. Altogether, on two counts, it was not a particularly auspicious ending to my first race as a Ferrari works driver.

I enjoyed being paired with Lodovico; he drove with me on several occasions and I enjoyed working with him. Although he was a member of a wealthy family – he was second cousin to Gianni Agnelli – he wasn't a particularly political character. He was just a good, solid sports car driver whom I always found I could depend on.

Soon after the Sebring race was over, we heard through the grapevine that a protest had reached the Press Office on behalf of the other works Ferrari entry, claiming that their car had covered more laps than we had. This was really quite laughable, because the only two complete lap charts which could be found were the organisers' and the one which my wife Pat had kept for Lodovico and myself. These two charts told the same story – namely, that we were the winners.

The lap scorers who were acting for Willy and Nino must have been psychic, because they spent half their time in the back of the pit with their feet up, possibly suffering from an over-indulgence in Florida oranges – or, more like it, Californian wine! Any resemblance between their chart and the official lap-by-lap positions could only have been coincidental. Throughout my time with Ferrari, Dragoni was never able to produce accurate lap charts or time-keeping. But that didn't stop him continuing on the offensive by stating to the press on his return to Rome airport that I hadn't really won the race!

After this episode, I think Dragoni quickly came to appreciate that I was not to be treated in the rather casual manner which he'd become used to with the Italian drivers. From then on, an uneasy calm would exist between us, occasionally exploding out of hand, but – until 1966 – always settled by some explanation or other by Mr Ferrari himself.

I think Dragoni particularly resented the fact that I didn't have to rely on him totally for lap times and information on how the other competitors were doing. With Pat doing all the teams' lap scoring and timing virtually the entire field, I had my own private source of information, which I'm not sure he was too happy about. In addition, he had played no part in recruiting me to Ferrari in the first place.

Dragoni had been on the motor racing sidelines before he took over the Ferrari team management after becoming involved with Scuderia St Ambroseus, which ran the car Maranello lent to the Italian federation in 1961. Giancarlo Baghetti drove this car and, of course, gained some temporary celebrity status by winning his very first Grand Prix, the French race at Reims.

By profession, Dragoni was a Milan industrialist, with interests in the pharmaceutical business, whose character I found extremely difficult to understand. Although he cared quite deeply for motor racing (or was it just a means to an end, or a big ego trip? I'm not sure), he demonstrated that typical Italian trait of indulging in sporting politics. He may have fitted in well with Ferrari on that score, but I believe that, as a team manager, he was incompetent and quite a liability to Maranello. He readily worked on the old Ferrari principle of trying to set one member of the driving team against the others off the track.

From the outset, I found that endurance racing required a technique very different from that employed behind the wheel of a Formula 1 car. In the first place, the cars were set up quite differently from a Grand Prix single-seater and, with the power on tap from a 3-litre V12 engine, the sensation of driving the 250P for the first time reminded me of the days when I tried the Aston Martin DBR1 and the Vanwall at Goodwood.

The 250P was, in my view, certainly a *simpatico* car to handle, but it must have weighed in at around 1900 lb, which meant it was no lightweight by racing standards and called for more manual effort than I had been used to exerting in motor racing. There was also a lot more noise. With enveloping bodywork surrounding the driver, he also tends to feel more remote from the road. Overall, though, it was not an unpleasant sensation and, once I got the hang of that very willing V12 engine, I began to get a big kick out of driving the Ferrari prototypes.

It's important to explain the word 'prototype' in connection with these cars, because the 3-litre Ferrari 250P and its successors, the 3.3-litre 275P and 4-litre 330P, were not built as sports cars in the manner of, for example, the Lotus 30 or Lola T70, and the other British lightweight 'Appendix C' – or Group 7, as it would later become – two-seaters with large American V8 engines. Instead, they were prototypes of potential Grand Touring cars of the future and the fact that they happened to have open bodywork was almost incidental. They were not sprint cars capable of putting in fantastically quick lap times in short-duration races and, as a consequence, did not always show up so well in these events, particularly when held on relatively slow and tight circuits. I think Enzo Ferrari and his team could feel justly proud of the fact that, during my first two years with them, although I lost several long-distance race victories through mechanical bothers, these were always due to some trivial fault – such as electrics – and not once the result of a major mechanical failure.

As far as the Formula 1 programme was concerned, I hadn't been a Ferrari works driver very long before I realised that we would not be able to keep to our planned schedule. The original scheme had been to use the uprated 156 which Mairesse had driven at the Nürburgring and Monza the previous year – and which had been the first Ferrari F1 car I tested at Modena – for Willy and I to drive in the first few races. These would be raced until the new semi-monocoque 156s were ready in about June.

I had also understood that, as part of our preparations for the World Championship, which started with the Monaco Grand Prix, we would be taking part in a few of the non-championship events in Britain and on the Continent in order to limber up for the main programme. However, things worked out a bit differently from what I had expected.

Mainly because of the factory's preoccupation with the sports cars, and their heavy early-season programme at Sebring, the Targa Florio and the Nürburgring 1000 Km – all of which led up to Le Mans – our F1 development programme fell well behind schedule. Consequently, while the opposition had about half a dozen such races in which to prepare themselves, we had to wait until 11 May for a pre-season warm-up at the BRDC Silverstone International Trophy race, only a fortnight prior to Monaco. We had had very little testing and, clearly, if anything went badly wrong in this race, we wouldn't be left with much time to get it sorted out for the first round of the championship.

Before starting on the F1 trail we had a busy time with the prototypes, taking the 250Ps to the Le Mans test weekend, where I was fastest, and the Targa Florio, the Sicilian road race which I was contesting for the first time. It could hardly have provided a more vivid contrast to the billiard table-smooth tarmac at Le Mans.

When I arrived at the 44-mile Madonie Piccolo circuit, the surface of which ranged from adequately good to quite diabolically bad, I was horrified at what I found. The usual plan was to hire a car in order to make a preliminary reconnaissance of the route before getting down to the serious business of practice.

I shared a Fiat 1100 with Mike Parkes, who had already been there for a few days, and was staggered to come across small groups of labourers laying down a few stone chippings here and there to fill in some of the more serious holes in the road. I must say it seemed inconceivable to me that we should be racing on this surface within a couple of days.

Of course, the circuit was so long that you could not possibly learn it all in the comparatively short spell allotted for official practice. You really did need nerves of steel to deal with it all; around every corner you could expect to find anything from workmen shovelling grit, a couple of peasants having a quiet chat in the middle of the road, or perhaps two farm trucks being driven, side by side, straight towards you to the odd donkey.

That said, there have been few races I have contested anywhere in the world which attracted such an enthusiastic local following. For this event I was paired with Parkes, who did the first stint, and I inherited quite a useful lead when he handed over the 250P, due in part to the fact that the Mairesse/Vaccarella car had retired.

Nino was a charming schoolteacher from Palermo, a local boy who could drive the circuit blindfold. He was 'Mr Targa Florio'. It was something to be seen, the way he could find his way round that circuit. He made me feel very humble, because I just didn't know where I was going!

He also did a good job in the sports car team generally: a reliable, sound sort who just quietly got on with it – just happy to come along, sit in the car and drive it as quickly as he could. However, on this occasion in the Targa, his luck was out. One of the cars he was driving was burnt out in practice, then the other landed heavily after taking off over a sharp bump, and flattened a fuel line in the process.

My race was quite a brief affair. About halfway round my second lap, I got on some loose gravel going into a right-hander. The car understeered straight off the road and ran down a bank. For a few moments I thought I would be able to get the car back on the road again – there were plenty of able bodies around, all anxious to help – but then I discovered the fuel tank had split.

Naturally I was very disappointed indeed, for Mike Parkes as much as for myself, and I was also concerned for the safety of the car. I didn't particularly want to spend the next few hours sitting on a bank guarding it somewhere in the middle of Sicily, yet I didn't want to abandon it either. That would have been an open invitation to the souvenir hunters.

In the end, I compromised and took a middle course. I entrusted it to the care of a policeman I luckily managed to find, who seemed suitably impressed by the honour bestowed on him, and hitched a lift back to the pits with a travelling marshal. The car was duly reclaimed intact!

On my return, Dragoni's first concern was for my own safety, which I thought was very considerate of him, and, after I had assured him that I was quite all right, he shrugged off the loss of the race very philosophically. It was not a very satisfactory meeting for us at all, because almost within sight of the line, our 2-litre car shared by Bandini, Mairesse and Scarfiotti was pipped for victory by the eight-cylinder Porsche of Jo Bonnier and Carlo Abate. Mairesse spun in a brief rain shower shortly before the finish and, although he sprinted to the line with the rear engine cover trailing, the incident had caused his advantage to evaporate.

Next on the agenda was the F1 debut at Silverstone where practice produced a few assorted bothers, the most serious of which concerned the new Bosch high-pressure direct fuel injection system which we just couldn't get to function consistently. When it was running properly, there was no doubt that it did a fine job, but at this stage of its development it proved extremely temperamental and, at times, made the car quite a handful.

The Ferrari V6 was now capable of being run to 10,500 rpm – 1000 rpm up on what had been permissible in 1962 – and we were working on a pretty narrow rev band, so it didn't help us at all when the engine would suddenly lapse onto four cylinders coming through a fast corner like Woodcote. In the circumstances, I suppose that we had cause to be grateful that the 156, although not the best-handling car on the track, was very forgiving. With a more precise-handling chassis, a sudden loss of power through a fast corner could have been quite tricky!

I qualified respectably on the inside of the second row, ahead of Jimmy Clark and Trevor Taylor in their Lotus 25s, while in front of us were Jack Brabham's Brabham, Bruce McLaren's Cooper, Graham Hill's BRM and surprise pole-position man Innes Ireland in the UDT Laystall Lotus 24 in which he had won at Goodwood a few weeks before.

Innes misjudged his start and I quickly got through to fourth place, moving into third behind Clark and McLaren after a couple of laps. It was encouraging to find the Ferrari running competitively, at least when the fuel injection was behaving itself, but I soon noticed that every time I went round a right-hand bend a tell-tale smokescreen built up, which was very worrying. This was later found to be leaking oil dripping onto a hot exhaust.

On lap ten I got up to second place where I stayed until lap 31 when the oil pressure finally vanished and I switched off the engine. Willy, meanwhile, had crashed into the ditch at Stowe Corner, rumpling his car quite badly, but although I had been forced to retire we had no real reason to feel despondent as the Ferrari had proved pretty competitive on this important occasion.

The following weekend the Nürburgring 1000 Km sports car meeting started off badly for us when Vaccarella wrote off a brand new 250P during practice which meant that we were down to two works prototypes, the second being shared by Scarfiotti and Mike Parkes.

If there was one driver who knew the Nürburgring really well it was the late Peter Lindner, who was to be killed at Montlhéry in '64 at the wheel of the lightweight Jaguar E-type he was using in this race. He operated a flourishing Jaguar agency in West Germany and was always extremely spectacular value at the 'Ring. At the start of the '63 race he got away brilliantly and led our two prototypes for the entire first 14-mile lap, although I went by as we passed the pits and Lodovico immediately followed me through.

Once ahead, we started to open up quite a lead, but then I suddenly noticed Lodovico was flashing his lights at me. I eased up to let him close the gap and he came alongside. I thought he was going to tell me something of great significance, but he just nodded his head and smiled.

I think he had just decided that I might be lonely out there on my own, and that, as we were both travelling in the same direction, we might as well keep each other company! So, for lap after lap, we went round in line-ahead formation, although not so close that we could involve each other in any trouble. Ironically, something of that kind was to happen later, but in a rather different fashion.

I completed my scheduled 14 laps, then pulled in to hand over to Willy, while Lodovico went through to complete 15 laps before handing over to Parkes. Theirs was a faster pit stop than ours, so that Mike had left the pits holding the lead before Willy reappeared at the end of his personal first lap. Then, suddenly, there was a lot of animated talk over the loudspeakers and we gathered that both Ferraris had crashed on the same corner!

You can imagine how we felt. A mixture of disappointment that the race, which had been going so well, was now lost; fear for the safety of the drivers, and anger that they had ruined our chances by indulging in a private dice, or so we imagined.

In fact, we were quite wrong on the last score. Mike had lost control of his car on the tight right-hander at Aremberg, hit the wall and torn off a rear wheel, suspension, driveshaft and several other bits and pieces. Willy, arriving on the scene seconds later, had run over some of the wreckage and punctured a tyre. He changed the tyre on the spot and cruised gently back to the pits, where another wheel change was needed to cure the lack of balance between the one original and one replacement tyre.

By this stage, Phil Hill was more than half a lap ahead in the lead with the eight-cylinder Porsche, so what had started out looking an easy race for us was clearly going to be a real challenge. Gradually Willy and I whittled down his advantage, but then we were handed the lead back on a plate when Phil left the road on the same right-hander which had claimed Parkes.

From then on, our nearest challengers were the Ferrari GTO of Pierre Noblet and Jean Guichet, and the E-type of Lindner and Peter Nocker, which later retired with engine trouble. At the chequered flag, we ended up with a lead of eight minutes over that GTO, which, on paper, looks like a very comfortable win. But if that race was anything at all, it was definitely not comfortable. I can't remember enjoying a hot bath so much in all my life as the one I had that evening!

The F1 team started off the Monaco weekend more than usually in the dark; the new 156 was very different to its predecessor from the 1962 season. With more power, a different rev band and revised suspension characteristics, it was quite a struggle. I suffered a cracked water manifold in the first session, was briefly fastest in the second and brushed the barrier at the chicane due to fading brakes in the third. Nevertheless, I wound up on the second row of the grid behind Clark's Lotus and Hill's BRM.

This was the first year for which the organisers had moved the start/finish line to its present position in front of the pits rather than just before the old Gasometer hairpin in what, today, is the Monaco pit lane. There had been a multiple pile-up on the first corner the previous year, so this very sensible revised arrangement was adopted, which presented the field with a long sprint to Ste Devote, the first corner and in those days a pretty quick right-hander.

From the start Hill and Richie Ginther went ahead in their BRMs, while I watched the action from just behind Clark in fourth place. On this occasion I was particularly interested to see that this was not the relaxed and calm Jimmy. He was having a really big go, at times getting the Lotus 25 very crossed up out of the corners, while the BRMs seemed to be pulling away much more cleanly, gaining useful yards on acceleration, particularly out of the two hairpins.

Eventually Jimmy got through to the front before retiring close to the end of the race with transmission trouble; I was hampered by fluctuating oil pressure again and was eventually quite satisfied to finish fourth behind both BRMs and Bruce McLaren's Cooper. On the very last lap I threw caution to the wind and established a new record of 1m 34.5s, which was a source of additional pleasure.

It was a bitter-sweet moment, though. My relief at having finished this gruelling race was tempered by the niggling thought that perhaps it was the oil pressure gauge, and not the engine, that was at fault on this occasion. But post-race scrutiny revealed that the gauge was correct and our problems had in fact been caused by bearing trouble.

Not that you would have reached that conclusion had you read the Italian press during the days that followed. I was blamed for throwing the race away through tiredness, and it was claimed that I was responsible for Ferrari not scoring a deserved victory. I need hardly add that the journalists concerned were not even present at the race, nor had they troubled to check a few facts with the factory before going into print. Such precautions seemed of secondary importance . . .

At least this incident enabled Enzo Ferrari to have a spot of fun at my expense. Before the race, one of his most attractive female customers had made herself known to me, and we were photographed together. Inevitably, the prints found their way onto Ferrari's desk at Maranello. After examining them at some length, he looked at me long and hard – with just the slightest sign of a twinkle in his eye – and said, 'On second thoughts, there could be some substance to these "tired driver" reports I have read in the Italian press!'

A batch of faulty brake cylinders, a pair of which were fitted to my 156 before practice started at Spa for the Belgian Grand Prix, left me with the interesting experience of absolutely no retardation coming into the fast Stavelot right-hander during practice. I just made it with my wheels virtually rubbing against the advertising hoardings. Again we had problems with the high-pressure fuel pump, constant running on full throttle apparently overheating the pumps and causing air locks to form in the system. I managed to get onto the front row alongside Hill's BRM and Dan Gurney's Brabham, but a recurrence of that injection trouble caused retirements in the race for both myself and Mairesse.

As the reader will have gathered, our European racing schedule was pretty hectic, even more so when one considers that we were still driving almost everywhere on the Continent. In that connection, I can well remember Mr Ferrari's rather withering reaction when I turned up at Maranello still driving my trusty old BMW 507 which was, by now, almost six years old.

At that time Mr Ferrari wasn't terribly enamoured of German cars. He was quite prepared to use companies such as Bosch to supply crucial components, although he preferred the British suppliers. But he definitely turned up his nose at the BMW. He told me I ought to be driving a Ferrari. There was no doubt in his mind. But there was no question of a free hand-out when it came to supplying one, as today's drivers might demand – in addition to their millions!

He wanted to sell me a Super America – I don't think they were selling too well. Personally, I was attracted to the little Lusso, but unfortunately it was just that – a little Lusso. So eventually I decided that the 330GT was most suited to my purposes, offering a reasonable amount of space for all my luggage and racing kit. I think I got a dealer discount of 15 per cent and paid somewhere in the region of £3000 for my first one, about the same as I'd paid for my BMW in 1957.

My first 330GT was a grey one, which I kept through to 1964, when I changed it for – what else – a red one, which never went quite so well, for some reason. The first one was subsequently sold to Henry Manney of *Road and Track* magazine, the second to Luigi Chinetti. I put about 30,000 miles on each of them and they performed reliably. The 330GT was not a true sports car, but that V12 was nice.

I had a close call with the second one, returning from Italy in the snow with Pat. Just before we got to the Swiss border, I lost control approaching a level crossing where a sheet of frozen water had built up on the road. We just slewed across the road, down a bank and hit a tree – luckily not too hard, but below there was a 500-foot drop. Neither of us was hurt and the car was repairable, even though it had been over on its roof.

Motoring in Europe, of course, was more of a pleasure in those days. I could leave Gallarate in the BMW, or Maranello in the Ferrari, at four o'clock in the morning and get back to England in a day, averaging 70 mph for the trip door to door. That involved using Silver City Airways and their Bristol Freighter service from Le Touquet to Lydd, in Kent, which left me only a short run up to our home in Limpsfield.

There was just no traffic around by today's standards. It really was a stress-free exercise. I never thought anything of driving home for three days, then driving back to Italy. Today, for all the motorways and autoroutes, a trip to Italy by road is a major undertaking.

When I was in Modena we used to stay in the Hotel Fini at 2000 lire a day, at a time when there were 1750 lire to the pound sterling, and we ate like lords in the Tucano Restaurant, where all the culinary delicacies of the Modenese region were available for 1000 lire a meal. These fringe benefits made for a very nice life which suited us down to the ground and made up for the poor money Ferrari paid their drivers.

Despite our disappointing showing at Spa, there was insufficient time available in the racing schedule for us to get down to any serious F1 testing. We had to be satisfied with a bit of bedding-in work before Zandvoort, where I had a new partner in Scarfiotti.

Willy Mairesse was briefly out of commission, having suffered burns at Le Mans when the 250P with which we were leading the race suddenly ignited following a pit stop due to excess fuel being slopped into the undertray during refuelling. With only a few hours to go, I had just handed over to him and, as he went to brake for the Esses on his first lap, it seems that a short circuit from the stop light switch may have ignited vaporising fuel in the undertray; the whole car just went up and he went off the road. That left Bandini and Scarfiotti with an easy win.

This was a great shame, for Willy had been driving quite well during the season up to that point, and, coming only a few weeks after our memorable victory at the Nürburgring, proved to be a turning-point in his fortunes.

As usual, once Le Mans was over, the Ferrari racing department began to concentrate more of its attention on the Grand Prix scene. After solving a slight chassis alignment problem during first practice in Holland, I finished the first session third fastest –

although I was still 1.2s slower than the best time I'd recorded in the Bowmaker Lola 12 months earlier. With a fresh engine installed, I managed to get onto the second row of the grid and finished a solid third in the race. But I was very concerned that we had been lapped by Clark's Lotus; a high placing is no real comfort when you know that your car is basically uncompetitive.

The French Grand Prix at Reims was unfortunate for Scarfiotti who crashed heavily in practice. The accident happened near the top of the hill between Muizon and Thillois, where the constant rain had caused a small rivulet to develop across the track. He slid sideways on this, careered off course, and demolished a whole line of telegraph poles. Although he must have been travelling at over 100 mph at the time, the Ferrari stayed on its wheels and Lodovico went to hospital with nothing worse than a damaged knee, bruises and a determination to announce his retirement from racing – which he later revoked.

I qualified on the inside of the second row behind Clark, Hill in the experimental monocoque BRM and Gurney's Brabham, only for the start to be rendered a total fiasco by the antics of 'Toto' Roche, the long-time Clerk of the Course who could usually be relied upon to produce pandemonium on the grid. This year was no exception.

Hill found that he couldn't start the BRM and raised his hand to warn everybody behind, expecting that he would be left on the grid. But M. Roche had other ideas. He ordered the BRM mechanics to push-start their car, which was against FIA rules, and as soon as the car had been pushed back into position he dropped the red flag which he happened to be holding at the time.

Everybody took that to mean the race was on, although according to the rule book the red flag means 'stop the race immediately'. It was a real carnival, and for Graham it ultimately meant the forfeiture of the points he thought he had won for third place, in addition to the 60-second penalty he was awarded during the race. It was all very complicated and unnecessary.

After the first few laps I managed to consolidate second place behind Jimmy, but after only nine laps the engine began to misfire and, three laps later, it packed up altogether and I came into the pits. The mechanics quickly found and replaced a blown fuse on the electric fuel pump, but it lasted only another half-lap on my return to the track, which told me that the problem was rather more deep-rooted than we had initially thought.

Subsequent examination revealed the problem to be in the fuel pump itself, one of a special batch which had been flown over from America in an attempt to cure the starvation problems we had experienced at Spa. In assembling the pump, one of the leads had been wrapped round a terminal, but not soldered onto it. The lead had just vibrated off.

After a spot of serious testing at the Nürburgring, where we managed a best lap of 8m 44s – well under the record – it was back to Silverstone for the British Grand Prix. With both Mairesse and Scarfiotti out of action, I was running 'solo' again at this race and had two cars to choose from, one a brand new chassis to replace the one lost at Reims.

During practice, when we did our fuel consumption calculations, we concluded that our existing tankage would be right on the danger line when it came to the 82-lap, 240-mile race. At first glance, it was not easy to see what might be done, because in those days of ultra-compact F1 cars it was extremely difficult to find any spare space for anything, let alone a bulky item like a fuel tank, but we decided that it would be possible to fit in a small, triangular-shaped tank under my legs and forward of the front bulkhead. The next problem was to build one!

After a lot of searching around, we managed to find a supply of galvanised iron sheeting from a garage in Brackley on the evening prior to the race. As I was the only one in our party who could weld, I had to roll up my sleeves and get to work with a torch. It proved quite a difficult job because all the galvanising had to be burnt off and the metal cleaned up before I could fabricate and weld it.

Eventually I managed to present the mechanics with a roughly triangular structure which – remarkably – managed to hold about 1½ gallons of petrol. It was a real backyard blacksmith's job, but it looked as though it would do the trick, and we linked it into the system via a T-piece between the two main tanks. As I climbed into bed at 2 a.m. on race morning, I hoped that all the hard work would pay off.

As things turned out, that extra fuel tankage played right into our hands. While Jimmy's Lotus steamed off into the distance, I was left dicing with Graham Hill's BRM for what eventually turned out to be second place. I was just about resigning myself to third when Graham's car hesitated, low on fuel, possibly, coming through Abbey Curve for the last time. I was able to sail past and finish second, reaping a harvest of good fortune which had been planted with that toil the previous evening.

After Silverstone, it was on to the Nürburgring, scene of possibly the biggest disappointment of my career up to that point. Twelve months earlier I think I can fairly say that I was robbed of my first Grand Prix victory on four wheels by the intervention of a slower car on the last lap. That day, I had finished an out-of-breath second, with the firm determination to go one better in 1963.

Willy Mairesse was back in the team for this race, now happily recovered from his Le Mans burns. He used my Silverstone car, while I took over a newer chassis fitted with new bolt-on wheels which, together with revised hubs, saved in the order of 4 lb unsprung weight on each corner.

Our earlier testing outing at the 'Ring paid dividends as we had already worked out a good chassis set-up and I managed to qualify a comfortable second to Clark, with Lorenzo Bandini emerging as one of the sensations of the weekend with the Scuderia Centro Sud BRM, qualifying third alongside me.

It was good to be on the front row, but I'm afraid I threw it all away by making a slow start. After a bit of sorting out I got past Clark and Ginther in the BRM to take the lead, and Jimmy quickly followed me through into second place. From then on we both chopped and changed for the lead, both of us suffering a spot of engine inconsistency. Jimmy's Lotus was intermittently lapsing onto seven cylinders, while the fuel bleeds on my tanks were tending to lose fuel, which was being drawn down the intakes, giving me four or five cylinders at times.

Thankfully, after a few laps this trouble died out and I was left feeling completely in command of the race. I was able to set a new lap record of 8m 47s, and still keep just that little bit in hand in case the pressure increased, but I don't mind admitting I felt pretty good. It wasn't really a walkover, either, because for several laps Jimmy kept right up with me, and it was not until the closing stages that he disappeared from my mirrors for good.

That final 15th lap seemed a particularly long one, but eventually the startline tower came into sight, and I surged over the brow for the last time to take the chequered flag. It was a wonderful moment. I had always believed that the good old V6 workhorse had it in it to win a World Championship Grand Prix in 1963 and, although we waited long enough for it, I was delighted that we finally demonstrated that ability on the toughest circuit of them all.

Basically, the V6 was a good little engine, but the problem with it was that it wasn't safe to rev it where it developed its full power. If you took it to 11,000 rpm it was fantastic, but going over 10,000 rpm meant that we risked running into piston and valve troubles, so, for practical purposes, we were down on power compared with the Climax or BRM V8s.

Swiss injection specialist Michael May had been appointed as a consultant on a 'no cure, no pay' basis and, with the development of special Bosch high-pressure direct injection, we began to make progress. Prior to the Nürburgring race we spent a week or so with Bosch trying to sort out the fuel injection, the original design of which hadn't been conceived with small-capacity engines in mind.

Getting precise fuel metering across a wide rev range was the biggest problem, but things were much improved by our testing in Germany, where we developed a new mechanical linkage to operate the metering system rather than the previous vacuum-operated arrangement. This allowed us to make a better compromise, rather like the Lucas mechanical injection system, in fact, which was mechanically operated by a cam on the stroke of the piston.

On the rough and ready circuits – like the Nürburgring – where you needed such a compromise in car setting, you could produce results, but where sheer power was involved we were at a bit of a loss. The tubular chassis's behaviour at places like the 'Ring was rather Cooper-ish; quite good handling, as regards predictability, but not very efficient in the sense of Colin Chapman's cars, for example, because it spent too much time travelling sideways and used too much road. As I said before, in connection with the difference between the Formula Junior Cooper and Lotus, Colin's cars managed to put their power down onto the road with the minimum loss of that power.

Another point to remember about circuits like the Nürburgring is that, with all the flexing over the bumps, it was quite common to find the fuel leaking over your legs, so you would finish the race with overalls soaked with petrol. The advent of monocoque chassis and bag tanks certainly represented a considerable improvement in terms of comfort and safety.

Ferrari had been talking about building a flat-12 for a long time, but in the meantime they introduced the V8, which I feel they should never have completed. It was never as quick as the V6 in its best form, although you could at least run it reliably, and, on balance, I think they should have gone directly from the V6 to the flat-12.

Sadly, Mairesse's return to F1 was brief; he crashed heavily at Flugplatz on the opening lap and was hospitalised for several months. It marked the end of his career with Ferrari, and also in Grand Prix racing.

A word about Willy: he was a quick driver, probably a little faster than Bandini at the time I joined the Ferrari team. But he was quite highly strung and, after the Nürburgring accident, his was a very sad story. He was quite talented, but there was an awful lot of tension and emotion inside him. Very sadly, he eventually committed suicide in 1969. His world was so shattered when motor racing finally gave him up, a few years later, that I imagine he felt there was nothing left to live for. It was a great tragedy, for I had real respect for his ability to handle a racing car.

Unfortunately, the Nürburgring was to be my sole Formula 1 victory of the 1963 season. A particular disappointment was Monza, where, after more work on the engine and chassis, I managed to qualify in pole position and set the pace among the leading bunch before engine failure caused me to retire after only 17 laps. The car I was using there was the new semi-monocoque Ferrari chassis which had been built to accept the new 90-degree V8 engine but, since it wasn't quite ready, the chassis was adapted to take the trusty V6.

Of course, this was not a true monocoque in the sense of a Lotus 25. I had wanted them to do a standard, conventional monocoque, but I think, firstly, there was something of a worry on the part of Mr Ferrari, which was certainly taken up by Forghieri, that they didn't want to follow that path. As a result, they pursued the path of manufacturing it from a skeleton of small tubes over which a stressed outer skin was applied: the Ferrari way of showing their individuality. It was certainly a lot better than the original tubular 156, however!

That race also saw Lorenzo Bandini return to the Ferrari F1 fold as my team-mate. He'd briefly driven for them in 1962 after Mairesse had been injured in a collision with Trevor Taylor's Lotus in the Belgian Grand Prix. I liked Lorenzo a lot. He was uncomplicated, cheerful and non-political. He just loved driving racing cars and, of course, developed into the best Italian driver of that era.

Lorenzo was often underrated by some people, but I thought highly of him. I don't think he was really number one material, or, come to that, ever wanted to be. He liked somebody in the team to relate to, to aim for, and to satisfy himself against an established bench-mark. He was an easy person to work with, and a good competitor.

The 1963 season also saw me make my first visit to the North American sports car series which would eventually blossom into the successful Can-Am Championship a few years later. These races were conveniently slipped into the calendar around the time of the United States and Mexican Grands Prix, so it made sense to make one big trip of it and fill the intervening weekends with some really good sports car racing.

The main problem was to find a suitable car. As previously mentioned, the Ferrari 250P was essentially a long-distance machine, not as fast as a genuine 'Appendix C' sports car. Nevertheless, I was convinced that a 250P could give quite a good account of itself if we could lop off a bit of excess weight, and I managed to persuade the *Commendatore* to release a car to me to run as a private entry in a programme of five sports car races.

Although I was loaned the 250P, Ferrari could not spare a mechanic, so I recruited Peter Bryant, who had been with me in the Bowmaker days, to look after the car on the other side of the Atlantic. Down at Maranello we took a close look at the car and removed all surplus equipment including the high screen, the heavy wiper motors and the air deflector behind the driver's head. We fitted F1-type elekton disc wheels and, in total, managed to reduce its all-up weight by about 100 lb.

David Yorke, who used to be Tony Vandervell's racing manager, agreed to handle the transportation side and general arrangements in North America, and the car was flown to New York; from there, Luigi Chinetti's NART team transported it up to Mosport Park, near Toronto, with Peter Bryant in attendance.

I finished practice for this first race on our programme – titled the Canadian Grand Prix – 1.5s slower than Dan Gurney's Lotus-Ford, which was really as much as we could hope for. Our V12 was developing about 270 bhp while the much lighter Lotus had more than 350 bhp from its 4.7-litre V8, which offered more torque with less weight. Even more worryingly, our fuel consumption calculations suggested strongly that we would have to make a pit stop to replenish the tank during the race.

I mentioned this to Chinetti, who was fielding his own 250P for Pedro Rodriguez in the same race, but he dismissed the whole thing quite casually, saying that he was sure the consumption would not be that high and we would get through OK. I wasn't convinced and decided to wait for an opportunity to take a close look at his car. Sure enough, hidden away under the bonnet was an auxiliary fuel tank!

Shades of the British Grand Prix! Suddenly we found ourselves facing the problem of installing an auxiliary tank at short notice. We rushed back 95 miles to Toronto where we found a canning factory which agreed to make up a tank to our exact specification, containing 9½ gallons, which would just fit into the scuttle area. Installing it was no great problem, but the question of fuel feed itself turned out to be a bit more tricky. However, we eventually got everything organised, only for the race to degenerate into something of a disappointment.

Everything went quite well at first. Rodriguez and I were able to pull away from the rest of the field at about a couple of seconds a lap, with Pedro leading for the first 12 laps before we began to swap places quite regularly. Just when it seemed as though I had it all sewn up, I had to retire at quarter-distance with overheating. That left Pedro an easy win, almost a full lap ahead of Graham Hill's Ian Walker-entered Lotus 23. The big V8s had all retired.

The plan now was for the 250P to be sent out to Riverside, California, while I stayed on to contest the United States Grand Prix at Watkins Glen, where I held the lead for most of the race before a sick engine forced me to retire in the closing stages. It was a bitter moment, not helped by the fact that I had been driving in great pain, having developed third-degree burns on my right foot due to the intense heat which had built up around the pedals.

The following weekend I was still in such discomfort that the doctors on the spot advised me not to race, but I was anxious to honour my contract with the organisers and went to the start at Riverside liberally dosed with pain-killing drugs. The race organisers were extremely sympathetic about it all, and declined my offer not to take my full starting money because I felt I wouldn't be able to produce anything like my best performance.

With the temperatures nudging the 90-degree mark, the favourite was clearly going to be Jim Hall's 5-litre V8-engined Chaparral-Chevrolet, with the 'King Cobras' of Dave McDonald and Bob Holbert from Carroll Shelby's stable also in with a chance. These specials were in fact Cooper-Monacos fitted with Ford V8 engines. All we could realistically hope for was a trouble-free run.

In the event, Jim Hall dominated the race until he was sidelined by an electrical fire, so Dave McDonald was handed a clear lead which he held to win from Roger Penske's Cooper-Zerex, Pedro Rodriguez in a Ford-engined Genie – a locally built lightweight spaceframe car – and myself in fourth.

Unfortunately, taking part in this race had badly aggravated the burns to my feet and there was no way I could drive the 250P at Laguna Seca the next weekend. I got in touch with the organisers and explained my predicament and they quite understood. Obviously, I now had to reappraise my whole North American tour, because the number one priority was to be sufficiently recovered for the Mexican Grand Prix on 3 November.

Immediately after the Mexican race, I was due to compete in the Nassau Speed Week, in the Bahamas, but I decided that I would have to miss these races in order to rest my foot for the South African Grand Prix at the end of the year. After all, my first priority was to Ferrari as a factory F1 driver, not to my own private racing programme. Consequently I asked David Yorke to write to 'Red' Crise, the Nassau race organiser, so he could negotiate for a substitute entry if need be.

Accordingly, David sent the following letter to Crise, dated 25 October 1963:

Dear Captain Crise,

I much regret to have to tell you that, due to reasons beyond our control, it will not be possible for John Surtees to compete in the Nassau speed week. I trust that notification at this date will enable you to enlist a substitute.

Yours Sincerely

David Yorke

I might add that the reasons for my non-appearance were perfectly well known to Crise, who had been following the West Coast races, and was fully acquainted with the fact that my septic foot had been the cause of my withdrawal from the Laguna Seca race at short notice. I heard nothing more until I returned home to receive a letter from Basil Tye, the RAC's Deputy Competitions Manager, which shook me rigid. The letter, dated 13 November 1963, read:

Dear Mr Surtees,

I have been advised by Captain S.F. Crise of the Bahamas Automobile Club that on August 22 last, you agreed to participate in the Bahamas Speed Week, having agreed and accepted the starting money offered to you.

I understand that you have now written to Capt. Crise cancelling your entry, and I should be pleased if you would confirm:

1. That you already agreed to enter for the event and,

2. Give me your reasons as to why you have now decided to cancel your entry as it would appear that there may be some possibility of a breach of RAC General Competition Rule no. 71. However, before deciding whether or not it is necessary for any further action in this matter, I would be pleased to have the facts from you.

Yours Sincerely

Basil Tye

I'm afraid I really blew my top at this and let Basil have it fair and square. Not content at unjustly smearing my name in print, Crise was now even threatening to disrupt my career. I was also shocked that the RAC should imagine that I would behave in such an unprofessional manner, as it was fairly clear from the tone of that first letter that they believed there to be some substance in Crise's complaint.

Anyway, I telephoned Basil Tye, explained the whole sequence of events to him, and left him in no doubt that I was extremely angry about the whole affair. Unfortunately there subsequently seemed to be a difference of opinion about what was said on the phone that day, but I insisted that I could see nothing to apologise to Crise for.

Basil obviously formed the impression that I would send a letter of apology, because in due course I received this letter from him, dated 24 February 1964:

Dear John,

Further to my letter of November 13, and the subsequent telephone call that you made to me at the Carlton, Bournemouth, concerning your non-participation in the Nassau Speed Week, 1963.

I am somewhat surprised to learn that although you undertook to write to Captain Crise a letter of apology, and giving your reasons for not competing in the event, it would appear that you have failed to do this.

Whilst I was in Nassau last December for the Speed Week, I was shown all the correspondence, etc., which had taken place concerning your entry for this event and, frankly, I have no doubt whatever in my mind that you had entered and this entry had in fact been accepted. I think, therefore, in the circumstances the organisers were entitled to be given reasonable explanation for the withdrawal of such entry, not just the short, curt note that was sent to them.

Following our telephone conversation, having advised Captain Crise that you were writing a personal letter of explanation to him, offering your apologies for having to withdraw the entry, I am somewhat surprised that this has not, in fact, been done and in the circumstances I would ask that you do this as soon as possible.

Captain Crise's address is PO Box 5031, Fort Lauderdale, Florida, USA. I would be grateful if you would send me a copy of the letter that you write to Captain Crise.

Yours Sincerely

Basil Tye
Deputy Manager, Competitions Dept.

By this stage, I was getting thoroughly sick of the matter. As I saw it, if any apologies were called for, they were from Crise's side. Nevertheless, I wrote to Basil Tye at some length, explaining the sequence of events once more, in the hope that it would bring the matter to an end.

Happily, this letter seemed to herald more or less the end of the affair – or so I thought. But Sebring, 1964, proved otherwise. There Crise put out a statement to the effect that I would not be permitted to take part in 'his' races at Nassau that year without his special consideration and monetary guarantees.

Naturally, I would not think of allowing myself to be subjected to such undignified treatment, and when Luigi Chinetti asked me, later in the year, whether I would take part in the North American sports car series I had to explain that I would only go to Nassau if Crise was no longer involved in the race – an amusing thought – or he apologised for bad-mouthing me the previous year. Neither eventuality arose and, in any case, his statement at Sebring made it clear that he didn't want me there.

We finished the 1963 season on a mixed note; front suspension failure at Mexico City prevented me from challenging Jimmy Clark after qualifying a strong second to his Lotus, then an outing in the non-title Rand Grand Prix at Kyalami in early December produced an easy 1-2 for myself and Lorenzo.

Then it was back down to sea level for the final race, against the backdrop of the Indian Ocean at East London. But I'm afraid our F1 season fizzled out in rather disappointing fashion in that South African Grand Prix, where I stopped with engine failure when running a distant third and Lorenzo was fifth, lapped by Clark and Gurney.

Chapter 6

Champion Again and Beyond

The 1964 season was the one in which I achieved another of my great ambitions, to add a motor racing World Championship to the seven I had won on motor cycles. Yet in some ways it was a year which I wanted to forget. It turned out to be a time of tremendous frustration, a year in which many things went wrong which had no right to go wrong and, more significantly, could have been avoided.

It was a year during which I had quite a serious accident, one in which I might never have been involved had I not relaxed my intention never to compete at the wheel of a 'class' car in a mixed-category race, as distinct from a potential outright winner. It was a year in which the Ferrari team became the centre of a lot of politics which saw me racing in American colours for the last two championship F1 races of the season. Finally, it was with some irony that I clinched the title on the last lap of what, for me, had been the most frustrating race of the year, due to the inability of my car to compete on level terms with the opposition when there was so much at stake.

The year's results speak for themselves. I competed in 18 important F1 or long-distance races, and won only three of them – all F1 events. All this despite leading ten of them at one time or another, including every race in which I drove a Ferrari prototype. I was second five times, third three times and retired seven times. It was not a record about which I was to become over-elated.

Looking back over the year, I concluded that one of the fundamental reasons for our comparative lack of success – despite winning the championship – was that, once again, too much was being attempted for the resources available. There was simply not the manpower – or, I now realise, money – available to run an intensive F1 and sports prototype programme without one or the other suffering from lack of attention.

Of course, by the start of 1964 I knew very well the importance which Mr Ferrari attached to the long-distance race programme. It was easy to understand that success in this field helped sell a lot of road cars, so it was quite reasonable that the maximum effort possible be made to sustain the company's decisive lead in the sports prototype class.

Yet we had suffered on several occasions during 1963 through our lack of preparedness on the F1 front, so I was determined to do everything I could to prevent a repetition of the situation in '64. I had a long, frank talk with Mr Ferrari on this subject at the turn of the year, and he gave me an assurance that everything would be all right. But it wasn't.

It was the same old story of preoccupation with the two-seaters to the extent that I didn't even sit in our F1 V8-engined monocoque until the eve of the non-title Syracuse Grand Prix in Sicily which, thanks to a wet track, I was able to win. However, in this case, our first place probably did more harm than good.

Some people at Maranello became so elated that the team's brand new and untried car had won on its first outing that they convinced themselves it was a world-beater, which, quite definitely, it was not. As a result, nowhere near sufficient time was spent on development testing and we were patently outclassed through the first half of the championship season. Even worse, we lacked reliability, and only managed to finish once – second at Zandvoort – in the first four Grands Prix.

I didn't even have the opportunity to use the new V8 in the Silverstone International Trophy race, the weekend prior to Monaco, and was obliged to race the older V6, only to retire with an injection blockage caused by dirt in the fuel. As you can imagine, I was not amused!

At Monaco it was a sad saga of faulty gearbox bearings. Only one V8-engined car was available, both Bandini's and the spare having the old V6 installed. Gearbox trouble in the first of the three practice sessions meant switching to the spare 156 for the second, and it was only when a fresh gearbox had been installed that I managed to return to the V8 for the third session.

I qualified on the second row and was embroiled in a five-car bunch chasing Clark at the front of the field when I felt the gearchange starting to play up. I briefly dropped back to sixth, then pulled into the pits for attention. I rejoined almost immediately, but soon found myself standing dejectedly by the Ferrari just before the tunnel, a reluctant spectator before even a quarter of the race had been run.

Bandini's car lasted for 68 of the 100 laps before it also succumbed to a similar failure and retired from fifth place. It was a most depressing way in which to kick off our World Championship programme, all the more so because, had we been able to test the cars properly prior to the race we would almost certainly have identified – and rectified – the root of the problem, which was caused by sub-standard components produced by an outside supplier.

A new V8-engined car was finished in time for the Dutch Grand Prix at Zandvoort, which was some comfort, and of course the gearbox problem had been overcome. Both Bandini and I had our troubles during the practice periods; at one time or another we were stopped by fuel injection gremlins, a broken radiator, an engine oil leak and brake balance problems. As a result, we did quite a lot of chopping and changing of cars.

Once again, I found myself on the second row of the grid, this time behind Gurney, Clark and Hill, and with McLaren's Cooper alongside me it was Brabham-Lotus-BRM-Ferrari-Cooper in the first five positions. I decided to use the new car with the regular nose cowling and, just before the start, Bandini was handed the other V8 fitted with the nose from the new car. Unfortunately for Lorenzo, the engine developed a misfire on the grid and he had a miserable race, retiring early on with fuel starvation trouble.

This turned out to be one of my more pleasant F1 drives of the 1964 season. After the initial rush I found myself in fifth place behind Clark, Hill, Gurney and Peter Arundell in the other Team Lotus 25, which I quickly overtook to grab fourth spot. Then I had quite a tussle with Dan's Brabham, got past him on lap ten, and set out after Hill in the BRM.

It was only when Graham's car developed vapour lock in its fuel system that I began to see any real chance of moving through into second place. Up to that time I had been very worried by fluctuating oil pressure and was consequently reluctant to press harder. But when the BRM began hesitating out of slow corners, I soon caught it and moved into second place. This turned out to be quite a break, because for the last few laps my oil pressure gauge was reading virtually zero, and I had to back off considerably. In the end, I was 53.6s behind Clark, the only other driver on the same lap.

But there was more frustration on the way. Spa had rarely been a happy circuit for Ferrari and that trend was continued on our visit for the '64 Belgian Grand Prix. Throughout practice, I had been in fuel-feed troubles. The car would run properly for only a few minutes at a time, preventing any opportunity of stringing together a really consistent lap. We never did find the root cause of the problem and, although I scraped onto the second row of the grid, I was anything but confident of my chances in the race.

For the first couple of laps everything went well. Arundell led away, soon to be overtaken by Gurney, while I slipped into third ahead of Clark. By lap three I was in the lead, but then it was the same old story all over again: fuel starvation, which this time led to a burnt piston. I limped into the pits and took off my crash helmet. Bandini in the other V8 joined me after another ten laps, alas out with engine trouble.

We were left to watch from the sidelines as Gurney's Brabham dominated the race only to run short of fuel on the last lap, stop for a top-up and find none was available. He ground to a standstill further round the lap, leaving Hill, McLaren and – finally – Clark to take the lead. Jimmy tore past Bruce's Cooper only a matter of yards from the chequered flag to score his Belgian Grand Prix hat-trick and one of the luckiest wins of his career!

If the Belgian Grand Prix had been a disappointment for us, the French Grand Prix which followed was a fiasco. The team was late in arriving at the Rouen-les-Essarts circuit and missed one of the official practice sessions. I remember very clearly thinking that that wasn't the way to go about winning major motor races.

Well, for once, I managed to get the V8 onto the front row alongside Clark and Gurney, with Lorenzo on the third row, but it had all been a bit too much of a scramble for my liking. I was not satisfied that the cars were in as good shape as they should have been and, sure enough, on the second lap I ran into engine trouble.

When I stopped at the pits, we found that an injector pump oil pipe had come adrift. There was oil everywhere and I lost seven laps before rejoining. Unfortunately, the fracture had occurred at the one place where the stream of escaping lubricant would spew all over the distributors. That messed up the electrics completely and the engine refused to run cleanly. I struggled round a few more miserable laps before realising that it was pointless to continue, so I came in to retire. Bandini stuggled home ninth in his V8, just as uncompetitively.

The V8 just wasn't a really competitive proposition. I'd talked to Engineer Bussi about it and he had reported that the disappointing power output on the test bed merely confirmed what I had felt from the cockpit. Although more reliable when revved hard, in real brake horsepower terms it wasn't as competitive as the V6.

On reflection, they should have jumped straight from the V6 to the flat-12, but I believe they had some long-term joint project with Fiat which gave them an interest in developing a race-winning V8. Many years later, of course, the Ferrari 308 road car appeared – the first Ferrari production car to use an eight-cylinder engine. Although it is not an identical design, I still wonder whether the future link with Fiat might have had something to do with their enthusiasm for the V8. Bearing in mind how long they persevered with it, when it was increasingly clear into 1965 that the flat-12 was a better long-term bet, I can't think of any other justification for it.

One finish and three early retirements from four World Championship Grands Prix: it was a depressing score, especially as I felt certain our basic Formula 1 material was pretty good. It just lacked careful development and preparation, and would continue to do so as long as the race team workforce were pulled away to work on other things. But after Rouen, there was one glimmer of hope. The race programme for the sports prototype cars had been completed at Le Mans, and if events followed their usual path there would now be a late effort to retrieve something from the F1 programme.

That's not to say our activities in the endurance races had exactly been an unqualified success, at least not so far as my cars were concerned. In fact, it had just been another catalogue of frustration. I led at Sebring, the Nürburgring and Le Mans, but hadn't managed a single win.

There was another dimension to take into account which aggravated matters. In an attempt to bolster the Ferrari challenge in the face of growing Ford opposition, selected independent entrants were able to purchase, or loan, works prototype cars. This was obviously an extremely attractive proposition for the independents, but very tough on the factory drivers.

In the first place, we were given the job of sorting out these customer cars and setting them up to ensure that they were all fully competitive, and competitive with ourselves. Secondly, the amount of attention and personnel available to look after the works cars was reduced. Thirdly, we in the works team did not enjoy any mechanical advantages and were actually getting paid less money than the private teams were paying their drivers. Rather a no-win situation!

The usual system which operated for the privateers was that the drivers took 50 per cent of the starting and prize money, and got out-of-pocket expenses, such as travel, paid as well. In our case, the team normally negotiated an overall fee covering the expenses of transporting the cars and the technical personnel to the races as well as the starting money, and the distribution after the race would be on the basis of what was left over from the negotiated fee, plus anything that had been picked up in the way of prize money.

But with works drivers being responsible for their own out-of-pocket expenses, it was quite conceivable that a race such as the Sebring 12 Hours would cost a works Ferrari driver money unless he and his partner won outright, whereas the driver of a private entry could reasonably expect to pick up a decent sum, regardless of whether he finished or not. Hardly a satisfactory situation!

Lorenzo and I shared the works 4-litre 330P at Sebring, qualifying fastest and leading most of the race, although we had quite a tight battle with the similar Maranello Concessionaires-entered car of Graham Hill and Jo Bonnier until they retired with transmission trouble in the ninth hour. After that, it seemed as though we had the race sewn up. Our nearest challengers were now our own team cars driven by Parkes/Umberto Maglioli and Scarfiotti/Vaccarella, although we were not expecting too much in the way of trouble from them!

Disappointingly, we then encountered lighting trouble. At Sebring, any car spotted without all its lights functioning after dark is immediately brought into the pits and kept there until the necessary repairs have been carried out. So we sat in the pits and watched our other two team cars build up an impregnable advantage, leaving Lorenzo and I in a disappointed third place at the finish. As I said, not much good if you're trying to make a living out of being a Ferrari works driver.

My luck was also out two months later in the Nürburgring 1000 Km where I qualified fastest in the works 3.3-litre 275P, ahead of the new Ford GT which Phil Hill and Bruce McLaren were sharing as part of their warm-up for Le Mans. But while practice had shown that the new car was certainly quick enough, even with two fine drivers behind the wheel I didn't expect it to offer much in the way of a threat on race day. Tackling the Nürburgring at race-winning speed calls for the sort of stamina I didn't imagine such a new car would be capable of showing. It came as no surprise when it ran competitively during the early part of the race but, equally, it was no shock to find it being wheeled back into the paddock quite early on with transmission trouble brought about by the failure of a chassis mounting.

Even after the Ford's departure, we still had a slight problem battling against the Maranello Concessionaires 275P driven by Graham Hill and Innes Ireland. Eventually it went out with a split fuel tank, but my efforts came to nought when I suddenly felt something let go at the rear end. The car slewed off the road and out of the race. A rear hub had sheared. And there was more of this frustrating medicine to come.

The Le Mans test weekend in April had demonstrated that there was little to choose between the 275P and 330P in terms of performance. The Ford GTs were also very quick, but proved worryingly unstable at high speeds. Both cars crashed during these trials and were obviously crying out for aerodynamic attention.

By the time the Le Mans race came round two months later, the Fords were obviously a lot better. In practice, Richie Ginther was timed at over 191 mph on the Mulsanne Straight. We took along four Ferrari prototypes – three 275Ps and a 330P for Lorenzo and myself – to combat the trio of 4.2-litre Ford GTs.

I'm pretty confident that many people in the Ford camp shared my doubts about the staying power of their cars and it didn't take long to recognise the sort of tactics they were employing. Ginther came through to lead in the opening laps, setting a pace during the first hour which was considerably quicker than that really needed to win the race. It was the sort of thing you do when you know you're not going to last the distance. If you're going to retire, then best be in the lead when you do so!

That's exactly how things worked out. Richie had built up a lead of almost a lap at one point before the Ford began to slip down the leaderboard. It eventually retired with gearbox failure before one-quarter distance. The Phil Hill/Bruce McLaren car lasted the longest, getting just beyond the halfway point before transmission trouble intervened, although it was not reading in the leading bunch by then.

Lorenzo and I felt confident, sticking rigidly to our pre-arranged schedule, and as a result sharing the race leadership with the 275P in which Vaccarella was paired with Guichet. Then we hit trouble, Bandini stopping with a fractured fuel line on the Mulsanne Straight when we were well in the lead and past the 20 hours mark. He made a temporary repair which got the car back to the pits, but by then we had slipped out of contact with the 275P.

What had happened was that the petrol pipe had broken off halfway down the fuel tank, so that after that fuel stop he had used up only half his fuel load when he effectively ran out of petrol. From then on we could only run half our fuel load between stops.

In addition, we also encountered quite a lot of clutch trouble and were unable to pile on the pressure necessary to make a decent counter-attack. In the end, we had to be satisfied with third place behind Guichet/Vaccarella and the Maranello Concessionaires 330P of Hill/Bonnier. Just one more of those things!

Although the factory did not contest it, I agreed to drive in the Reims 12-hour race in a 330LM entered by Luigi Chinetti's North American Racing Team, sharing it with Lorenzo again. In the early stages of the race I had no real difficulty matching the pace set by Ginther in the Ford GT. This was extremely satisfying in itself because, although the LM was quite a good car, it didn't have the precise handling of the works prototypes and there were a couple of points around Reims where crisp high-speed handling was an absolute priority.

Once again, the Ford challenge was spent early on, so the race settled down into a private duel between our NART car and the Maranello Concessionaires entry. It was all really close-fought stuff. Neither car had an appreciable advantage over the other, and it seemed to me that if neither car wilted under the pressure it would be a fight to the very last lap.

Into the closing stages and I began to feel we were establishing a slight edge over the other Ferrari, but I got quite a shock when Bandini handed the NART car over to me with about two hours to go. He mentioned that the brakes were getting a bit low, but I soon discovered that that was something of an understatement.

They were virtually completely shot, and another pit stop to replace the front pads put us just out of realistic challenging distance. But we were still managing to pick up between two and three seconds a lap on Bonnier when I collected a puncture. That meant limping slowly back to the pits and the realisation that we would have to accept second place, five miles behind Graham and Jo, but no fewer than eighty miles ahead of the third-place GTO shared by Parkes and Scarfiotti.

There was more than a touch of nostalgia for me about the 1964 British Grand Prix, held six days after the Reims race. For the first time it was to be held at Brands Hatch, a very different circuit, of course, from the one which I had known from my earliest motor cycling days. Nevertheless, I still regarded it as my home circuit, only 15 miles or so from my home at Limpsfield.

I felt confident we could give a reasonable account of ourselves on this challenging 2.65-mile circuit, although the team started off at a bit of a disadvantage when only a single V6-engined car was ready in time for first practice. My V8 was still on its way from Maranello, which meant that I took the 156 and Lorenzo had to kick his heels on the pit counter.

However, I managed to get down to a very reasonable 1m 39s best, only six-tenths of a second away from Dan Gurney's fastest which earned him the additional reward of 100 bottles of champagne. It would have been interesting to see how close I might have come to the champers that day had the V8 been available! When my 158 arrived I managed to qualify on the inside of the second row, quite happy with the car's handling, but still painfully aware that we were short of power by comparison with the Lotus, BRM and Brabham which Clark, Hill and Gurney had used to button up the front row.

Jimmy got the best start and, at the end of the opening lap, I was sandwiched between Hill and Brabham in fourth place. On the third lap, we all moved up a position when Gurney suddenly threw up his hand and slowed with smoke pouring from his Brabham's transistor box. I just managed to avoid ploughing into the back of him and then settled down to consolidate third place, unable to stay with the Lotus and BRM in front.

So that's where I finished and, with Lorenzo coming home a strong fifth after a fierce battle with Jack Brabham, it was encouraging to record that both cars had remained totally reliable throughout what had been quite a tough race. As events were later to prove, the British Grand Prix at Brands Hatch was something of a major turning-point, at least as far as my World Championship aspirations were concerned.

I had finally brought my modest points score up to double figures, but Jimmy's 30 points from three outright victories and one fourth place looked pretty formidable against my ten from one second and a third. But I was comforted by the thought that we might do pretty well at the Nürburgring, where the German Grand Prix would be the next championship round on the calendar. Meanwhile, there was a non-championship outing at that other fine German circuit, Solitude, near Stuttgart which, in fact, fell at a particularly convenient time for the Ferrari team.

This non-title event was extremely useful for the purposes of carrying out some experiments with our fuel-injection system and, with the Bosch factory close at hand, Solitude was probably the most suitable circuit imaginable. All season, the V8 had been bugged by poor pick-up out of slow corners and we concluded that the problem was probably due to a delay in the actuation of the rack on the injection pump. After trying a number of experiments, we rigged up a little electrically operated servo unit to assist the action of the diaphragm, and so eliminate the lag.

In an attempt to assess the relative performance of our cars in relation to the opposition, we decided to station two men out on the circuit to time our cars and those of our chief rivals from the bottom hairpin to the top of the hill beyond. They came back with some very interesting evidence. My V8 was losing between 0.6s and 0.8s to Clark's Lotus on this section alone, yet by the end of the final practice session I was only 0.2s slower over the entire lap. That certainly gave the Ferrari and Bosch technicians something to think about!

The race itself started in heavy rain, a stark contrast to the scorching heat of practice. Clark had the most grip at the start and I found myself going through the first corner in third place, immediately behind Hill's BRM. I managed to pass him about halfway round the lap and pushed past the Lotus to take the lead before we came past the pits for the first time.

Little did I know of the trouble which had taken place behind us. On that first lap there had been a chain-reaction collision in the middle of the field, when the pack was still tightly bunched on the slippery surface. Among others, this involved Brabham and Bandini, while Graham had his own accident and wrecked the BRM separately. Thankfully, nobody was hurt.

This meant that Clark and I were left right out on our own and, for the next hour and a half, we indulged in a private dice during the course of which we succeeded in lapping the remainder of the field. When the rain was at its worst, I managed to pull out a lead of around 20s, but as the sun began to dry the track this advantage dwindled.

It was when the circuit was only partly dry that I found myself experiencing the most trouble. In those circumstances I was unable to keep the revs up to compensate for the poor engine pick-up characteristics. At about half-distance, Clark came through in the lead, although I managed to repass him again a couple of laps later. After another four laps, he came past for good and there was nothing I could do about it. He won by ten seconds, but at least the Ferrari V8 had performed better than usual and I felt confident we had learned something about our fuel-feed troubles.

On to the Nürburgring, then, with a determination to repeat our success of the previous year. On this occasion there was a spare Ferrari 158 on hand in case anything went wrong with my regular car and, I must say, that Solitude accident certainly hadn't done any harm to Lorenzo's determination. Just as he'd done with the Centro Sud BRM 12 months before, he made the outside of the front row with the Ferrari 156.

For once, I started the V8 from pole position with Clark and Gurney between me and Lorenzo. My team-mate made the most of his grid position, too, and led away through South Curve and up behind the pits. Jimmy went through into the lead going into North Curve and I was soon behind him.

At the end of the opening lap I was right on Jimmy's tail and ducked through into the lead going into South Curve. Gurney and Hill were close behind and, for a change, it was to be Dan rather than Jimmy who proved my strongest rival on this occasion.

Dan swept past the Lotus and before long he was right on my tail. This was the start of a really fine wheel-to-wheel battle which lasted several laps. On a couple of occasions Dan managed to edge past briefly, but I felt I had the measure of the Brabham and would be able to pull out just a little bit extra should it become necessary.

As things turned out, there was no need. After about seven laps, Dan began to fall back slightly with overheating trouble caused, no doubt, by the large sheet of newspaper which had somehow caught up in his Brabham's radiator cowling.

Once he had fallen away, I had no further serious opposition, for Graham was over a minute behind in the BRM, and falling back. Brabham and Bandini were another five minutes behind him, battling over third place. Jack eventually retired with transmission trouble, so Lorenzo ended up with a firm third place, half a minute ahead of Jo Siffert in Rob Walker's Brabham-BRM. The World Championship table was now led by Graham Hill on 32 points, followed by Clark, still on 30, while I had now climbed up to third on 19.

There followed a three-week gap before the Austrian Grand Prix which had been granted World Championship status for the first time. Zeltweg wasn't the best of circuits, by any means, as it used the runways and perimeter roads of an operational military airfield, the surface of which was hardly up to normal Grand Prix standards.

The facility was only available to the organisers for a few days each year, allowing the absolute minimum of time to get the circuit organised. Under the circumstances, I think the local automobile club did a very fine job to stage the race at all, although I wasn't sorry that we didn't return to that particular track because of all the suspension breakages that its bumpy surface produced. It would be another six years before we were back at the splendid Österreichring, a couple of miles away, for the next Austrian Grand Prix to count towards the World Championship.

Graham's BRM was on pole with my Ferrari 158, Gurney and Clark completing the front row. Dan and I made the best starts with Lorenzo bursting through in great style from the second row to run third, behind us, from the start.

On the second lap I went through into the lead and pulled away. There were 105 laps to be completed, so there was plenty of time. As things turned out, there wasn't anywhere near as long as I had anticipated. As I braked for the hairpin on lap eight, the car promptly sat down on a rear corner as a suspension ball joint broke. So that was that!

It looked as though this failure might have done mortal damage to my championship prospects, but I was soon to discover that I wasn't the only front-runner in trouble. Graham retired the BRM with a sheared distributor drive and Jimmy was to join us before half-distance with a broken driveshaft.

After I stopped, it looked as though Dan would walk away with the nine points for victory, but his Brabham eventually succumbed to a suspension breakage, leaving Lorenzo at the front of the field. We all spent a very anxious few moments, hoping that his 156 would stand the pace. Happily it did, and Lorenzo drove a very cool race, refusing to be flustered by Richie Ginther's late challenge in the second BRM.

The whole team was naturally delighted for Lorenzo to have scored his first Grand Prix victory, and while I was sorry not to have collected another nine championship points I honestly couldn't think of anybody I would have preferred to see wearing the winner's garland.

A few days later, I broke one of my own very firm rules of motor racing – and paid dearly for it. I have always believed that the only sensible way of taking part in a long-distance race is to drive a potential outright winner. There is little point in going for a class win as it adds considerably to the danger factor when you are in a position of having to overtake perhaps as many cars as you yourself stand to be overtaken by.

Having almost always been in the position where I could pick and choose which cars I drove, I had always gone for a car which had a reasonable chance of outright victory; until, that is, I was talked into driving something else in the '64 Goodwood Tourist Trophy.

It was pretty clear from the outset that the race was going to be won by Jim Clark's Lotus 30, Bruce McLaren's Cooper-Oldsmobile or the Maranello Concessionaires Ferrari 330P driven by Graham Hill. Ferrari were not entering any works cars, so I was without a drive until I was offered the wheel of a NART Ferrari GTO, one of four contesting the GT category against five AC Cobras.

The Cobras were proving a big threat to Ferrari's grasp on the GT World Championship, and perhaps this fact helped to influence me. Anyway, from the viewpoint of outright victory, I knew that I was starting the race in a car which, short of a near-miracle, had no chance of winning.

As anticipated, the big-engined sports cars went straight out into the lead and the race was eventually won by Graham's 330P after Bruce and Jimmy had retired. From the start I found myself boxed in among a group of midfield runners. It took me about six or seven laps before I was able to make real headway and begin climbing through the field. And then it happened.

Going into St Mary's on the eighth lap, I found Tony Lanfranchi's Elva-BMW in front of me, taking a tight line through the first, right-hand section of the ess-bend. I moved over to the left, intending to pass him on a wider line which would leave me well placed for the left-hander that followed.

Everything would have been OK except that Innes, in the Maranello Concessionaires GTO, clipped Roger Nathan's Brabham BT8 and spun right in front of Lanfranchi. Tony obviously hadn't noticed that I was virtually alongside him and, in an attempt to avoid Innes, moved right across my nose.

My GTO went straight over the top of him and spun off into the bank on the left-hand side of the track. It was one hell of an impact!

I had been held firmly in place by my seat harness, but the whiplash effect moment-arily knocked me unconscious. I came to, climbed out of the car . . . and passed out again. The next thing I can recall is being taken to the first-aid room by the circuit entrance. The doctors decided I was slightly concussed and I was sent off to Chichester General Hospital for a precautionary check-up.

After all the usual tests, I was kept in through the following day and only released on the Monday on the strict understanding that Pat would drive me home very gently and that I would then go straight to bed. With the Italian Grand Prix less than a week away, I was obviously very worried. Not only was this a crucial race for my championship chances, but it was also the most important event on the calendar from the viewpoint of Ferrari prestige.

I had to do everything possible to get fit in time. I called my own doctor and it was arranged that I should go up to King's College Hospital for a further check-up. I felt much better by the Tuesday morning, but the medical people were hardly enthusiastic when I mentioned the prospect of flying to Milan and racing at Monza a few days later.

Eventually I managed to persuade them that I should make the trip to Italy and, on my arrival, duly started practice only for a protest to come from BRM over my fitness. At this point Dragoni stepped in and arranged for me to see Sig. Marghiere, a world-renowned neurological specialist who has been attached to the NASA space programme. It was only after his test that the organisers allowed me to compete.

It was a great relief all round when he reported that the only obvious trouble was slight bruising around the back of the neck. He recommended that, providing there was no adverse reaction to the physical effort of driving the car, I should be given the OK to race.

For Lorenzo's home Grand Prix, he was assigned the second V8, while Monza also marked the first appearance of the new flat-12 engine. Lorenzo briefly tried it in practice, but it was insufficiently developed to contemplate racing it at this early stage. There was also a third works entry, one of the older V6s, for Scarfiotti to handle.

Thankfully, the Ferrari 158 was running very well, and my best lap on the first day was good enough for pole position. Monza's characteristics in those pre-chicane days particularly suited me as high-speed corners were my personal forte. They also removed the problem with the V8's power curve inasmuch as it was possible to keep the engine running in the high rev band – and, anyway, the team usually had its engines run-ning better by Monza, now that the pressures of Le Mans were a long away behind.

Dan's Brabham-Climax wound up second ahead of Graham's BRM, with Jimmy's Lotus back on the second row for once. Graham's clutch withdrawal mechanism failed on the line and Bruce McLaren dodged his Cooper round the stationary BRM to catch Dan and I off our guard and lead round the opening lap as far as the Vialone curves.

Both Dan and I were ahead of the Cooper by the end of the first lap, leaving Bruce to slip in behind with Jimmy to form a tight-bunched quartet contesting first place. A whole gaggle of ten or more other cars got together to fight out fifth place onwards, but the only time I saw any of them was when I came up to lap those of them that were left during the second half of the race.

For the first 25 laps or so it was a real slipstreaming special at the front, but Dan's Brabham and my Ferrari spent most of the time actually leading. From then on, Clark began to fall away and before much longer his Lotus was out with a sick engine. Bruce had by now lost touch and, just as at the Nürburgring, I was saved having to race Dan to the finish when electrical fuel pump trouble intervened to delay him.

All this left me a clear run through to victory, over a minute ahead of Bruce's Cooper. With Lorenzo just taking third in a photo-finish from Ginther's BRM, and Lodovico coming home ninth, it was a 100 per cent finishing record for Maranello and the vast crowd responded with all the emotional enthusiasm which is always reserved for a Ferrari win at home.

Only when it was all over, and I had notched up another nine points to keep me in the championship battle, did I suddenly appreciate just how much the race had taken out of me. Suddenly I felt very tired indeed.

I seem to remember that it was early to bed that night, for the next day we went back to Modena for some testing with the new flat-12 car. But just the sound of the engine being run up in the pits was sufficient to send my head spinning, and I realised that I would have to take a few days off, right there and then!

Pat drove us both down to a very pleasant Mediterranean resort called Punt-Ala, where we soaked up some sunshine, as a result of which I soon felt much better. Nevertheless, it was to be more than a year before I finally got rid of those headaches completely – by which time I had rather more serious medical problems on my mind. I didn't realise it at the time but, having been unable to test the flat-12 Ferrari 1512 at Modena, it would be all of ten months before I was even to sit in its cockpit again!

Satisfying though victory at Monza undoubtedly was, the Italian Grand Prix had been conducted under something of a cloud due to a dispute between Enzo Ferrari and the AC d'Italia, the country's national automobile club. This dispute arose out of the club's refusal to accept the Ferrari 250LM for homologation as a GT car. On paper, in order to validate the LM as a GT car, it was necessary to prove that 100 cars had been either produced or laid down.

The ACI said that the car had not met these production requirements and refused to forward the homologation application to the CSI, the sport's governing body. Ferrari was livid. Everybody knew that 100 LMs hadn't been built, but, equally, everybody knew there were quite a number of so-called homologated GT cars running around which had been produced in far fewer numbers than this particular Ferrari.

At the time, the CSI was taking a very lenient attitude, to say the least, to the production qualification and seemed content to admit cars which were clearly in series production and on sale to the general public.

Ferrari was outraged, threw in his competition licence and said that he would never race his works cars in Italy again, as well as decreeing that when they raced abroad they would no longer be painted in Italian racing red.

It was a threat he kept up until the end of the year, by which time the homologation business was well on the way to being sorted out. The 250LM was eventually accepted into a new sports car category requiring the manufacture of 50 examples, while the GT production requirement was raised to 500 cars per year.

As a consequence of Mr Ferrari's threats, when Bandini and I turned up at Watkins Glen for the United States Grand Prix, our cars were painted blue and white – the US international racing colours – and entered by Luigi Chinetti's North American Racing Team. The Monza success had put us back into the championship equation with a slender chance and, despite lengthy debates back in Italy, Ferrari agreed to send over a full-strength team with a choice of two V8-engined cars for myself, the flat-12 for Bandini, and a V6 as the spare.

I qualified alongside Graham's BRM on the front row, and things went quite well from the start. I managed to take the lead on the opening lap, but by lap six Jimmy's Lotus was alongside me and edging ahead. Gurney's Brabham had by this time come up to join us and for some laps the order settled down with Clark, myself, Hill, Gurney and Mike Spence in the second Lotus pulling clear from the rest.

I suddenly began to find myself about 200 rpm down on the long straights, so there was nothing I could do about Jimmy, but that problem solved itself just before half-distance when he began to slip back through the field. Later he took over Spence's car, thereby sacrificing any championship points he might earn, but with the prospect of preventing any other driver from collecting the points accruing to his car for the place it occupied at the finish. But this didn't work out and the second Lotus also retired a few laps later.

From then on, Graham began to consolidate first place with the BRM; I knew that if I was to have a hope of winning, I would have to hang on in his slipstream for a big go on the last lap. As it happened, things didn't turn out this way.

Trying to stay with the BRM as we cut our way through traffic, I missed a gear and went sailing off the circuit on a long right-hander at the end of the back straight. By the time I recovered, Dan had slipped past into second place, but he retired with engine trouble shortly afterwards, with the result that I was able to trail home second behind the BRM.

The effect of this result was really to tighten up the championship struggle going into the final race of the year in Mexico City. Hill now had 41 points, of which he could count 39, I had 34 and Clark 30. For Jimmy to take the title, he had to win in Mexico with me finishing lower than second and Graham lower than fourth. This would give Jimmy 39 points – equal with Graham – and he would get the verdict because he had scored the greater number of victories.

If I won the race, I would be certain of the championship, but could also take the title by finishing second, provided that Graham was not in the first three. It was all very complicated.

The Magdalena Mixhuca circuit was basically not a bad track, but the surface was extremely bumpy. We'd strengthened all the suspension after the ball joint failure at Zeltweg – a very rare breakage on a Ferrari in those days – had cost us nine points.

The problems we had experienced over the previous couple of years with the metering of the fuel injection system manifested themselves when we came to the 7000 ft altitude of Mexico City as we were unable to get the injection set up properly. You've got to remember these pumps were originally designed for 2½-litre engines and we had trouble getting the metering correct.

The flat-12 didn't suffer this problem because it, like the Climax and BRM V8s, was using Lucas injection, which was more of a compromise and had a wider range of adjustment; the worry about using this engine in Mexico was not its high fuel consumption, as the mixture could be run very lean at this altitude, but its high oil consumption. On those long curves, particularly the Peralta banked right-hander before the pits, we faced a very real problem of oil surge. So we thought it was too risky to use the 12 except as a hare.

So the silly thing was that I had to use the V8, which was less competitive in absolute terms but more likely to get to the finish. I had quite a depressing first practice: one V8 engine broke and the other proved well below par. I was over a second slower than Clark's Lotus, but things seemed to get worse on the second day when I was unable to get within a second of my earlier time. In the end, I found myself in fourth place – on the second row of the grid – behind Clark, Gurney and Bandini.

What a race of changing fortunes this turned out to be! Things almost went wrong a few seconds after the start: I made quite a reasonable getaway from the second row, and was moving away nicely, when the engine suddenly cut dead. For an agonising second or so, I hung back as everybody started to pass me.

Fortunately it picked up again, but by this time I had completely lost any advantage I might have earned from my good start. Graham had also been slow off the mark; he'd had a spot of trouble with his goggles just as the flag was dropped, so we both faced a hard fight as Clark disappeared into the distance on a clear track.

At the end of the opening lap I was 13th out of the 19 starters and Graham not much better off in tenth. The only real consolation was that Bandini was holding a really strong third behind Dan Gurney's Brabham, the flat-12 going very well indeed. For myself, it was just a question of getting my head down and moving through the pack as quickly as possible.

The whole course of the race was changed dramatically by an incident which took place shortly before half-distance. After battling together for many laps, Hill's BRM and Bandini's Ferrari touched at the hairpin. I was able to witness the whole thing from beginning to end, having pulled through from that initial 13th place right onto their tail. I was mainly concerned about keeping Graham in sight as he was my main championship rival.

Hill had previously overtaken Bandini into third place, but Lorenzo was hanging on to him very closely, challenging strongly as they went into the corners. Graham was playing it very shrewdly, leading into the hairpin on a very tight – and slower – line which gave Lorenzo no opportunity to push through.

However, Graham was being given pit signals which told him that I was also closing in and it was pretty clear to me, watching him for a few more laps, that he started taking a wider approach line to the hairpin in an effort to increase his lap speed a fraction. Of course, that strategy left the door open for Bandini.

After several near-misses, the inevitable happened. The BRM and Ferrari locked wheels and spun, and I went straight through into third place. Bandini recovered quickly and resumed racing behind me, slipping past soon afterwards, but Hill's BRM suffered damaged exhaust pipes and he had to call at his pit for attention. This virtually

CHAMPION AGAIN AND BEYOND

wiped out any chance he had of taking the title.

In the aftermath of the accident, a lot of people started gunning for Lorenzo, suggesting that he had driven recklessly in order to help me. Most of these critics were, of course, a good way from the incident and in no position to judge it for themselves. Lorenzo may have occasionally tended towards over-exuberance, but never indulged in dirty tactics; he and Graham shook hands over the whole business very soon after the event and there was no lasting animosity between them.

The other point the anti-Bandini brigade had overlooked was that, had Clark gone on to win the race, he would have been World Champion anyway. As things turned out, the title only slipped into my grasp on the very last lap!

A few laps earlier, a trail of oil had begun to appear round the circuit. Those of us who remained in the hunt all began to take peculiar lines on at least one of the corners, trying to establish whether we were the one with the problem.

It didn't take Jimmy long to realise that he was the unlucky one. Gurney swept by into the lead as Jimmy slowed to a crawl going into that final lap and I repassed Lorenzo. Contrary to what was written at the time, this was not a back-off situation as far as Bandini was concerned. The flat-12 slowed up on the last lap because of the oil consumption situation. Had Lorenzo run without problem to the end, I have no idea whether or not he would have backed off, and I may have passed him anyway.

Suddenly it was all over. Dan had won the race after Jimmy's retirement. My second place meant that we'd won the World Championship; it all took quite a while to sink in. A day that had started with such slim hopes, which were almost totally nullified when the engine cut out on the run to the first corner, had been transformed by the incredible sequence of events later in the race. It was almost too much to take in.

Immediately after the race, I shook hands with more people than I can remember, including Prince Phillip, who had been in Mexico for the Olympic Games. I had at last realised that ambition to win my eighth World Championship – the first on four wheels – yet it had come at the end of a season in which I would have given little enough for our chances. Even that final race, despite its satisfactory outcome, had provided further proof that, more often than not, we had been racing with an uncompetitive car throughout 1964.

At the official prizegiving that evening, I was presented with a beautiful gold Longines watch from the President of Mexico – which Her Majesty's Customs later kept for a couple of months! That was more than I actually got for winning the World Championship, as all I received from the sport's governing body was a diploma!

Then we got together a bit of a party and went off to dinner at the rooftop restaurant of the Hilton Hotel. It was, I suppose, an appropriate place to eat, because that night I really did feel on top of the world.

During the 1964 season, I had become increasingly aware of the way the Ferrari team was isolated. The days of competing against other Italian teams were over. Previously, you'd had Maserati and Lancia in business as well and the amount of knowledge circulating would be quite considerable, not only between the manufacturers but also among all the accessory suppliers.

What we now lacked was this general sharing of information which tended to go on all round the British scene from which our strongest competitors were springing. We were in danger of getting out of touch.

I wasn't earning much money with Ferrari, and there were opportunities of competing in the Can-Am races in the closing months of the year. So the question of racing sports cars arose and, after discussing it with Mr Ferrari, he said, 'in the classes we don't make cars for, OK'.

So I started to give serious thought to how I could expand and develop my motor racing career in fresh directions, and at the same time keep myself abreast of what was going on in the outside world. It would be better for me, better for Ferrari.

The expansion I had in mind was something I had been considering for some time: to form Team Surtees. Initally the idea was to expand my sports car racing programme beyond the limits of my Ferrari commitments into the North American sports car field, where I had dipped my feet into the competitive waters with the lightened 250P at the end of the previous season.

Over the previous couple of years, I had kept in close touch with Eric Broadley and discussed with him the prospect of building a purpose-built sports racing car which could accommodate a variety of American V8 engines. It seemed as though we could put together a good partnership. I would benefit from having a competitive machine, and he would gain the advantage of somebody to carry out test and development work for his new project.

Right from the outset, I discussed the matter with Mr Ferrari. I reasoned that the technical information such a project might produce could only be beneficial to my programme with Ferrari. Working with Firestone, I would get some insight into what the opposition was doing on the tyre front, and there was plenty to be learned from all the component suppliers who were involved in developing the new car. This was the start of the Lola T70 story.

Mr Ferrari was broadly sympathetic towards my suggestions, although it was rightly understood that my commitments to his team would take precedence. As a result, the winter months were to prove extremely busy because, apart from getting the Lola programme under way and taking part in the South African Grand Prix on New Year's Day, I was also asked to assist with some track testing of the new Formula 2 engine which BMC had under development. In addition, there was also a certain amount of testing to be carried out on the F2 Lola T60 which was to be entered by the Midland Racing Partnership with works assistance.

The BMC engine project was virtually over before it started, as things turned out. I'm afraid it cost a lot of money, most of which went straight down the drain. It really was a lost cause. I raced the Cooper-BMC for Ken Tyrrell on only one occasion, at Crystal Palace on Whit Monday, and that outing ended in retirement during the first heat with a thrown connecting rod. There wasn't much we could do about that in the paddock between heats. To take part had meant dashing home overnight from Mosport Park where I'd won the Player's 200 race the previous day in the Lola T70. It was a lot of effort for no result whatsoever.

My second F2 race was one of the supporting events for the Guards International Trophy race on August Bank Holiday Monday. I ran with the leaders until I encountered some gearchange problems and then went off round the back of the circuit on the last lap. At least I managed to win both heats of the main race in the T70, which was the most important business of the day.

The most successful F2 outing came a week later when I won the International Gold Cup at Oulton Park after 40 laps of really fighting with Denny Hulme, Jochen Rindt, Jimmy, Graham and Alan Rees. We were swapping places from start to finish and, at the chequered flag, Denny was only one-fifth of a second behind me in second place. Then it was straight back onto an airliner and across the Atlantic again to win the sports car race at Ste Jovite!

The Grand Prix season had kicked off in South Africa – a country I have come to like enormously – on New Year's Day and I must say it was nice to see our Ferraris back in their familiar red livery. Mr Ferrari had made his peace with the Italian Automobile Club, but there wasn't much in the way of progress to be reported from the V8 which I was to use in the race, nor indeed from Bandini's flat-12.

I finished the Grand Prix in second place to Jimmy Clark but, while my Ferrari proved competitive with Hill's BRM, the V8 certainly wasn't in the same class as Clark's Climax engine. As usual, any development on the F1 front was to be a low priority for the next couple of months as the factory concentrated on the sports prototype programme.

In the face of the Ford threat, the new P2 was a much improved car. The main difference was that the V12 engine now had twin overhead camshafts on each bank. Now the 4-litre version – the 330P2 – developed about 380 bhp at 7600 rpm, and the 3.3-litre 275P2 around 340 bhp at 8000 rpm. The chassis retained its multi-tubular construction, but featured a much improved double wishbone suspension system, similar in layout to that used on the Grand Prix cars.

The bodywork was smartened up, producing a more efficient aerodynamic profile, and we felt that a programme of development would enable us to match anything thrown against us.

Although we decided to give Sebring a miss after the organisers made their event less attractive for sports prototypes by opening the entry list to lightweight sports racers, we did send a car along to Daytona in February. If nothing else, it proved to us, a month earlier than Sebring would have done, that the P2 had a major tyre problem.

But for this, I believe Pedro Rodriguez and I could have won the race over the 3.8-mile mixture of Daytona banking and infield. During the early part of the race I swapped the lead with Dan Gurney's Lotus 19B, which was powered by a 5-litre Ford V8, so I was feeling quite confident. In the event I managed to struggle back to the pits after a very nasty moment when the tyre failed at speed and, although we got going again, transmission problems eventually caused our retirement.

Our first F1 race of the season was at Brands Hatch on 13 March, the first Race of Champions to be staged. It was an extremely frustrating affair. The factory made available just a single 158 which hit engine trouble in practice. We didn't even have a spare V8 to hand and, when we made the inevitable panic phone call to Maranello for help, they rushed over an engine minus its fuel injection equipment.

We had to strip the broken engine of all its injection equipment and transfer it to the replacement. We couldn't do much about resetting all the adjustments correctly. It was quite a panic and we hoped for the best. 'The best' didn't amount to much, as things transpired, and after struggling through to finish sixth in the first heat we retired early on in the second when the engine went badly off-song again.

Still, at least we left the circuit with our car intact. Jimmy crashed his Lotus 33 during the second heat while under strong pressure from Dan Gurney's Brabham. He got onto the grass coming out of Bottom Bend and slammed into an earth bank. Jimmy was extremely fortunate to climb out of the wreckage with just a sore knee to show for his troubles.

At Brands Hatch we had enjoyed warm spring sunshine, but the following weekend at Silverstone it lashed down with torrential rain to the point where the meeting had to be abandoned after the second race. This was my first outing with the Lola T70 and, having spun my car at least seven times during the race in question, I sympathised with the decision of the officials!

Initially, we had fitted the car with a 4.7-litre Chevrolet V8, but this was meant as a stop-gap before we dropped a 5.3-litre unit in for the race. The contest developed into a speedboat race between me and Jimmy in the Lotus 30. After my final spin I decided to retreat into the pit lane to check for damage, but as I did so I noticed that the chequered flag had been produced at the start/finish line. That meant I had completed 18 laps, finishing second to Clark who continued on to complete another lap and win the battle. To be honest, we were all very happy when it was over that we were all in one piece.

The month of April opened at sunny Syracuse in Sicily, giving me the first serious opportunity to stretch the Formula 1 Ferrari's legs since the South African Grand Prix. Not being a World Championship race, Syracuse didn't attract many works teams, but Team Lotus were on hand with cars for Jimmy and Mike Spence, so it was hardly going to be a Ferrari pushover.

I was still persevering with a pair of V8-engined cars with direct fuel injection, while Bandini continued to use the newer flat-12 which, equipped with Lucas port-type injection, seemed to be working very well indeed.

This race marked the appearance of English-style glass-fibre bodywork on one of the 158s, something I had instigated by getting Peter Jackson of Specialised Mouldings involved with the programme. We were planning to set up a joint venture in the old Colotti gearbox factory. Mr Ferrari knew about all this, and had given his tacit approval, but the next thing I discovered was that he had set up his own similar operation in small premises behind the Scaglietti coachworks. I was a bit taken aback when he did this, but said nothing. I simply chalked it down to another lesson learned!

The Syracuse race developed into a three-way battle between Jimmy, myself and Jo Siffert in Rob Walker's Brabham-BRM. I tailed the Brabham for the first ten laps, then moved ahead but I was unable to pull away. At the half-distance mark, Siffert was still right with me and in fact came past me again before I managed to squeeze back in front.

By this time I was being very badly troubled by a lack of brakes and, with my engine also beginning to lose its edge, it was becoming increasingly difficult to hold the Brabham. I began to realise that a private entry was on the verge of beating the works teams, which was more than a little embarrassing, but it was not to be Siffert's day after all.

With about ten laps to go, he timed a gearchange just as his car's rear wheels hopped off the ground over a bump. The revs shot sky-high and, inevitably, the engine blew up. Although his retirement put me back into the lead, there was no doubt in my mind that this was one race that Siffert certainly deserved to win.

Sadly for me, my brake problems got so bad that Clark went by quite easily to score

I drove for Ferrari in 1963 and was immediately given the job of testing the new V12-engined sports car. This in fact was one of the previous year's V6-engined machines, slightly lengthened, and fitted with a 3-litre V12 engine. These cars, later fitted with new bodywork, became the successful 250Ps.

Below right: *I was soon to learn that at Ferrari the single-seaters came after the sports cars in the list of priorities. My second job was to test a modified 1962 F1 car powered by a 120-degree V6*

Below: *With my mother and father in the pits at Monaco, 1963. Despite a few problems in practice (bottom), I finished fourth in my first Grand Prix for Ferrari.*

A rare shot of Mr Ferrari, together with Giuseppe Bacciagaluppi of Monza, during the first test away from Modena for the 1963 Ferrari 158.

Below: The Ferrari team. Me in the background with Forghieri, Engineer Bussi, who was then in charge of engine development but was later abducted in Sardinia and never seen again, and Franco Rocchi, the mainstay of all engine design during that period.

The beautiful Spa circuit and the Ferrari 156 as it finally appeared for the 1963 season.

Just remember, as far as car preparation was concerned, this group represents the F1 team, the sports car team and, at times, the customer sports car team!

In discussion with Mauro Forghieri

Above: *Yours truly with Willy Mairesse: a great enthusiast and a very capable driver to whom racing meant too much.*

Pat handles the stop-watch. It must have been a good lap!

JOHN SURTEES

Right: *Solitude, 1964. A very important race, as we made considerable headway with the V8 fuel injection system; if it had stayed wet a little longer, we might even have won.*

Above: *Just look at that crowd! Heading up towards North Curve at the old Nürburgring at the start of the 1000 Km, with one of the works 250Ps.*

On the victory rostrum at the 1965 Nürburgring 1000 Km (below) *with Lodovico Scarfiotti.*

Above: *The Ferrari 158 in the 1964 German Grand Prix, now benefiting from its development race at Solitude. With the help of the Nürburgring, I was able to control the race from the front from Jimmy Clark and Dan Gurney, seen here tucked in behind me.*

Left: *The two factory-prepared Ferrari 250Ps at Sebring, the works car driven by myself and the other entered by Maranello Concessionaires for Graham Hill.*

The championship would have been that much easier, if only . . . But racing is all about 'ifs and buts' and I, for one, would not have expected a ball joint to break on the Ferrari's rear suspension, losing me the lead of the '64 Austrian Grand Prix on the Zeltweg aerodrome.

Above: *With the other main contenders of the time and drivers it was a pleasure to be on the track with: Dan Gurney, Jim Clark and Graham Hill, prior to the 1964 Mexican Grand Prix.*

Above right: *It was fortuitous that HRH The Duke of Edinburgh was in Mexico City at the time of the '64 Grand Prix. Here he congratulates Dan Gurney and myself on our wins in the race and the World Championship respectively.*

What, a works Ferrari not painted red? After falling out with the Italian federation over the homologation of the 250LM sports car, our cars ran the last two races of 1964 in the American colours of blue and white, Mr Ferrari entering them under the North American Racing Team banner of his old confederate Luigi Chinetti. Here I take the Ferrari 158 to second place in the Mexican Grand Prix – and the title.

Right: *Giving Jimmy Clark a lift back to the pits during practice for the 1965 French Grand Prix at Clermont-Ferrand.*

Centre: *A fine picture. The V8 Ferrari in more conventional pose at the same circuit.*

Bottom right: *My 1965 European season opened at Syracuse where I had quite a dice with Jo Siffert's Rob Walker Brabham and Jimmy Clark's Lotus. Siffert over-revved, my Ferrari lost brake fluid when leading and Jimmy won.*

Left: *The 1965 American sports car series started well with a win at Ste Jovite, then it was back to England for an F2 win at Oulton Park; but then came disaster at Mosport Park. I had just been asked to test the other team car and am seen here making my notes in the pits shortly before going out and losing a wheel. The rest we know . . .*

In 1965 we took a 330P2 to Daytona (below) where I shared it with Pedro Rodriguez. Here it leads the pack in the opening stages.

Above: *Leading Jim Clark's Lotus 30 on my way to victory at the Player's 200 meeting, June 1965.*

The 1½-litre 1965 flat-12 Ferrari in action at Silverstone – without the revised cylinder heads which were to be introduced at Monza. Note the low induction tracts.

an unchallenged victory. My engine was getting rougher and rougher by the lap, so I dropped back and just scraped home second by a few seconds from Lorenzo. There were one or two sheepish faces in the Ferrari pit when I explained that I usually liked racing with brakes operating on both ends of the car – not just the rear wheels. Close examination revealed that the cover on one of the brake fluid reservoirs had been over-tightened with a spanner, causing it to distort and allow the fluid to leak away during the race. Thereafter, the mechanics had strict instructions only to tighten those reservoir covers by hand!

After the Le Mans test weekend, where my fastest lap in the 330P2 was some seven seconds quicker than our '64 best, it was back to England for the Easter Monday Goodwood meeting. There was no F1 Ferrari to hand for the main race and, following engine trouble, we had to withdraw the Lola T70 from the supporting sports car race, so I was happy to return to the warmth of Italy for the Monza 1000 Km and some motor racing in the sun.

For this first direct clash of the year with the Ford team in Europe, we faced up to two 4.7-litre Ford GTs driven by Bruce McLaren/Ken Miles and Chris Amon/Umberto Maglioli. I shared a 330P2 with Scarfiotti, and there was a sister car for Bandini/Vaccarella and a 275P2 for Parkes and Guichet. In addition, the race marked the debut of the very promising little Dino 166P driven by Giancarlo Baghetti and Giampiero Biscaldi.

I was pretty confident that we would do well in the race, having lapped about six seconds faster than the Fords during practice. The battle began with a flying start following an Indianapolis-style pace lap around the combined ten-kilometre road and banked circuit, making a race distance of exactly 100 laps and a duration of around five hours.

I set the pace from the start in my 330P2, but we faced an early setback when Bandini suffered broken suspension and had a nasty spin on the banking, nearly collecting one of the Fords as he slid down the slope into retirement. Then, after about ten laps, I suddenly hit major tyre trouble and had to come in for a wheel change.

That dropped me well down the field, and when I started to press hard in an effort to make up places the P2 encountered more serious tyre-wear problems. It seemed I had the choice between motoring on at a steady pace, which would not significantly improve my position, and driving flat out to regain time, only to risk losing it again with another stop.

It developed into an extremely frustrating race, although Lodovico and I managed to climb back to an eventual second place some two minutes behind the leading 275P2 of Parkes and Guichet. Ford lost one of their cars when Amon's broke its front suspension late in the race, so the final order was a Ferrari 1-2 with Ford third and a Porsche fourth.

The race was saddened by a fatal accident to the Swiss driver Tommy Spychiger at the wheel of a Ferrari 365P entered by Scuderia Filipinetti. A few days later we lost a potential Ferrari team driver on the same circuit during a period of private testing. This was Bruno Deserti, who had been quite successful in Formula Junior and was one of several drivers being given a trial in a works P2. He crashed heavily at the Curva Grande and, quite understandably, testing was suspended. This tragic accident was one of the contributory reasons we failed to carry out our customary 24-hour endurance test before going to Le Mans.

Persistent steering problems with the Lola T70 deprived me yet again of a possible success in the Tourist Trophy, held this year at Oulton Park, and, although I didn't take part in the Targa Florio, I was to have a busy schedule on 15 May driving both the F1 Ferrari and the Lola T70 at the Silverstone International Trophy meeting.

With Jimmy away qualifying for Indianapolis, my only real opposition in the sports car race came from Bruce McLaren's McLaren-Oldsmobile. From the start, it turned into a two-horse race but, soon after I overtook him into the lead, my engine began to overheat worryingly. I eased back, allowing Bruce to counter-attack, and when he repassed me I had to back off even more to allow plenty of clean air into my radiator. Eventually a misfire told me that a head gasket had failed and, by the time I went off-course to avoid a wayward wheel shed by a back-marker, my engine was boiling like a kettle and I called it a day.

In the Formula 1 race, after Jack Brabham had retired from a commanding lead – having coated my goggles with oil film – I was left chasing Jackie Stewart's BRM. The Scottish new boy drove very well indeed to hold his first place and, while the gap between us varied between one and three seconds, depending on our luck in passing slower cars, I realised that Stewart would have to make an error of judgement if the places were to be reversed.

Well, he made no error on that day and, on his performance as I saw it, I thought he had worked well for and had thoroughly deserved his first Formula 1 win. Psychologically, it must have done him a great deal of good, coming as it did on the eve of the European section of the championship battle.

For myself, I was not so bothered that I had finished second to the BRM as by the fact that Brabham had proved so quick. It was not too comforting, either, to know that Bandini's flat-12 had finished a distant seventh. Once again, we were suffering badly from a lack of testing.

One of the high points in a year of very mixed fortunes turned out to be the Nürburgring 1000-km race, the weekend after Silverstone. In fact, everything went so completely smoothly and according to plan that I can sum it up in a very few words. I was paired with Lodovico in a 330P2 and we also had the works 275P2 for Parkes and Guichet, plus the little Dino for Bandini and Vaccarella. The factory had also loaned a 330P2 to Maranello Concessionaires for Hill and Jackie Stewart, and we were ranged against a four-car Ford attack, three having 4.7-litre engines and one a 5.3-litre unit. They were to offer us little in the way of trouble.

I started from pole, some seven seconds faster than the best Ford driven by McLaren and Phil Hill – the 5.3-litre version – and we led almost all the way. Parkes and Guichet held second place for virtually the entire race, and the little Dino was even up to third overall at one point, although it fell back with a sick engine towards the finish, ending up fourth behind the 2-litre Porsche of Jo Bonnier and Jochen Rindt. The sole surviving Ford trailed home eighth.

Then it was off to Monaco for a race which would prove about as tough as I have ever experienced on this gruelling, round-the-houses track. There was still no sign of my getting hold of a flat-12, so again I was provided with a choice of V8s. On this circuit, perhaps more than any other, the advantage of the new engine, with its improved pick-up out of the slow corners, was very noticeable and I had to work exceedingly hard in practice to match Lorenzo's times.

In the end, he beat me by one-fifth of a second, which was sufficient to put him on the second row, leaving me on the third. With Clark and Gurney racing at Indianapolis, Jack Brabham made good use of the latest 32-valve Coventry Climax V8 to join Graham Hill on the front row of the grid. Stewart was ahead of Bandini, and I shared row three with Dickie Attwood, easily the best of the non-works drivers in the Parnell team Lotus-BRM.

The way the two BRMs shot away during the opening laps was quite disturbing, and I found myself in a rather embarrassing position behind Bandini. He definitely had the faster car, and could use his advantage away from the corners, so that even when I was able to close the gap under braking I was never close enough to draw level with him.

This was the pattern of the race until just after quarter-distance, when we came down to the harbour front to find Graham Hill wheeling his BRM back onto the track. He'd wisely chosen the escape road when he found Bob Anderson's lame Brabham cruising back to the pits. Stewart was now in the lead but soon afterwards he spun at Ste Devote, which left the order Bandini, Brabham and myself in the first three places.

Jack didn't take long to get ahead of Lorenzo, only to retire with an oil leak just before half-distance. Bandini then went ahead again, with Graham now hard on my heels after mounting a very determined recovery from his earlier incident.

Graham came past me into second place, then set about pressuring Lorenzo. Eventually, on lap 65, he nipped past to regain the lead he had originally lost almost 40 laps earlier. I redoubled my efforts to pass Bandini, which I finally managed to do with about 20 laps left to run. I then did my best to close the gap to Graham, but he responded with a new lap record which my car was quite incapable of equalling, let alone beating.

Just when it seemed as though second place was buttoned up, the V8 began spluttering midway round the 99th lap. With one lap to go it finally died and, as I coasted to a halt, I was faced with the mortifying sight of Bandini and Stewart going by to take second and third places.

It was a terrible disappointment, resulting from a fuel consumption miscalculation, and I suddenly felt very low. I had done the best I could with the machinery at my disposal and felt badly let down, just when I should have been feeling a certain measure of personal satisfaction.

Happily, a week later in Canada, I experienced a very different story when I won the Player's 200 sports car race at Mosport Park in our 6-litre-engined Lola-Chevy. In practice, Jim Hall's automatic-transmission Chaparral, Bruce McLaren's McLaren-Oldsmobile and I managed to lap the circuit at an average of over 100 mph for the first time and Bruce set the pace from the start. I ran second ahead of Hall, but after about ten laps I noticed that my water temperature needle was creeping ominously across the dial. Of all things, a fan belt had flown off, so I had lost my generator as well!

Hall began to press quite hard at this point, coming past me on a couple of occasions, although I managed to retake him quite quickly. Nevertheless, I appreciated that the important thing was to get through to the end of the 40-lap heat with the car still in good shape, so I could do something about making up the leeway in the second race.

In the end, after Bruce had gone into the pits with boiling brake fluid, I finished second, some 40 seconds behind Hall with Hugh Dibley's Lola T70 in third place. With a fresh fan belt fitted, and carefully adjusted, I went out on the warming-up lap for the second race feeling reasonably confident that we could put on a decent show.

To my horror, I suddenly found I couldn't select any gears, so went straight back into the pits at the end of the warm-up lap. A pin had dropped out of the gear linkage, so a replacement was fitted and I shot out onto the circuit with the rest of the field already halfway round the opening lap!

I quickly cut my way through the tail-enders and, by lap 15, was up to fourth behind McLaren, Dibley and Charlie Hayes in a Cooper. Jim Hall was back in the pits by this time, with a manifold falling off the Chaparral as well as gear linkage problems, so things were beginning to look up. Eventually I moved up into second place and, when Bruce slowed with a broken transmission, swept into a lead which had seemed pretty unlikely when I left the pit lane at the start of the race.

Back across the Atlantic at Spa, I was to have a short Belgian Grand Prix when my Ferrari V8 broke its engine after only six laps. I was lying third behind Clark and Stewart at the time, but if I had had to retire early from any race that season this had been a pretty good one to choose. The weather was absolutely appalling; it rained incessantly and most of the few laps I completed involved driving blind through a wall of spray thrown up by the other competitors. All decidedly unpleasant.

It is now a matter of history that the 1965 Le Mans 24 Hours produced the last Ferrari victory to date, but only because there were a couple of good private entries in play when the works cars ran into trouble. Masten Gregory and Jochen Rindt emerged as the winners in a NART Ferrari 275LM, taking the lead from a similar Belgian-entered car at around lunchtime on Sunday.

In my view, the reason the factory team failed to win was our failure to carry out that pre-race 24-hour test at Monza, plans for which had been curtailed by Bruno Deserti's distressing fatal accident. Had we done so, we should no doubt have discovered the cracking problem which we were to encounter with the ventilated disc brakes employed on the P2. One by one, at around the halfway mark, these started to fracture and, towards the end of the 24 hours, the P2s were running with a mixture of replacement discs, some ventilated, some solid.

As far as my car was concerned, this was not the only problem. It broke a front spring and eventually retired on Sunday morning with gearbox failure. The other 4-litre P2 also succumbed to transmission failure, while the 3.3-litre car broke its engine. Yet by midnight on the Saturday we had been leading the race and Ferraris had filled the first half-dozen places.

By then the Ford challenge had been completely broken. Transmission problems had sidelined their two 7-litre cars and the 4.7-litre machines hadn't offered us anything by way of a threat while they were running. Yet the satisfaction at having overcome the Ford effort was diluted by the fact that our works cars also failed to last the distance. So much for giving the prototypes priority over the Formula 1 programme during the preceding weeks and months!

In 1965 there was a new venue for the French Grand Prix: the tortuous and undulating five-mile road circuit in the hills above Clermont-Ferrand. This was a real drivers' circuit and, in some respects, like a miniature Nürburgring. Its only real problem was that, lying in the foothills of heavily wooded mountains, it tended to attract quite a lot of mist, something which we learned all about during the practice sessions.

Just before the start of practice, Dragoni rather took the wind out of my sails when he offered me the flat-12-engined car literally minutes before the start of practice. This was quite a surprise, as I had not exactly been encouraged to show much interest in the car during the previous three months.

Prudently, I declined. I didn't think an official practice session was the moment to take on the business of testing what, for me, was effectively a brand new car. However, although the Italian press made quite a meal of my declining to use the car, I made it clear that I would very much like to drive it in the British Grand Prix, which was the next event on the calendar.

Clark, Stewart and Bandini made up the front row of the grid, Lorenzo and I having lapped in exactly the same time. However, since he did his time before me, I was consigned to the second row alongside Gurney's Brabham. Clark shot away at the start and, on the second lap, Stewart nipped by Bandini to take second place.

It took another lap before Dan and I managed to get ahead of Lorenzo, by which time the leading bunch was well strung out. Eventually, on lap 14, my engine started to stammer and splutter, so I shot into the pits where it was discovered that the rectifier had pulled loose and was only being held on by its wires.

The wires were cut and I resumed with the alternator operating without the rectifier, the engine sounding as sick as ever. Under the circumstances, to come home third behind Jimmy and Jackie was quite satisfying. It was the first time since South Africa that I had actually been running in a Grand Prix car when the chequered flag fell!

After another second-place finish in the Reims 12-hour race – where Mike Parkes and I were unlucky enough to be delayed by a rare broken rocker arm on our 4.4-litre Maranello Concessionaires P2 – I took over the flat-12-engined Ferrari 1512 for the British Grand Prix at Silverstone. To be frank, at this stage of its development, I didn't feel there was much to choose between this and the V8 when it was running well.

I qualified on the inside of the second row, with Clark, Hill, Richie Ginther in the Honda and Stewart on the front row ahead of me. Ginther led away, but Jimmy got past him before the end of the first lap. I ran fourth in the early stages, but it soon became clear to me that the flat-12 definitely lacked power compared with the Coventry Climax, and we were sadly missing the new cylinder heads which had been prepared but not machined in time for the race owing to the pressure of the sports car programme.

The day finished with Clark winning from Hill; I was in third place, a few seconds ahead of Spence in the other works Lotus. Poor Lorenzo, incidentally, was out after only three laps with a blown V8 in his car.

Quite simply, the 1512 was underdeveloped. From the start of the season we should have forgotten about the V8 and put all our eggs in one basket to concentrate on the flat-12. As it was, the policy seemed to be: 'well, let him use the reliable V8 for the first few races, then we'll get down to some serious flat-12 development after Le Mans. That should see him winning the later races, which are the ones which count.' This was, of course, totally the wrong way to go about things. With a bit more foresight and planning we could have retained our World Championship.

Zandvoort was a typical example of how we came unstuck through lack of testing. Earlier in the year, Dunlop had come up with a new tyre – the R7 – which we had used on the sports car, but hadn't tried on the F1. Had we done so, we might have discovered that it presented certain specific problems and something could have been done to resolve matters. As it was, it wasn't until practice for the Dutch Grand Prix that we were able to come to grips with them.

We tried all manner of tyre combinations and suspension adjustments to make the flat-12 handle and, eventually, concluded that the best compromise would be to use the older R6s at the front and R7s at the rear. In the end, however, taking into account that the new tyres had a different construction, it was better to use them all round. We had encountered overheating problems with the sports cars, but we didn't expect these difficulties to occur with the much lighter F1 chassis. Little did we know . . .

After five laps on full tanks in the race, the car felt as though it was running on four plates of jelly. I had started fourth on the grid, as was becoming customary, but could do no better than seventh at the finish. When I got the car back to the paddock, I found you could get hold of the tyres and pull lumps of the tread off with your bare hands. It was just as if they were made of Bostick. It was a terrible slip-up, and we were as much to blame as anybody for failing to carry out the requisite tyre testing.

The disappointing trend continued through to the German Grand Prix at the Nürburgring where I was aiming for a hat-trick of victories. We still didn't have the new cylinder heads for the flat-12, but at least I had a spare car and managed to qualify fourth behind Hill, Stewart and Clark, lining up on the outside of the front row.

For all the good it did me, I might as well have started from the back row! Accelerating away from the start, I ran into gear selection problems and had to hobble round the long 14-mile lap before being able to stop at the pits for attention. I lost two laps while the jammed selectors were freed, and then set off again for a very lonely 11 laps before the problem repeated itself and I pulled in to retire.

Although the month of August had started badly, it ended well with a comfortable win in both heats of the International Guards Trophy sports car race at Brands Hatch. For this event I drove an improved version of the Lola T70, a little lighter, with changes to the suspension geometry. We had also detuned the 5.3-litre Chevrolet V8s in the interests of reliability and the result tended to speak for itself.

Behind me, Bruce McLaren took second place in his McLaren-Oldsmobile, with Jackie Stewart third in my regular Team Surtees T70. We went home feeling extremely satisfied about the reliability factor, and also that the new car had gone so well. This was the Lola which I intended to use in the forthcoming series of North American sports car races which were scheduled to start at Ste Jovite, near Montreal, a week after the Italian Grand Prix.

As usual, of course, Ferrari were out in force for their home event at Monza. We had a total of four cars on hand: three flat-12s and a V8. Lorenzo and I were to drive the 12s, with Vaccarella nominated to handle the 158. Thankfully, we also had the long-awaited new cylinder heads available. These gave us an extra 7 bhp or so – not a whole world of difference, maybe, but, with considerably improved mid-range torque, just sufficient to make all the difference between being competitive and trailing as an also-ran.

For this race I was sandwiched between Clark and Stewart on the front row of the grid. But, as at the Nürburgring, I was unable to make much use of this good position. This time it was clutch trouble. I thought the hydraulics were playing up during the warm-up lap, but everything seemed in order as I arrived on the dummy grid, before moving up to take the start.

But as soon as I wound up the engine and let in the clutch, it began to slip badly, and at the end of the first lap I had dropped back in among the second half of the field. By this time the clutch had stopped slipping, but would now no longer disengage. This meant changing gear without the clutch, but at least with a bit of luck I would be able to keep running. I managed to extricate myself from a whole gaggle of cars and set off at high speed after the leaders.

It didn't take me very long to get in among them – Clark, Gurney, Bandini, Stewart, Siffert and Spence – and I was very pleased indeed with the way the engine was performing. In retrospect, for all that was written, it was the only time during my Ferrari Formula 1 career that I felt I had equipment which was the equal of the opposition, even possibly with a slight edge.

From then on, the race settled down into a scrap between Clark, Hill, Stewart and me, with Gurney and Bandini close behind. If I had been totally confident in the transmission, I would have attempted to make a break for it, but I opted to stay in the leading bunch and hope that the clutch would hold and I could then use the slight power edge I had on the others in the closing stages. But it was not to be . . .

To my immense disappointment, just before half-distance the clutch began slipping again. And this time it kept on slipping. I cruised round another slow lap and came in to retire. Stewart went on to score his first championship race win and Bandini finished fourth, about a minute and a quarter behind the triumphant BRM. Little did I know it at the time, but this was to be my last race under the 1½-litre Formula 1 rules.

Also, I could hardly have known that my plans to run a modified car with a 2.4-litre Dino V6 engine, entered under the Team Surtees banner, in the Tasman Championship the following winter were to be thwarted by an accident in Canada on the very day that this single-seater was to be given its first test run in Italy.

It was to prove an expensive accident in more ways than one, because it postponed and prevented a number of developments I was putting into operation, including plans to run a Dino sports car in 1966 as part of an enlarged Team Surtees, to house which I was negotiating for new premises.

All these things were about to be demolished by the biggest accident it had been my misfortune to suffer at any time during my racing career.

Chapter 7
The Accident and its Aftermath

After the Italian Grand Prix at Monza I had flown directly from Milan to Montreal in preparation for the following Sunday's Can-Am race at Ste Jovite, that beautiful track situated in the Laurentian Mountains. I spent Tuesday checking over the Lola T70s which Jackie Stewart and I were scheduled to drive in the race.

There was a reversal of the cars within the team, Jackie having made some comments about my having raced the new car at Brands Hatch, where I had won, so the cars were swapped and he was to have the new one. I qualified the original car on Wednesday and flew back to London for the Oulton Park Gold Cup, which involved practice on Saturday. In this race I drove the Midland Racing Partnership Lola T60, on which I had worked with Eric Broadley, to victory, then flew back to Canada for the Sunday race.

The effort and vast mileage covered in this logistical shuttle were rewarded with two wins on two continents. With the Lola T70 now proving reliable, and F1 prospects looking up with that improved performance from the flat-12 Ferrari, I approached the following series of races in North America with some confidence.

Sadly for me, the change of fortune promised by the wins at Ste Jovite and Oulton Park was short-lived. On the following Friday, 24 September 1965, a twist of fate brought me face to face with the most serious accident it had ever been my misfortune to encounter.

In practice at Mosport Park, I had settled in, but Jackie was not totally happy and therefore asked me to give his car a run. I remember climbing into the car, but recall nothing more until about four days later. It was later pieced together that, accelerating past the pits, heading towards the downhill right-hander, I lost a front wheel.

The car ploughed into a barrier, somersaulted over it and landed on top of me. I'm told that, on my way to the hospital, I briefly regained consciousness. Frankly, I don't know. It wasn't until four days later that I recall anything. As I say, the last recollection I have is of getting in the car to go out to practise.

The car was fitted with a harness, but whether the mountings pulled out of the chassis or not I just don't know. All I do know is that one of the marshals who pulled me out of the wreck came to see me in hospital and explained that their biggest worry was fire. I was doused in petrol from head to toe. Mercifully, it didn't catch fire.

It was something of a relief when Rob Rusbrook of Lola brought news that a suspension failure had been pin-pointed as the cause of the accident. Rob had been helping our very small team, which was effectively run single-handedly on the mechanical side by Malcolm Malone. He was assisted by reliable and enthusiastic local helpers at the various venues, and in Canada this was no problem.

Rob's news was, in itself, very reassuring because at least it gave me the consolation of knowing I wasn't laid up in hospital through any error of my own. He was also very helpful in assisting Malcolm to clear up all the racing equipment after the accident.

It was, of course, very important for me to know that it hadn't been my fault. The most frightening thing for a racing driver is the unknown. You've got to have reasons. You need to know whether it's your mistake, somebody else's mistake or a mechanical failure. This is crucial for the sub-conscious mind which partly runs you when you are under extreme tension.

As a racing driver becomes more experienced, he develops a certain instinctive way of doing things which comes extremely naturally. When I first drove a racing car, every single move was not pre-programmed but programmed from moment to moment as I made it. I was having to rely on my instant reactions because I had no mental data bank, no experience, to relate to. This made car racing mentally exhausting in those early days because of the intense concentration I expended competing at that level with no previous experience.

Having become experienced, you increasingly rely on this sixth sense which allows you to do everything at a slower mental pace. When you start, 120 mph seems like 160 mph. With experience, that 120 mph seems more like 60 mph. The difference between the absolute top-liner – like Senna today – and the average driver is that it's all happening slower for the former. The whole thing is unfolding in slow motion.

Ironically, it wasn't even a Lola component which had broken! At that time Eric had been discussing with Texan car owner John Mecom the possibility of producing the T70, and some other Lola cars, under licence in the USA. The plan was to use a certain number of English parts and a certain number of components manufactured in America. A trial upright had been sent over and, when my T70 had been built, it had inadvertently found its way onto the new car. It was a clanger. What had happened was that the core had moved during the casting process. The upright had been on the car when I won at Brands Hatch, but chose this moment at Mosport to fall apart.

I had ended up in the wrong place at the wrong time. Mind you, if it hadn't happened to me, it would have happened to Jackie and, since it was my team, I suppose it was only right that I should have been the one to suffer this misfortune!

Four days later, I didn't really know the extent of my injuries. I was later to learn that the decision had been made that nothing should be touched; it was just in the hands of God what would happen to the ruptured kidneys from which I was losing so much blood.

The kidneys had been ruptured because my pelvis had been split in the middle and my left side had literally been pushed up by about four inches. In turn, the kidneys had ruptured and the breakage had broken off the transverse processes on the base of the spine.

The orthopaedic side was just at a standstill. Everything depended on whether or not the kidneys sealed themselves. The alternative was surgery, but they didn't want to use the knife unless it was absolutely the last resort. This was the difference, they explained, between the medical attitude which existed in the USA and the Canadian outlook, which was, perhaps, slightly more European. The doctor concerned was from the Montreal area and I think that was a very important thing for me.

During this period Tony Vandervell – who was on a business trip to Canada at the time and came bustling along to the hospital when he heard the news – and many others from the racing fraternity were in and out, but I don't really remember much about it. Nor do I recall Pat and my mother- and father-in-law arriving on the day after the accident. Their arrival was organised by the *Sunday Mirror*, for which I was writing some articles at the time, and I must say the paper really came up trumps. The whole scene was extremely critical, of course, and they had been told it was touch-and-go whether I actually pulled through.

My first firm recollection of the aftermath is of waking up and finding that I wasn't quite as mobile as I might have been. Quite rightly, the doctors steered clear of discussing my problems with me in too much detail at this early stage. I wasn't too worried about cars or motor racing at that time, just concerned about hanging on.

Forghieri and the Ferrari team came straight to see me once they arrived for the US Grand Prix at Watkins Glen. Although I don't remember it, I'm told I went rambling on at Dragoni, telling him to get my car ready for the Mexican Grand Prix. I had been so excited about the possibility of racing what was, for the first time during my years with Ferrari, a truly competitive car. I believed from what I had experienced at Monza that the flat-12 had at last come good with those Rocchi-designed cylinder heads and that, frankly, we were going to do ourselves justice.

Tactfully, Dragoni adopted his familiar 'we'll wait and see' policy, which was quite correct, because it wasn't until the initial effects of the drugs began to diminish that I really started to experience the excruciating pain.

They were not keen on having me too heavily sedated for too long because they wanted my body to fight anything naturally. So, obviously, coming to and seeing myself surrounded by all the transfusion equipment and so on was something of a shock. I must say that the whole affair put me in mind of my father's accident when he'd been into that quarry and smashed his femur at the time he was travelling backwards and forwards to Catterick. History seemed to be repeating itself!

When it appeared that the blood loss from my kidneys was beginning to stop, we started chatting with the doctors about what was to happen next. They said that they didn't think they were really qualified to take – or wanted to get involved in – the responsibility of putting a sportsman together again.

They offered me the choice of two places where the best-qualified medical attention was available: America and Europe. Once my condition had stabilised, it didn't really take too long to realise the extent of my injuries. It quickly became an obvious priority to get me to not only a top specialist, but to one who really understood the mentality of the racing driver: somebody who didn't simply regard him as a damn fool, but understood that his natural competitiveness enables him to force the pace of a recovery rather quicker than normal folk.

As Tony Vandervell suggested, the obvious thing to do was to get through to England, so Pat contacted Stirling Moss and got the name of Mr Urquhart at St Thomas's Hospital, who'd looked after him after his accident at Goodwood in 1962. So we got in touch with him and he said, 'Don't let those Americans get their hands on you; they'll use the knife. Get back here as soon as it is safe to travel.'

They fixed it all up and, as soon as it was considered safe for me to travel, good old Tony Vandervell pulled out all the stops and got in touch with BOAC to arrange for a row of seats in the first-class cabin of one of their Boeing 707s to be blocked off to take me, as a stretcher case, back to London.

The return journey was finally arranged for 18 October, barely three weeks after the accident. I was literally mummified in bandages from head to toe, with splints down each side of me, tied down to a stretcher and whisked off to the airport. There was no question of any movement at all. In fact, the flight was very good, except for a little turbulence over the Irish Sea which shook me up a bit.

Looking back, the most laughable thing, if it hadn't been so serious, was the journey from Heathrow to St Thomas's Hospital. I had been collected from the Toronto hospital in one of the latest, super-streamlined American ambulances in which the stretcher slid in and locked in place, and it just glided away with its automatic transmission and soothingly soft suspension.

This was a dramatic contrast to the St John's Ambulance vehicle which picked me up at the other end of the journey. Let me say at once that they provide a wonderful service and, as recently as this year (1991), we planned to take part in a fund-raising operation for them at Brands Hatch.

But that journey, from the moment the clutch was let out, allowed every little ripple in the road to be transmitted through my body. It was agony. My trip in what I can only describe as this English antique through the mid-morning London traffic subjected me to an involuntary, and unwanted, vibro-massage.

The driver did his very best, but these vehicles were really not up to the level required for transporting the sick and injured. I was later to find out that the design had been standardised in 1928 and that these ambulances were still being turned out on effectively the same chassis.

This all came out when I was asked to contribute some articles about my experiences to the *Sunday Mirror* and it didn't bring me too many favourable comments from the powers that be at the St John's Ambulance headquarters. But if by any chance those remarks spurred them on towards insisting on a slightly more advanced design for their ambulances – which I'm now assured was the case – then perhaps it did some good.

When I arrived at St Thomas's they began checking me over after a couple of days to recover from the flight. I met Mr Urquhart and was immediately impressed with his attitude. He didn't think we were head-cases for racing around on motor cycles or in cars. He looked upon it as a challenge and even understood somebody who perhaps wanted to start it all again.

Of course, to be quite frank, I wasn't ranting and raving, or even talking, about motor sport. Lots of messages were coming in asking whether I would race again, but I just replied that it was absolutely pointless to speculate about it. Until I was fit, there was no point in saying yes, no or maybe.

Then one day Mr Urquhart presented himself. He said, 'Right, time's getting on. You're in a bit of a sorry state, but everything else is stable, so we've got to try and straighten you up. We've got to get your left side down a bit to match your right side. I thought you might like to know about that, because tomorrow me and my colleague are going to stick you on the table. He'll get one end, I'll get the other and we'll pull like bloody hell.

We'll get you somewhere near!'

And that's just what they did! They got the differential down to about half an inch, which is still what it is today. Afterwards, I had some special shoes made to prop up my left side, and stupidly let the matter lapse, which cost me later trouble with bending of the spine and other problems.

It didn't take long for the drugs to wear off after this initial treatment, but I tried to take my mind off the aches and pains by exercising the upper half of my body by lifting myself up on what I called the monkey rope slung above my bed.

Within the same hospital wing, the television broadcaster Richard Dimbleby was a patient, battling against the cancer to which he would sadly succumb even before I left. There were a number of really cheerful Australian nurses on the ward, really good sorts who did an enormous amount to boost my spirits, and I remember one day they came up and said, 'Ah, Mr Dimbleby sent up this champagne for you. He's got enough.'

Although he was battling against stomach cancer, the doctors allowed him champagne and I was grateful to receive some of his surplus supply. It was the same for me. With my kidney damage, champagne was regarded as no problem. They even told me it could do some good and, either way, it was certainly calculated to raise my spirits!

Eventually the pin came out of my injured left leg and I started a competition with the physiotherapist and specialist concerning how quickly I could lift it on my own. They would say, 'We reckon you'll be working that leg on your own in about a week's time,' so I replied, 'Let's see if we can't do it in five days.' This spirit was wonderful; they were all tremendous, with the nurses pitching in to do everything possible to help.

Eventually the day came when they wheeled me down to the physiotherapy pool and the relief of being put into that lovely warm water, and the buoyancy that went with it, was more wonderful than I can explain. I obviously wasn't allowed to put any weight on my left leg, even in the pool, but I could stand again on my right leg and, from then on, I would spend an hour in the pool every morning. By the time I returned to my room, I felt as though I had driven the Le Mans 24-hour race single-handed!

Nowadays, you hear about all the vast expense necessary for this sort of installation, that sort of equipment. But what had the specialists at St Thomas's done? Many people will recall the corrugated-iron water tanks provided for the fire services during wartime – straightforward corrugated-iron sheets bolted together. The specialists had taken one of these down into the cellars at St Thomas's, re-erected it and this was their orthopaedic pool. And I don't doubt that they had every bit as much success with it as many hospitals with more elaborate, tailor-made equipment.

This process continued until 24 November, which was something of a red-letter day in the recovery process. They said, 'Right, today we're going to try and get you walking on one leg.' A pair of crutches was produced, I was lifted out of bed and reminded firmly again that under no circumstances was I to try putting any weight on my left leg. I managed precisely three steps before virtually passing out. That day I wrote in my diary: 'feeling very poor and depressed'.

The following day I reckoned I really had to do better than that, so I got up in the morning and managed to complete eight steps before pegging out. By 26 November I was able to take 83 steps and, because I had a bet with my physiotherapist on the basis of double or quits, managed 400 steps on the morning of 28 November.

On 9 December I had some more X-rays done and the following day I started work in the gymnasium. By now I was settled into a regular regime: mornings in the pool, followed by heat treatment and gym work in the afternoon. Next I started exercising on a stationary bicycle and gradually built up sufficient strength to start putting weight back on my injured leg, and tackle the obvious incidental challenge of building up the muscles which had wasted away during almost two months spent flat on my back. I was also using the old spring compressors to keep my wrists in shape, much as I had after damaging my scaphoid in that motor cycle accident in the Isle of Man many years earlier.

After toning up with a programme of 'stationary' table tennis and squash – as I couldn't move around I was riveted to one spot, but used the exercise to move round my upper torso – I took the advice of my specialists, who kept reminding me that warmth and exercise was the best recipe for recuperation.

I was finally able to leave hospital early in the New Year and, shortly afterwards, Pat and I flew off for a convalescent holiday in Guadeloupe, in the French West Indies. We had consulted Harry Myers, who had been a partner of Stirling Moss's in a travel agency, and asked him to recommend somewhere suitable. Our requirements were a hotel on the water, warm sea, shallow beach and not too much expense!

The shallow beach was quite important because Mr Urquhart suggested one worthwhile therapy was to lie in the water, put a plank on my leg and then work it in the water to build up the muscles. We stayed in the Caravelle Hotel, as it then was, and found it was just the job.

It was the first time I had been out to that part of the world, but in a way Guadeloupe was somewhat depressing because it had no real character of its own. It had been a French colony, so any Caribbean culture tended to be imported. I found it a little sad from that point of view, although for my purposes the food was good, the weather was right and I could continue my convalescence.

Just prior to this holiday, I had gone out to Italy to discuss future prospects with Enzo Ferrari, who had never stopped insisting that they would wait until I was fit and not contemplate getting another driver. Although I was still hobbling round on a stick, I was extremely anxious to let them know that I was very determined to race for them again in 1966.

The Italians may have their strange ways, but the honest and sincere manner in which I was greeted on my return to Maranello gave me a great boost. Fiat loaned me a car which I drove up the autostrada from Milan to Modena – which didn't involve me having to use my left foot too much – and I was very touched when everybody I met when I arrived at the factory seemed to have tears in their eyes.

I spent some time looking around at all the cars, and going through the drawing office, and then Pat and I went off to dinner with Mr Ferrari, chewing over all the racing gossip and chat that had arisen in the weeks since my accident. Right from the start, in the immediate aftermath of the crash, Mr Ferrari had been extremely positive, even to the point of shrugging aside news of the injuries to my left leg by assuring me that, if necessary, they would rig up some sort of automatic transmission to accommodate me. That wasn't going to be necessary, of course, but their mood of optimistic encouragement and concern was a great morale-booster during those difficult weeks.

What's more, despite the fact that I didn't have the accident in a Ferrari car (although

I was driving my Lola totally with their knowledge and permission), their insurance policy covered me. The sum involved wasn't a great deal, something like £1000, but I had no insurance policies at the time and their action on this was very much appreciated. They looked after the hospital and everything else. They gave me an enormous amount of support. The same thing happened to Didier Pironi after his accident at Hockenheim in 1982, though of course he was in a Ferrari, but he told me they'd been fantastic.

To digress slightly, I always felt very sorry about that Hockenheim crash – which ended Pironi's career – and his subsequent death in a powerboat racing accident. I got to know him through his half-brother José Dolhem, who has also sadly passed away. Didier was obviously a fantastic driver, but was too often regarded in the shadow of Gilles Villeneuve. But whereas Villeneuve always seemed to me to be just waiting for an accident, Pironi was every bit as quick and much more of a thinker.

I find it amusing to think what would be said if Senna drove like Villeneuve, indulging in all those off-track excursions. Almost everybody would take the chance of condemning him for not using his brain. I think Villeneuve certainly had speed, but didn't channel his talent correctly.

To return to 1966, when I got back to the factory for the first time, all the mechanics were crying. I obviously had pretty limited mobility as I was still wrestling with those crutches, so they got hold of one of those little hoists that they used to move the engines about, and they winched me into the Tasman Dino 246 which was still there waiting for me. The car stayed at the factory after my accident and I used it as a training car to get myself back into the groove again.

Preparing for the new season, which, let's not forget, marked the start of the new 3-litre regulations, I went round and round Modena in that little 246, one of the V8/V6-type semi-monocoque 1965 F1 cars fitted with a 2.4-litre version of the V6 engine.

At this time, Mr Ferrari raised another significant point. He asked me whether I would take on even more responsibilities within the team and, with that in mind, whether I would consider living in Italy. I agreed that I would. I wanted to get more involved in Italy as a whole and become more fluent in the language because, although I could speak it well enough to discuss anything to do with cars and motor cycles pretty well, frankly my general Italian would not stand up in every circumstance.

Living there was the obvious answer. So Ferrari agreed to give me one of his flats, just up the road from the home of Lina Lardi, the mother of his second son, Piero, who in 1991 took over control of the F1 team after the dismissal of Cesare Fiorio.

Of course, up above Mrs Lardi, somebody had rather strategically placed themselves in a flat higher up in the same building. This was Mike Parkes, who would later share the flat with Brenda Vernor, who had come to Modena as an English teacher and in turn was to become Piero's English tutor. Much later again, after I had left, Brenda became secretary to the racing department.

My flat was very nice indeed, and I remember going with Pat to some of the little furniture makers in Maranello; the area abounded with little factories turning out lovely material. In fact, in my study today I have a cabinet which, to look at the detail of its marquetry, you might believe was very ancient. But, in fact, it is a piece from Maranello made in the 1950s. The craftsmanship was absolutely superb.

On my first trip back to Maranello, I went round to touch base with everybody in the racing department to see how things were progressing for the new season. Well, suffice it to say that it was a familiar story. The F1 project was a long way behind schedule. The pressure of competition from Ford in endurance racing meant that priority was given to the prototypes, and I suppose the personal competition which now existed between Enzo Ferrari and Henry Ford after their abortive talks about Ford taking over the company made things even more intense.

So the F1, despite the fact that it held out hopes of a renaissance for Ferrari, took second place. I knew that it was a four-overhead-camshaft V12, but was very disappointed to find that it was to be basically a short-stroke sports car engine. I was assured there were lots of other developments in the pipeline.

The 312 V12 was wheeled out and it looked absolutely enormous alongside the Tasman Dino, my 'convalescence car'. Everybody was making optimistic noises, saying that the 3-litre Ferrari would walk the championship, that Surtees had no problems. So I took this thing out and it was two and a half seconds slower round Modena than the 2.4-litre V6.

It just didn't want to go. It was very drivable, but it was heavy and didn't have the power. The engine was still a straightforward aluminium block, with aluminium heads, with the same external dimensions as the sports car engine.

Everybody was saying, 'Poor old Jack Brabham has only got about 290 bhp from his Repco V8,' whereas in reality our V12 was only developing 270 bhp, as well as being way over the weight limit. I started the F1 season with a win at Syracuse, but I had to row it along like mad to beat Lorenzo in the little V6. Luckily Syracuse had some fast twiddly bits round the back where I was able to pick up some time.

Then we were beaten roundly by Brabham in the Silverstone International Trophy which, frankly, was no surprise to me at all. We wore tyres out at a great rate and simply couldn't compete on speed with the Brabham-Repco – or even the 2.2-litre BRM V8s, come to that.

I told Forghieri and Franco Rocchi what I thought about this gutless V12 and they went very quiet. They admitted that the team couldn't really afford the time or, I believe, the money to build a totally new engine and had to streamline the technical operation, making components which were interchangeable with the sports car programme. So I made it quite clear to them just how hard I had had to wind the thing up in order to finish second at Silverstone, but they inwardly knew the truth of the matter and that I used to go into the engine test house to see exactly what sort of power outputs the engines were giving. I was really struggling to get within two seconds of my best time with the V6 round Modena, so I went to the Old Man and told him it was pointless, and that I wanted the 246 to drive at Monaco. I went to that race with expectations of driving it, only for Dragoni to start lecturing everybody with 'we make 12-cylinder road cars so you've got to race the V12', which hardly went down well with me.

I replied that I thought we were going to Monaco to try and win the race, but he just shrugged my remarks aside by saying, 'Oh, you'll win the race all right.' So I told him that, yes, we would probably stay in front for a few laps, 'and I'll tell you what will happen then: the bloody thing will break its gearbox because I'll be driving it so hard to stay there'.

As everybody knows, that's exactly what happened. I held the lead for a few laps and then it went *crunch*. Jackie Stewart was handed the race on a plate, although I had had to drive pretty hard to stay in front of him. Lorenzo came through to finish second with the V6, strengthening my feeling that we could have won if I'd used it. Even if the V12 hadn't retired, I don't believe it had sufficient fuel capacity to last us through to the finish.

Ferrari's press chief Franco Gozzi recounted to me in a fairly recent conversation how the reports filtered back to Mr Ferrari, and this fits in with my own thoughts about the events leading up to my departure from the team. Dragoni had always been in the semi-limelight since being hailed as the saviour of Italian racing drivers after he discovered Giancarlo Baghetti. On the basis of that, and his Scuderia St Ambroseus, which was basically a club made up of wealthy, enthusiastic racing car owners, he was, I suppose, attempting to find another Ascari or Nuvolari after Baghetti had come and gone.

In some ways, Dragoni disliked the close personal relationship I enjoyed with Mr Ferrari, which was extremely straightforward and based on mutual respect for each other's positions. To a lesser extent I had a problem with Forghieri, who had his nose put slightly out of joint with my Lola involvement and some of the suggestions and criticisms that I was bringing back to the Ferrari technical side.

It all came back to the fact that they had created a technical oasis tucked away in Italy, away from the centre of the F1 action in England. In addition, Mike Parkes had always been slightly overshadowed by my presence and never had any real involvement as a driver in the sports car programme at all when it came to either design or development and testing.

I think Dragoni was quite happy that we didn't have a competitive car to start with, because it could easily suggest that JS was not performing that well after his accident. He was also pleased that there was only one V12 initially, so that there could be no direct comparison with Bandini.

A second V12 was ready in time for Monaco and the reports that Dr Gozzi received at the factory suggested that I had demanded both the V6 and both the V12s for my personal use, which would have left poor Bandini without a drive. My response to this was 'total, utter rubbish'. All I wanted was the V6, but this hadn't been the message transmitted back to Mr Ferrari.

What you've also got to remember is that there wasn't a great deal of F1 television coverage at the time, so Mr Ferrari just had to rely on whatever news was filtered back to him by his acolytes. There was nobody there to contradict this information. In my view, the V6 could have won every race up until I left the team, including Spa, which was a wet race.

Also, on my return to the team, I soon got an inkling that Dragoni and, to a lesser extent, Mike Parkes had become extremely active on the political front. However, I would like to think that Bandini was not involved in this apparent campaign to undermine my position.

Lorenzo wanted me to stay. I think he was a very good driver, but at that stage in his career he needed another driver in the team to aim at. In some ways he was rather like John Watson who, in my view, was not strong as a team leader in his own right. He didn't have the ability to inspire himself. But put him in a team with somebody who could motivate him – like Niki Lauda did for him at McLaren – and he could raise the standard of his game.

Although I believe Lorenzo had a rather stronger personality than John, he still thrived in a situation where I gave him a standard to aim for. He quite liked the car set up in the way I did, so we felt comfortable together. It was a rather pleasant relationship. He was a nice man, straightforward and uncomplicated, a good person to work with. We didn't live in each other's pockets, but we got on well and there was a mutual respect between us which I think was very important.

In fact, I don't honestly believe that Scarfiotti was naturally political either. But he was drawn into the political scene simply by virtue of his position as a relation of Mr Agnelli. I think Dragoni used this fact, holding out the potential of the later, more powerful V12 engines, to hint at the possibility of an Italian driving renaissance in which Lodovico would play an important part. But I never had any animosity towards Scarfiotti and we had had some good drives together in sports cars.

I think Mike Parkes gave Dragoni something of a helping hand, mainly, perhaps, because he felt rather overshadowed with me there in the team because I was gaining a lot of the publicity. On my return, we had a confrontation about the set-up of the Ferrari 330P3 sports car for the 1966 Monza 1000 Km, which was due to be my first race back in the team after the accident.

I took the car out for testing at Monza and, after a few laps, came into the pits and said, 'Well, I don't understand this. He's been testing this car and, going into both the Curva Grande and Curva Ascari, the back end wanted to snap round and overtake the front.' I talked to Forghieri about this and expressed the view that the problem was mainly aerodynamic.

I thought the root of the problem was the effect that the large windscreen, demanded by the latest regulations, was having on the car as a whole. We made some minor changes to the nose section and, sure enough, it became a very drivable car which you could get through those really quick corners with a degree of confidence.

This didn't put me in very good odour with Mike, who had done the initial testing. Then, come the race itself, which we won, the P3's windscreen wiper failed and the story was reported back to Mr Ferrari that I had wanted to retire the car and that Parkes had been the one who insisted on continuing.

This was complete and utter nonsense. I was the one who quickly realised that if we cracked on hard, because of the P3's aerodynamics, the screen would remain comparatively clear. If we slowed, we couldn't see a thing. These silly twists were the last things we wanted in the team at the time. If only there had been more television coverage, Mr Ferrari would not have been so isolated, but that's the way it was.

Coming back to the Grand Prix programme, I still say to this day that we could have run the 2.4-litre V6 right through to the point that the three-valve heads were ready for the V12, and won the championship. As it was, with respect to Jack Brabham, I was very unfortunate not to win the title.

For the Belgian Grand Prix at Spa, I had taken pole position and made a good start in what was to be a race which had a tremendous impact not only on me but on motor sport as a whole. Going down towards Burnenville on the opening lap, I was suddenly aware of the odd spot of rain and thought to myself, 'Take care.'

Going round Burnenville I tried to stay well off the racing line to avoid the build-up of rubber which had been laid during practice and was likely to be very slippery if rain was falling onto it. It was well known at Spa that if it was raining lightly at that point on the circuit, it could well be pouring by the time you reached Stavelot.

Sure enough, a little further round the lap we hit the rain storm. The leading bunch got through, but several cars spun wildly off the circuit, including Jackie Stewart's BRM. Jackie was trapped for some time in the wrecked car, thankfully emerging with light injuries, but it was an experience which was to put him off Spa for good.

It was one of those races which you try and win as slowly as you can. At the height of the downpour, Jochen Rindt got ahead with his Cooper-Maserati, running on deep-grooved Dunlop all-weather tyres, so I was content to follow him round, effectively keeping in his wheel tracks as he cleared the circuit for me. For a number of laps this involved running blind in the spray cloud behind the Cooper and just praying that Jochen didn't make a mistake!

We were running on lightly grooved Firestones at that time, the link with the American tyre company developing after our blow-outs on Dunlops at Monza during the previous year's sports car race. Following that episode, I had contacted Mr McCreary of Firestone and asked him to come and see Ferrari and we arranged to run on their tyres for 1966.

Towards the end, the rain eased and the time came to repass Jochen on the entry to the Burnenville curve, and I went on to score a comfortable win. Lorenzo was third, more than a lap behind in the little V6.

None of this, however, seemed to please Dragoni, who criticised me strongly for spending too long following the Cooper-Maserati, and this was the story duly relayed to Mr Ferrari. I told Dragoni, 'Look, when you tell me how to drive my races, that will be the day. Winning is the only thing that matters.' His reply was that with the forthcoming new three-valve cylinder heads, which were under development for the V12, the team would be able to use lesser drivers and win anyway.

To compound this situation, it turned out that Dragoni also reported that the Cooper was suffering differential problems in the closing stages and this was the only reason I managed to repass it. I had speeded up. Jochen didn't go any quicker!

In retrospect, I think I concluded after this race, when I got no congratulations at all on winning from the team management, although the mechanics were happy, of course, that the crunch time was coming.

My life at Ferrari was not such a partnership as before, when Pat had played such an essential role. This later manifested itself in the form of problems within our marriage, but at that time it was expressed as worries about Dragoni being obstructive in connection with whether or not she could sit in the pits to do the timing and claims that one of the engineers had been making passes at her. I obviously found this unsettling.

I was totally involved in trying to overcome my injuries, and recommit myself to racing again, but I think the strains of the accident had been quite severe on Pat. All this built up to the point where I felt pressure coming at me from all sides and, after the Belgian Grand Prix, I felt it was time to cry enough.

The fact that I got totally involved in trying to recommit myself to racing after the accident perhaps made Pat feel slightly uneasy and brought about a certain feeling of insecurity. Although there was nothing else in her life apart from racing and the life that went with it, those early months of 1966 were definitely a stressful period for her and it all blew up out of control.

In any normal company, I feel I could have sorted everything out on a man-to-man basis, but Ferrari, with all its intrigue, was not a normal company and the only way to resolve the problem in such a situation was to make a clean break of it, no matter how much it hurt in the short term.

In any event, the racing programme didn't allow sufficient time to sort it out and now it was a question of going off to Le Mans. During the Le Mans test days the 7-litre Fords had really started to come good and Dragoni had come up to me and said, 'John, you're the only one who can do it; you've got to go out and post fastest time.' So I did just that.

Despite our dismal showing the previous year, the Ferrari sports cars were basically very sound machines and the real question mark was whether the Fords could last. In my view, we had to have at least one car which tried to act as a hare and go out in front from the start. It wasn't the intention that this car should run so hard that it would break, but we had to match any similar tactics which Ford might throw at us. Anyway, we had used this formula in the past and we knew it worked well.

In every single sports car race that I had done for Ferrari, the pattern of the team's race had been set by me because I was the fastest driver in the line-up. We had experienced clutch problems at the Nürburgring, where Phil Hill and Jo Bonnier had won in the Chaparral, but we were confident about our prospects in the 24 Hours.

On my arrival at Le Mans, Dragoni told me that Mr Agnelli was coming and, as a result, I would be taking the second stint to allow Scarfiotti to start the race. I replied that Lodovico was not going to be able to mix it with the fastest Ford drivers in the early stages. He replied, 'Oh, well, we thought if we let Lodovico start it would give you an easier time. Perhaps you might be tired.'

He also mentioned that there was a third driver, Jean Guichet, nominated as reserve. I reminded him who he had asked to try and set a time faster than the Fords at the test day, and who was the fastest driver in the team. I told him that whatever was behind his thinking it was not in the interests of the team and the main job in hand, namely that of beating Ford and winning the race, and that I was tired of being constantly sabotaged in my efforts to win by decisions that made no sense. Therefore he had best count me out.

Eoin Young was one of the first people I came into contact with and so, having a high regard for his ability and integrity, I explained the situation and said that I felt I ought not to be alone. We therefore piled into the 330GT and drove off to Maranello. We first saw Valerio, Mr Ferrari's secretary, and Dr Gozzi and then Mr Ferrari himself. Obviously the wires had been humming.

I do not know to this day quite what relationship existed between Mr Ferrari and Dragoni. Frankly there must have been some deep involvement somewhere, probably attached to funding. There was a lot of political activity, particularly with regard to the Fiat involvement, so perhaps the answer lies there. Well, I put my case that the team was throwing away its opportunities and misusing the abilities which were available by playing absurd politics both in the factory and at the circuit . . . politics where the best car was not necessarily used for an event. Mr Ferrari showed considerable emotion, not anger – in fact certain things were discussed during that meeting which to my mind showed that he genuinely felt very hemmed in by the whole situation. He made comments that explained a lot, things that he never talked about again during his lifetime, so I am certainly not going to raise them after his death. But the end result was that, as he joked with me in later years, there had to be a divorce.

I have seen remarks made by Mr Ferrari and even a comment in his book taken totally out of context and misrepresented to suggest that my leaving Ferrari was all to do with my putting to use knowledge of chassis and engine design gained at Maranello to form my own team. It just goes to show how little the people concerned know. My main preoccupation at the time was how much knowledge we could obtain from the English scene, as Ferrari were suffering from being isolated and not benefiting from the wealth of knowledge that was generated by the teams operating in England. I had tried to be a link with the modern world, widening my experience with the Lola sports car project and introducing numerous experts and components such as Peter Jackson on fibre glass products, Firestone tyres and so on.

On the engineering side I had a good relationship with Franco Rocchi and his small team who were mainly responsible for all new design work, and with Engineer Bussi on the engine side. With Mauro Forghieri, things were somewhat strained because he had started to take a little more responsibility on design and because I was being so very critical of first the new prototype and then the 3-litre Formula 1 car. Obviously this placed him in a difficult position. Mike Parkes I hadn't really come across other than as a driver in the prototype team, but I had crossed swords with him rather seriously over my less than complimentary remarks about the new GTB road car that he had been closely associated with, particularly as these remarks had been made directly to Mr Ferrari, who had asked me to give my opinion, and subsequently, on my return to the team after my Canadian accident, my equally scathing comments about the sorting or lack of it on the 330P3.

Therefore what emerged was Dragoni, who had been busy for some time trying to undermine my position, now getting support from Parkes and, somewhat unwillingly I believe, Scarfiotti, both of whom were promised Formula 1 drives. Forghieri was also in there somewhere, no doubt thinking that soon we will have the three-valve engine and a lot of horsepower and if we win with Parkes, Scarfiotti or in turn Bandini, who was obviously the most likely, we will get the credit, not Surtees.

My mind was made up, so Eoin and I walked out of the factory, bringing to an end a very special period in my life. The divorce of Ferrari and myself was agreed. I was to move out of the flat in Modena, which I had only just got settled into, and leave. If I had been more politically minded, or less sure of my own ability, I could probably have turned the tables on those parties who were against me. But I was hungry for success, particularly after my accident.

I just wanted to race, and to try and win. I had always been convinced that Ferrari had been his own worst enemy when it came to gaining consistent success. This latest political upheaval, on top of my accident, brought me to a point where I just wanted to get back to a simple way of life and be a racing driver without being involved in all this intrigue.

And it was a difficult decision, because I knew how much was in the pipeline at Maranello. With a bit of luck, if they'd kept at it, we could have had two championship years in 1966 and '67. For certain we could have won in '66, perhaps even in the next two years.

What made it even sadder was that, at the time of the accident, I was on the verge of committing myself even more deeply to Ferrari, with the intention of spending more time living in Italy to do so. I felt very much as though Ferrari would probably provide me with a racing home, so to speak, for the rest of my career.

Still, that was quickly to become water under the bridge. On one of the last occasions I met the Old Man before his death, he virtually admitted that our splitting up had been an opportunity lost. But, as he said, we shouldn't dwell on the bad times in the past, only the good, and in that respect I believe he was quite right.

On the other hand, you have to say that any problems at Ferrari had to be laid firmly at Mr Ferrari's door. It is easy enough to blame Dragoni, to blame this and to blame that, but at the end of the day it came down to Mr Ferrari, who was a very political animal, never really happy unless he was causing a bit of aggravation. He believed this was a major motivating factor.

He'd fought his way to the top of his chosen business by hook and by crook, and I don't think he'd been too concerned about playing by the rules on the way. He was rather like a puppeteer: he liked to have all the strings in his hands, everybody dancing to his tune. That quality lives on with Ferrari to this day, almost because people expect the team to conform to this established pattern. Enzo Ferrari may have gone, but the attitude of the Italian press, for example, certainly doesn't seem to have changed.

The Italian press, of course, was – and remains – extremely powerful, and Ferrari used to hand out awards to the people who stirred up the most trouble. He encouraged them to stir up Forghieri, to stir up Surtees, or whomever. It was ludicrous!

Later, when I had a team of my own, and began dealing with drivers, I started to understand many things which were a mystery to me when I was at Maranello. I was, to be frank, rather naïve, in that the basic ambition to compete for competition's sake was something I took for granted within drivers' characters.

Later, I realised this was not always the case, and that many of them spent far too much time involved in totally pointless political intrigue rather than having purely the racing at heart. This had perhaps influenced Mr Ferrari and made him, at times, very wary, although I believe we had a very good and honest relationship. All the good times we spent together, whether relaxing at his villa on the Adriatic coast or simply having a meal down in Maranello, were special moments which were not common in his relationships.

Of all my time in car racing, I probably endured the deepest depression and lowest morale – as well as the greatest satisfaction – during my years with Ferrari. The sad thing was that I was very happy for the majority of my time at Maranello, despite my inner knowledge that we could have achieved much better results together than we in fact managed.

Immediately after my final rift with Ferrari, I received an approach from Roy Salvadori on behalf of the Cooper-Maserati team – he had been my team-mate, of course, in the Bowmaker Lola days. Roy had always been serious about his motor racing and, in my view, never quite realised his full potential as a Grand Prix driver, mainly because he was waiting in the wings while Aston Martin were being so slow in developing their DBR4 in 1959.

The fact that I was quicker when I joined him in the Bowmaker team was not openly resented by him. I heard comments made to the effect that I had the best car and so on, but I had no reason to believe that Roy ever actually committed himself to saying such things. He was certainly a good and considerate team-mate and was keen to arrange a seat for me at Cooper in 1966.

I was also very grateful for the way in which Shell, to whom I was contracted as a Ferrari driver, had no hesitation in releasing me to Cooper, who ran on BP. There was no other Shell team available and I thought the Cooper-Maserati offered the most obvious berth with plenty of potential. Keith Ballisat of Shell and Dennis Druitt of BP quickly put their heads together and arranged the necessary release in order for me to make the switch.

One of the first things we did after I joined Cooper was to get Maserati to change to Marelli ignition, which made the V12 a little less prone to oiling its plugs. The Cooper T81 chassis was pretty good, although it was a little heavy, perhaps.

Working with their engineer Derrick White, we made detail changes to the suspension which improved the Cooper's traction but, although the Maserati had about the same power as the two-valve Ferrari I had driven at Spa, it was bulky and lacked refinement. This was the cause of many of the little problems we experienced which cost us races. But, on the whole, I enjoyed a good season with the team. With Jochen backing me up, we were in with a good chance, but we would clearly have to rely heavily on racecraft and out-driving the Ferrari opposition to achieve any success.

I qualified second for the French Grand Prix at Reims and got away first at the start, but fuel vaporisation trouble going into the first corner spelled the end of that outing. I had a good battle with Jack Brabham at the Nürburgring in the wet, but had to give best to him after losing the clutch and finished in second place.

Monza, of course, was down to slipstreaming and very much a question of how effectively you could get through the Curva Grande and the Lesmos, trying to sustain sufficient momentum to prevent anybody picking up your tow. In practice, the new Ferrari three-valve engines – which were reputedly developing around 360 bhp – were extremely quick and I remembered Dragoni's remarks about being able to win with lesser drivers.

The Cooper, however, was in with a very good chance, but suddenly I found myself sitting in a bath of fuel after the tank ruptured. That was a real shame, because to pull off a win at Monza would have been very satisfying.

At Watkins Glen, I set a succession of fastest laps in the United States Grand Prix which I'm sure we would have won if Peter Arundell hadn't virtually driven straight out of the pits into the side of me while I was running an easy second within a few feet of Lorenzo's Ferrari. I made a precautionary pit stop and, while the mechanics checked the cars over, my emotions got the better of me and I ran down the pits and told Arundell what I thought of him. The silly thing is that that collision probably lost me a victory, but on the other hand if I hadn't been taking a tactical approach, just sitting behind Lorenzo's Ferrari, being kind to the car, and had instead tried to lead from the start, I might well have been past the point where I tangled with Arundell before the Lotus left the pits!

As it was I then came back to finish third behind Jimmy Clark in the Lotus-BRM H16 and my team-mate Jochen Rindt, then we rounded off the year with a very gratifying win at Mexico City which meant that I ended up second to Jack Brabham in the Drivers'

World Championship.

I started the Mexican race with a freshly installed engine after my Maserati V12 had gone pop just before the end of practice and, with no race morning warm-up sessions in those days to sort things out, we got special dispensation to run the car back and forth along the Peralta banked corner just before the start.

We set up the injection settings almost by guesswork and, as I went off the line, it went as flat as a pancake for the first few laps. Obviously we'd got the mixture a bit too weak but, when it got to the point where the engine just about boiled, it chimed in and away we went. I was able to dominate the race from that point onwards which was a tremendously satisfying way to finish the season.

Cooper, of course, were owned by Marks and Spencer heir Jonathan Sieff, and at the time of the Mexican Grand Prix there was considerable uncertainty as to what the team's future might hold, particularly whether they would retain supplies of the Maserati engine.

In the event, the team continued with Jochen and Pedro Rodriguez driving, and Maserati continued to supply their engines, developing a four-valve head for the V12 which worked pretty well. But at that time they were not in a position to be totally specific to me about 1967. And it was in Mexico City that I first made the acquaintance of Honda's Yoshio Nakamura.

Naka-san had been in charge of Honda's Formula 1 programme ever since they made their first tentative appearance at the 1964 German Grand Prix with a car for Ronnie Bucknum. They'd returned with a full-scale effort the following year and were rewarded when Richie Ginther won the Mexican Grand Prix, the final race held under the 1½-litre regulations. They had then returned with a 3-litre V12 for three races in the first season of the new formula, but little success had come their way and, by the time I spoke to Nakamura in Mexico City, the Honda camp was in a rather dejected frame of mind.

Although the V12 engine was reputedly developing in the region of 320 bhp, the chassis was extremely heavy at 600 kg, with the result that Ginther had suffered a burst tyre in their first race at Monza and crashed heavily.

Nakamura virtually told me that the company had decided to stop F1, but that they would probably change their minds if I agreed to join and could make arrangements to run the car on their behalf. We had already set up Team Surtees to run the Lola sports cars so, after giving the matter considerable thought, and once again being ruled by my heart rather than my head, I considered what Honda had achieved in motor cycle racing and decided to take on the project.

What I hadn't bargained for was the way in which the Japanese would behave. I was about to enter a political situation rather similar to that which I had experienced with Ferrari and, just as I felt we were on the verge of producing a really competitive machine, based round a lightweight V12, the whole project was quashed at the end of 1968 after Mr Honda had gone off at a tangent with the ill-fated air/oil-cooled V8-powered car in which poor Jo Schlesser was later killed in the French Grand Prix.

Looking at Honda's F1 involvement with McLaren at the start of the 1990s, you've got to remember that, by comparison, we had a really tiny operation, with only a handful of people involved. Honda were very much in a transitional stage between bikes and cars and had a lot of financial pressures on them. Their first road cars were very much at the bottom end of the market, so I found myself having to go round doing sponsorship deals with people such as Firestone in order to keep the project afloat.

I had originally brought Firestone to Ferrari after using their tyres on the Lola T70s, then gone back to Dunlop during my spell with Cooper. Honda had been on Goodyear up until the end of 1966, but I made the switch to Firestone when I set up their operation in preparation for 1967. I also recruited Jimmy Potton, who'd worked for Aston Martin and later joined me on the Lola T70s and, briefly, at Cooper, to take over as chief mechanic.

I went out to Japan to try the two original chassis, one wide-track and one narrow-track, at Suzuka, but plans for a modified car never quite came about and we began the 1967 season armed with effectively the same RA273 Ginther had used at the end of the previous year. We had only three V12s for the programme to start with, plus a lightweight magnesium-cylinder head version which we soon lost as it proved extremely trouble-some. In addition, there were no facilities in England to rebuild the engines and the budget was so marginal that we didn't always have enough money to air-freight the engines back to Japan for their scheduled overhauls. Mr Nakamura had to regulate how much the engines ran, bearing in mind their crankshaft life.

In charge of engine developments and modifications back in Japan in '67 was Nobuhiko Kawamoto, who is today President of the Honda Motor Company, with Tadashi Kume, who became President of the company immediately prior to his colleague. In conjunction with Kume and Kawamoto, an outline drawing for a new, compact, lightweight V12 and transmission was prepared at the Team Surtees base at Slough. Mr Kume returned to Japan to progress the design and, so I thought, initiate its manufacture, but the project was effectively shelved as Mr Honda forced him to design that wretched V8.

The original V12 engine had been the responsibility of Soichiro Irimajiri, who later became a Vice-President of the Honda Motor Company and, in March 1991, was appointed head of the company's research and development programme.

In that respect, you have to say that Honda certainly believed in the benefits of a racing programme, and those involved in it had no trouble in gaining advancement within the management structure. Looking back on it now, that fact appears very praiseworthy, but life certainly seemed extremely frustrating at the start of the '67 season.

Whatever one might think about Japanese products, how nice it is to see people who have started quite near the bottom of the pile going right through to the top of their company. They are engineers running an engineering company, rather than accountants – who are never creative people in the true sense of the word – as we might find in England or the USA, which has been to the detriment of the engineering business as a whole. Too few engineering companies, I believe, have sufficient input from those who design and manufacture the seed corn of their company's products.

I used to fume when Honda seemed to turn over staff so quickly on the F1 project, but from their viewpoint, in terms of getting the necessary experience into the company, they did themselves an immense amount of good. The results on the track may not have been so clever in 1967/68, because of the political pressures involved, but I am gratified to say that the success Honda have enjoyed in recent years with the Williams and McLaren teams tends to back up my original confidence in their long-term capability. It's just a bit late for me to benefit now, but I always believed they had the ability to achieve these excellent results.

In particular, I was very touched after Nigel Mansell's victory with the Williams-Honda in the 1986 British Grand Prix when I received a telegram from Mr Kume saying, 'Without your contribution, none of this would have been possible.' That was very nice and quite unique in my experience; I can never recall anybody else responding in that way!

The basic problem with the Honda V12 was that the first RA273 chassis was tremendously heavy. It felt like a tank and was built as solidly as the Forth Bridge. The engine was also very heavy. But it's quite interesting to see that the latest F1 Porsche V12 has adopted a similar central power take-off to that employed on the first 3-litre Honda.

Our car started the season something like 400 lb heavier than anything else on the grid at 1500 lb, compared with the 1130 lb of the Brabham BT24-Repco and the amazing 1105 lb claimed for the Lotus 49 which made its debut mid-season. We were also hampered by the use of low-pressure fuel injection thanks to a strict directive from Mr Honda. In many ways it was a repeat of the Vanwall and Ferrari story inasmuch as the engine was very vulnerable and sensitive to changes in ambient temperature and general climatic conditions.

This low-pressure system would have been fine on methanol, but with pump petrol it just wasn't sufficiently precise, with the result that there was a lot of variation in the power curve. Later on, the Honda engineers managed to improve this by increasing the pressure slightly, but for political reasons the fuel pressure gauge had to remain calibrated as if we had retained the original system!

On our debut outing at Kyalami we struggled home third behind Pedro Rodriguez in the Cooper-Maserati and the private 2.7-litre four-cylinder Cooper-Climax driven by John Love. I crossed the line with a chronic misfire, the low-pressure fuel system being particularly vulnerable to the effects of high altitude and vaporisation problems, in addition to which one rear tyre was completely bald and the other on the verge of total deflation.

I suppose it was a moderately promising start, but things got significantly worse over the next few months. At Monaco I stopped with engine trouble while running fourth. That, of course, was the tragic Sunday on which Lorenzo Bandini's Ferrari crashed and caught fire at the waterfront chicane. Lorenzo died from his injuries a few days later, depriving motor racing of a really nice man whose pleasant personality I will always remember.

I can't help feeling that one cause of this accident was the additional responsibility which had been thrust on Lorenzo's shoulders.

On to Zandvoort, where the dreaded sand got into the needle rollers of the throttle slides and jammed the throttles open, then to Spa, where we were unable to give the sort of performance that we thought was possible because of fuel starvation problems produced by the sustained high-speed nature of the circuit. In the race, the engine broke its crankshaft on the opening lap!

Then we missed the French Grand Prix at the Le Mans Bugatti circuit due to a shortage of engines, before managing nothing better than sixth in the British race at Silverstone. Although I would finish fourth in the German Grand Prix at the Nürburgring three weeks later, it had become crystal clear that we had to take the initiative and do something about the chassis side in order to get more progress with the engine, as Honda in

Japan were not progressing as quickly as we had hoped in terms of lightening the existing RA273 chassis. So we asked for the OK to develop a new chassis with engineer Shoichi Sano working in conjunction with Eric Broadley. Hence the 'Hondola' was born.

Of course, our team was based in Slough, just round the corner from Lola, where we had in fact based Team Surtees and Lola Racing. Mr Nakamura and his team of Japanese assistants stayed in a small flat in Slough town centre.

So the question came up of how we should move on from here. The solution was found after discussing the matter with Eric Broadley: namely the adaptation of the Lola Indianapolis car to meet F1 regulations and take the Honda engine and gearbox. So we worked away to produce this new car, a joint venture between Eric's little team, our group round the corner and Honda. In so doing, we missed the Canadian Grand Prix at Mosport Park, but it was certainly worth the effort.

The decision to adapt the Indy car design came about as the long-term consequence of an invitation, back in 1965, from USAC engineer George Bignotti, who asked me whether I would be interested in doing an Indianapolis project in conjunction with car owner John Mecom. I went out there and talked over a programme with them, did a little testing, and agreed to drive at Indy in 1966, subject to Ferrari's agreement.

I then landed up in hospital and suggested that Graham Hill should drive in my place – and he won the race. I was subsequently invited to drive Bignotti's Lola in the Rex Mays 300 at Riverside in November 1967. Apart from the fact that the Offenhauser engine had great big holes in its power curve compared with an F1 engine, it was quite a nice car to drive. It was my involvement with this project which set me thinking that the Lola Indy chassis might be a good basis for redeveloping the Honda.

The fruit of our endeavours was dubbed the RA300. It weighed in 100 lb lighter than its predecessor, using a number of titanium components manufactured in Japan, but not the 200 lb lighter that we would have liked. This was because of the engine size and design, for with the central power take-off Honda found it necessary to use a three-shaft gearbox, so the restricting factor was the mass of those two units. However, the new car was aerodynamically better, and easier on the tyres. And, of course, we took it to Monza for its race debut where I managed to win, squeezing out Jack Brabham's Brabham-Repco in a last-lap sprint to the line.

No, we were not steaming away from the opposition down the straights by any stretch of the imagination. Running high gears for good maximum speed, we were only building up to that competitive velocity at the very end of the Monza straights. It took Honda a long time to learn the value of useable mid-range power and torque of the kind demonstrated by the Cosworth DFV, but they have certainly managed it with their latest products which, I believe, have been winning races as much due to their mid-range performance as their out-and-out horsepower.

The Honda engine had rather strange characteristics in a car that was very much overweight, but it was surprising how well you could get it to go round places such as Monte Carlo. Certainly, it took quite a lot of physical effort but, by running it with very low gears and letting the engine rev for short periods to 10,500 rpm, it could put up a respectable show.

Where we encountered a problem at Monza was that the terminal speed was high so we had to fit a suitable gear to achieve that speed, which still left us with the problem of not getting up to that speed early enough. If anybody has watched any film of that race they will see, for instance, that for two-thirds of the straight coming out of Parabolica, Brabham could pull away from the Honda, only for me to start clawing back his advantage as we approached the Curva Grande.

In this race I took one of the biggest gambles ever coming up to the last corner of the last lap. Earlier, Graham Hill's Lotus 49 had blown up and laid an oil slick on the approach to the corner, but with the benefit of a slipstream through the Curva Ascari this was an ideal place for overtaking.

Jack, of course, was one of the few people to have a go at anything, so was I to take a blocking line, put myself partly on the oil and slow up my exit, or was I to take the conventional line and try to tempt Jack up the inside, onto the oil, and hope that the cement which had been laid would do a good enough job?

I left my braking as late as possible and stayed on the line. Jack came up as expected and locked up, so I was able to nip through on the inside and just make it to the line ahead, scoring my first win for the satisfied Honda personnel.

I personally had no doubt that we had been promised some new developments for the start of the 1968 season, and Derrick White had been recruited from Cooper to design a new chassis which would be built in England to accept an updated engine.

As it was, we started the year with a slightly modified V12 incorporating a revised cylinder head with torsion bar valve springs of the type developed by Engineer Kume for use on the Honda engines raced by Brabham in F2, plus a magnesium engine block. In the end, I think we got one magnesium-block engine, which ran into trouble, although the new cylinder heads worked fine and we could now use more revs with safety and gear the car so that we could use the power for longer periods and cut out a few gearchanges.

This was to be followed by a new, smaller V12, but Mr Honda and the company were clearly under some pressure back in Japan as their range of small-capacity cars were not progressing as expected and the air-cooled N600 saloons were about to be launched on the European market.

As a result, he came up with the concept of the air- and oil-cooled V8 which relied on airflow through the engine keeping the oil temperature sufficiently low to cool the engine as a whole. As well as being a technical dead-end, its development delayed the testing of the new RA301 chassis, which managed only two days at Suzuka before being despatched to Jarama for the Spanish Grand Prix.

The V8 programme was all very secret. Suddenly this new engine and car, the RA302, appeared at Slough without any advance warning. All the Honda engineers began shaking their heads apologetically. Well, I thought we had to make the best of it, so I gave it a preliminary test and reported back to Honda that there was no point in even talking about racing it.

We did about two laps on the Silverstone club circuit before all the oil blew out. I didn't drive one again until Monza. It wasn't much better. Accelerating up to speed you'd hear a high-pitched 'ping' as the cylinder head bolts started breaking due to overheating, and the engine just cooked.

Prior to this, at the Silverstone test, the large air duct that was part of the oil-cooling system into the crankcase, from which all the oil came out, was blocked off but, again, rather like the fuel pressure gauge on the V12, this had to be kept very quiet.

Nakamura agreed with us that there was no way in which we should take the RA302 racing, so we tucked it away in a corner of the Slough workshop and tried to forget about it. Then one morning, we arrived and it was gone. The previous night, representatives from Honda France had arrived and taken it away.

The next time I saw it was in the pit lane at Rouen where there were effectively two teams at opposite ends of the paddock. Jo Schlesser had been talked into driving it in the French Grand Prix and, of course, it all ended in tragedy when he crashed heavily on the second lap. The car was totally consumed by fire and he didn't stand a chance. But they had made two of these cars . . .

The sad thing was that the RA302 was small and light but, rather like the way in which Mr Ferrari would say, 'Make an engine with this bore and stroke,' or 'Make an enormous single-cylinder engine,' as he once did, Mr Honda had stopped the development of the Kume/Kawamoto lightweight, compact V12, and in so doing had brought ever closer a sad end to the Honda F1 programme.

My initial reaction to all this was to stop the programme completely unless everything was done as originally agreed from that point onwards. But it was too late. For the rest of the year we raced on under a cloud of uncertainty and eventually a very sad Mr Nakamura said, 'John-san. It's the end.'

Yet, paradoxically, it was also the beginning of a new Honda. From that point on, and with the virtual failure of the production air/oil-cooled vehicles, their R & D department turned over to developing what must be regarded as one of the world's great little cars, the Civic. I also believe that Mr Honda took a step back and let future decisions be shouldered more by his management than by himself personally.

All in all, I was very disheartened. I'd spent two more years of my career putting together something which I looked on rather in the way I'd regarded Ferrari: the team with which I would stay for the rest of my career. Now it was over and I had to look elsewhere.

The '68 season hadn't yielded any more victories for Honda, but we'd certainly shown some promise and competitiveness. I was easily leading the Belgian Grand Prix at Spa when a rear suspension bracket – made in England, unfortunately – broke, I finished second in the rain in the sad French Grand Prix and ran with the leaders at Monza before going off on oil dropped by Chris Amon's Ferrari.

Rather like Watkins Glen in 1966, I was sitting just behind Chris with everything nicely in hand when the most freakish of accidents occurred. Amon's Ferrari was running an adjustable rear spoiler controlled from a lever in the cockpit by means of a hydraulic pump. Going into Lesmo, he operated the wing, a pipe blew off the system and sprayed hydraulic fluid over his left-rear tyre – and straight onto the road where I was sitting a few feet behind him. He went off, and over the barrier, and I slid into it.

One race where perhaps the weight wouldn't count so much, and where I had been able to overcome a few car problems the previous year, was the German Grand Prix at the Nürburgring, held in appalling conditions of torrential rain and mist. This was a race in which I believe we could reasonably have been expected to do something rather special. As things turned out, the start was delayed for about nine minutes due to the bad weather, the engine overheated and most of its water was lost.

Much as I haven't approved of many things Jackie Stewart has done during his career, probably the one result that gives his views credibility was the way he was able to drive this race in the Tyrrell Matra. It was a performance which I would have been proud to have produced myself. I have to give him an awful lot of credit for that.

After the final race of the season at Mexico City, Honda took the RA300 to Indianapolis. I had originally intended to go, but eventually had to get Ronnie Bucknum to do the job. He lapped it at 172 mph, but nothing more came of rumours that the company was considering an Indy car programme. Honda's motor racing involvement was scrubbed, completely and totally.

So that was the end of another two wasted years. I was 34 years old and, in my view, still capable of competing with the best as far as out-and-out speed was concerned. I didn't really know what to do, although I'd received overtures from Louis Stanley, who was trying to persuade me to join BRM for 1969. So I started to talk it through seriously, but I made it clear that the only conditions on which I would consider his offer were if the team planned a down-to-earth, straightforward race programme.

I didn't want to get embroiled in a complicated long-term programme with any sort of revised H16 engine. I wanted an uncomplicated chassis with the V12 engine. Stanley replied that BRM were totally dedicated to working as a team; Sir Alfred Owen, Big Lou himself, Jean Stanley . . . they were all going to pull in the same direction. Or so it seemed.

By this stage, morale was pretty low up at BRM's headquarters in Bourne. The previous season's Len Terry-designed car was much like a Formula 5000 chassis I'd commissioned his Leda Cars company to make on behalf of the actor James Garner, who was planning to start his own racing team. I had had to put together a team at Slough to take over this particular project when the car had not performed or held together as it should have done. It was eventually developed into the Surtees TS5 Formula 5000 car, so there was a direct blood-line between this and the BRM P139 which we were planning to use in the 1969 World Championship.

On the face of it, BRM's V12 engine seemed to be developing a reasonable amount of power, so after various board meetings I agreed to drive for them. But, almost from the start, we were in trouble. The V12 regularly lost power progressively after a few laps and it took virtually the entire season to pin-point the problem: the water wasn't circulating round the cylinder head correctly.

Tony Rudd was still keen on developing a lightweight version of the H16 with four valves per cylinder. In an ideal world, perhaps development could have continued as a separate entity, but there was neither the personnel nor the money available.

One of the technical staff at the time, of course, was Peter Wright, who went on to develop the concept of ground-effect aerodynamics to give Team Lotus a winning edge almost a decade later. In 1969 he already had all these drawings for a ground-effect car, but BRM's budget was too restrictive for him to be allowed a free hand, so it was agreed that Peter Wright's concept would be something of a second-stage development of the P139.

Tony Rudd left the team after Zandvoort, where I trailed round to an uncompetitive ninth place, and we missed the French race at Clermont-Ferrand in an effort to pull the team into some sort of shape. It wasn't easy!

Just prior to the British Grand Prix at Silverstone I suggested putting revised Surtees

TS5 geometry onto the P139 and, in fact, it certainly handled better during practice. I qualified on the inside of the second row, made a good start and went diving into Stowe on the first lap in third place behind Jochen Rindt's Lotus 49B and Jackie Stewart's Tyrrell Matra.

Then the front suspension broke and I ground to a halt. Someone at Bourne had slipped up. The components had simply not been welded. They had been tacked, but not welded. I was not amused. Looking on the bright side, the car had performed better. A board meeting had said, 'Yes, get on and test and get the chassis right.'

Then, after the Silverstone race, I got one of my early-morning calls from Louis Stanley saying that my team-mate Jack Oliver was unhappy, that really the poor boy should have a second car modified and that, in order to do this, there wouldn't be time to do any more work on the first car, or to do any testing.

This was totally contrary to what had been agreed, and contrary to the team's interests – in my mind, at least. I replied that this was totally and utterly contrary to our agreed programme. The idea was to build a second car only when we had completed the emergency development programme; Silverstone was just a first step in trying to get some sense into the project.

That was the story of BRM. We would have a meeting to decide our strategy, then the whole thing would be overturned by a telephone call – usually at about 1.30 in the morning – from Louis Stanley. The next day you'd have a call from Sir Alfred saying, 'I'm not sure that I agree with Mr Stanley, but I'm in a difficult position because of my sister. But couldn't we do this . . .' Sir Alfred's sister was, of course, Mrs Stanley.

We obviously also needed another engineer, so I suggested Tony Southgate, with whom I'd worked at Lola. He was then in the USA working for Dan Gurney's All American Racers, but I didn't think he was very happy there. He wanted to return to the UK, so I arranged for him to join BRM. The deal was, as I understood it, that he and Peter Wright would work on a new generation of cars. But nothing more happened regarding the development of the P139.

At the same time, Jim Hall had approached me about driving for the Chaparral Can-Am team. He told me he had something quite unique in the pipeline, and he was right! It had de Dion-type suspension, allowing a very narrow rear track, something like 20-inch wheel rims and special Firestone tyres. The driving position was such that you looked through a virtually horizontal screen. This was the Chaparral 2H which had been under development for more than a year.

I asked, 'How are you supposed to see out of this thing?' They rather shuffled their feet and said, well, it should work OK. To start the season, they bought a customer McLaren M12 and fitted it with one of their lightweight alloy Chevy V8 engines, the idea being that we should switch to the Chaparral when it was competitive.

In honesty, I think they only bought the McLaren to placate me; their hearts were never in it. Eventually we had to get the Chaparral out and racing, and I can only say, while I've driven some strange cars in my time, this one was probably the strangest. It was immensely difficult to handle; when you got it up to speed it began pivoting round its nose, so their answer to that was to fit bigger and bigger rear wings, which in turn killed its straightline speed.

Eventually, to improve the visibility, they raised the driving position so that my helmet stuck through the top, further messing up the aerodynamics. But at least you could see a little. That car was the worst I have ever driven in my life. It was frightening. But I had a contract, so I persevered.

Finally, I said to Jim Hall, 'This is ridiculous. I'm not doing any good for you, I'm not doing any good for myself. I'm just turning myself into a nervous wreck. It's just not a car you can drive properly. There's too much wrong with it.' All the time, of course, they were under pressure from General Motors, who had long used Jim Hall's operation as a front for development work and race experience. The idea then arose, so I was told, that perhaps a driver with much less experience and less used to conventional cars might be the answer. I had already stepped away. The next time the car went out, it was just about destroyed in a huge shunt. That was the end of the project.

What with BRM on one side of the Atlantic and the Chaparral on the other, it was enough to drive anybody to a nervous breakdown. And, in fact, just prior to the US Grand Prix, I was overtaken by what appeared to be a very bad attack of flu. This manifested itself in a really bad fever and was eventually diagnosed as viral pneumonia.

At the same time, I developed a lot of ulcers on my legs, where I'd been subjected to fuel burns during my time at Ferrari. Nevertheless, in the race we came home a moderately promising third behind Rindt's Lotus and Piers Courage in Frank Williams's Brabham, benefiting from some major revisions to the lubrication and cooling systems which had been initiated in the run-up to the event.

At the end of the season, I was absolutely drained and didn't feel at all well. My doctors in England attributed the viral pneumonia partly to acute mental stress and the skin problems to a generally run-down state. I was only to find out ten years later that something else was behind these problems.

I thought, enough is enough. This wasn't the BRM that had turned out so many well-engineered and successful cars in the early 1960s. It was just a pale shadow of its former self.

Consequently, I decided that I wasn't going to get involved in anybody else's political F1 projects and, since the Surtees TS5 was going pretty well in Formula 5000, we decided to take the plunge for 1970 and build our own Grand Prix car.

Chapter 8
Going it Alone

The first step we took in establishing our own F1 operation was to move Team Surtees's base from Slough to a little factory I had acquired in Edenbridge, a few miles from my home in Limpsfield. The Slough set-up was very expensive, not to mention a long way to travel in those days before the M25 was built.

So the plan was to build a new F1 car, the TS7, and a Formula 5000 derivative, the TS8, which would replace the TS5 which had been so successful in the hands of David Hobbs and Trevor Taylor in both England and the USA during 1969.

Of course, to a large extent, Team Surtees was born out of our partnership with Eric Broadley and Lola Racing, whereby Team Surtees had a contract to test, develop and race Lola products. That arrangement started in 1965 with the T70s and later expanded to include the F2 T100s which Chris Irwin and I ran during 1967 using Cosworth FVA and BMW Apfelbeck radial-valve engines.

This technology could have enabled BMW to effect an early entry into F1. To judge by all reports on the Apfelbeck engine's cylinder head flow, it was considered to have the potential to produce extremely high power outputs. But whereas it had the potential to be very high-revving, the mechanical efficiency of the valvegear did not allow the engine to be revved to where the cylinder head was really effective.

Yet BMW were very optimistic about it and, at one time, they were planning a mock-up of a 3-litre racing engine, using one of the aluminium cylinder blocks derived from the 507 road car range. A considerable number of drawings were done of a proposed V8 F1 engine using the Apfelbeck principle.

On quitting Ferrari, I found that one of the things I particularly missed was driving the prototype cars. Eric Broadley, of course, had been the spark that fired the Ford sports car challenge, because it was his Lola-Ford coupé which ran at Le Mans in 1963 which was the forerunner of the GT40 design. We had demonstrated with the T70 that we had a very competitive Group 7 sports car, and for 1967 we came up with the coupé version for long-distance racing.

This set me thinking about how we could mount an all-British challenge, not only for Le Mans, but for all the other major endurance races on the calendar. There was quite a lot of talk at the time about the Aston Martin V8, developed by Tadek Marek, so I discussed its potential with Eric and we agreed to go and have a close look at it to see if it was worth a try.

There was talk about taking the engine out to 5 litres and, as I recall, we were hoping

The new 1966 3-litre F1 V12 is wheeled out at Maranello. I wish they hadn't bothered!

My first race after my accident in Canada was the 1966 Monza 1000 Km in which I shared a Ferrari 330P3 with Mike Parkes. The windscreen wiper broke and we had to go faster than we wanted in order to see!

As very occasionally happened, although not during my time with them, Ferrari pulled something special out of the hat in 1966. They brought out the new three-valve V12 engine which immediately gave them an extra 50 bhp. Despite this, we were still in with a chance, and here I sit in close company with them at Monza with the Cooper-Maserati prior to the fuel tank splitting.

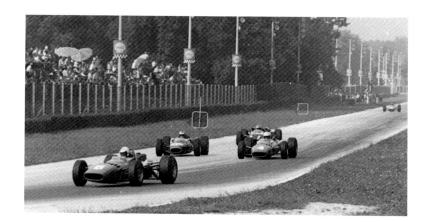

There I was, sitting on Bandini's tail at Watkins Glen, confident that I had everything in hand. Then Peter Arundell's Lotus came out of the pit road . . . I could have killed him, and had it in my mind when I ran down the pit lane at my ensuing stop, losing valuable time as I did so.

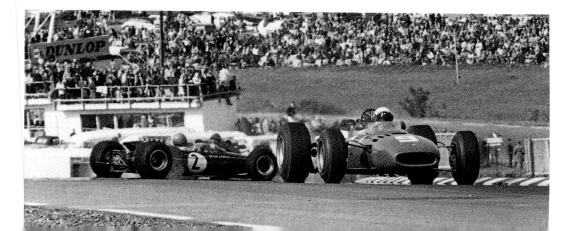

Above: *A Chevy van, trailer, my mechanic Malcolm Malone, a single Lola T70, two Traco-built Chevrolet V8 engines and myself brought us the 1966 Can-Am Championship. There was further success at home in events such as the Guards Trophy at Brands Hatch* (above left).

The first outing for the Honda RA300 brought success when I just beat Jack Brabham to the line in the Italian Grand Prix at Monza. Here I am seen leading Chris Amon's Ferrari and Bruce McLaren's McLaren-BRM V12 in the early stages. Below: *The eyes show my determination as I urge the Honda into the last lap.*

The only Indy car race of my career was the Rex Mays 300 at Riverside in November 1967 (above). Driving George Bignotti's Lola T90, I held sixth place before electrical trouble caused my retirement.

The Lola-Aston Martin project: perhaps just another of my dreams, but it should have worked and was only let down by the engine development team.

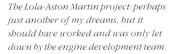

I share a joke with Lorenzo Bandini.

The 1968 season saw the appearance of the
Honda RA301, designed at Slough by ex-
Cooper man Derrick White and Honda
engineer Soicho Sano, with a slightly revised
engine featuring outside exhaust pipes which
was developed by the Honda team headed by
Nobuhiko Kawamoto and Tadashi Kume.

Oh dear! High wings, who said they were
dangerous? Well, they certainly were when they
fell off. This is the Honda at Brands Hatch
during the 1968 British Grand Prix.

Right: Probably the most
difficult car I ever raced,
the Chaparral 2H I drove
for Jim Hall in 1969. By
this stage they had raised
the driving position so I
could see out, but it still
didn't handle . . .

By 1969, BRM had
reached what must have
been the lowest point of
their F1 career. At that
stage, they truly
represented all that was
bad about British
management.

JOHN SURTEES

Right: *The Surtees TS7; me winning the 1970 Oulton Park Gold Cup.*

With the Team Surtees McLaren in which I set the fastest lap during the 1970 South African Grand Prix at Kyalami, but failed to finish the race.

With the Surtees TS10 (right) which allowed me to finish my professional career on a winning note with success at Imola and in the Japanese Grand Prix at Fuji.

Posing outside the Edenbridge factory in the early Seventies.

My last car race win in fact came at Oulton Park driving Anthony Bamford's short-wheelbase Maserati 250F.

Trying Mike Hailwood's 500 Honda four-cylinder. This I would have considered a real challenge to sort out. I might even have had second thoughts about going car racing if I had known it was in the pipeline.

With Jane and Edwina (then aged eight months) at Misano in June 1988.

Above: The new team and the future. With my wife Jane and our three children, Edwina Ann, born in 1987, Leonora Dorothy, born in 1989, and Henry John, who was born in 1991.

that it would develop somewhere in the region of 400 bhp. The agreement was that they would do a certain number of engines and we would prepare the T70s, running a single car in most races but probably two at Le Mans.

First and foremost, the engine was late. Secondly, it wasn't producing the power and we ran into numerous initial problems. In the end we got an engine which developed around 380 bhp, took it down to Goodwood and completed about ten hours' hard running. I then went to the Nürburgring, where in fact we ran quite quickly in the leading bunch before a rear suspension breakage caused my retirement, and – at least while it rained – at the Le Mans test weekend we put the fear of hell into Ferrari, setting the fastest time.

We knew we couldn't compete on maximum power, but, overall, it was quite a nice-handling package, so we thought if we could keep the thing going we might have a chance. As it turned out, the car I was sharing with David Hobbs lasted about one lap, the other, driven by Chris Irwin and Peter de Klerk, about half a dozen.

What had happened was that, after the Goodwood test, because Marek had decided there was some likelihood of cylinder head gasket problems, they had changed the design and specification in preparation for Le Mans. We didn't discover this until after the race.

So that was the end of the Aston Martin partnership. We came back to base, the engines were returned to Astons and the chassis were re-adapted to take Chevy V8s again.

I only got involved in race car manufacturing totally and utterly by mistake. While in Los Angeles in 1968 for the Can-Am, I was at a garage on Sepulveda Boulevard owned by a man called Scooter Patrick. James Garner, the film actor, was keen to establish a Formula 5000 team and he approached us to build a car.

So I spoke on his behalf to Len Terry of Leda Cars, who had John Lambert working on a Formula 5000 car; he was talking about selling the complete project. The whole thing looked neat and tidy, so, as I mentioned in the previous chapter, a deal was arranged whereby Garner would operate a race team and market the cars in the USA, Len Terry would build the cars and Team Surtees would simply act as agents, looking after things at this end and giving the benefit of our experience in the testing of the cars.

Firstly, the cars were a little late. Secondly, when we went to Oulton Park for a preliminary test, a number of brackets and components broke off. In the meantime, Bill Grainger, one of our mechanics, had gone to the USA to run the two cars for Garner and they ran into similar problems. It just wasn't good enough.

So we took the basic Leda, sorted it out and developed it into the Surtees TS5. We got David Hobbs to drive one, Trevor Taylor to drive another. We subsequently took over the Garner cars and ran them in the USA, finishing second in the 1969 SCCA F5000 Championship to prove to Garner that they were not all bad.

We initially intended to make a batch of 12 TS5s, but in the event we manufactured something like 25 and they were pretty successful. Our competitors in 1969 and '70 included McLaren, Trojan and Lola, who had used a lot of T70 components to build their first F5000 car, the T142. They subsequently produced the T190 for 1970, with which Mike Hailwood had so much trouble, and I eventually said, 'Come on, Mike, let's get together. We'll understand you,' and he joined up to drive the Surtees TS8 F5000 car for us in 1971.

Obviously I had known Mike and Stan Hailwood very well for many years. Mike had followed my tracks to a large extent, dabbling in F1 way back in 1964 with Tim Parnell, but that hadn't turned out very well and he'd returned to bike racing with Honda for the rest of the decade.

Mike was quite different from me in terms of personality, but we had pretty similar attitudes as soon as we put our foot over a bike or sat in a car. We were both fairly aggressive, both wanted to win. Mike brought a certain simplicity and honesty to the team. He just wanted to drive and didn't want to get involved in politics, or create any.

He had to be treated pretty carefully, though. In 1972, the year he won the European F2 Championship for us, Mike could be a bag of nerves before the start of a race. Everything would come together when the flag came down, but on the night before a race he would gain a reputation as a man-about-town, something of a playboy. Frankly, it wasn't really the case. Had he just lain in bed, he would have sweated himself to pieces.

It was far better for him to be occupied and involved, and a good friend of mine, Terry Regan, who had been a great help as a go-between trying to sort out various sponsorship projects, often went along with Mike virtually as his minder. He made sure Mike didn't get into too much trouble and at least got to the race the following day!

It was a great shame when I had to part company with Mike at the end of 1973. However, the team, with all its trials and tribulations, particularly after I stopped driving, is another story for another day.

To return to the development of the first Surtees F1, in order to maintain a presence in Grand Prix racing while the prototype TS7 was under development, we bought an M7 chassis from Bruce McLaren's team, fitted Surtees wheels and modified the monocoque by fitting a couple of panniers between the wheels to enlarge its fuel capacity. With that, I was lying fourth at Kyalami, having set fastest lap, when the engine failed, suffered transmission problems at Jarama and went out early on at Monaco with more engine troubles. After missing the Belgian race at Spa, we came sixth at Zandvoort and then sold the McLaren to concentrate on preparing the TS7 for its debut in the British Grand Prix at Brands Hatch.

We took on a couple of draughtsmen who had just graduated from Loughborough College – one of whom was Ken Sears, who stayed with us to the end – and a couple of local sheet metal workers and welders. We didn't have a lot of equipment, but the plan was to do as much of the manufacture as possible ourselves.

With the equipment we had, we couldn't really build a traditionally curvaceous monocoque – which I thought was outdated anyway – so, with a view to building in more torsional stiffness, we came up with a square-cut chassis. Using L72 aluminium sheet, with bulkheads from Reynolds square-section tube, similar to that employed to make the front sub-frame of the Jaguar E-type, we built up a strong and simple little chassis which became the first TS7.

It was ready just before the British Grand Prix, getting up to fourth place before running its bearings due to a problem with our oil tank. At Hockenheim we lost a certain third place through engine failure only four laps from the finish, and at the Österreichring broke a valve spring while lying sixth.

Happily, things were better in the non-championship Oulton Park Gold Cup where I managed to win the two-heat race. The opposition on this occasion included Rindt's Lotus 72, Oliver in the BRM P153 and Jackie Stewart in the new Tyrrell. I beat Rindt by just over 12 seconds in the first heat and finished just under ten seconds behind him in the second to make sure of overall aggregate victory.

We had completed a spare TS7 in time for the Italian Grand Prix at Monza, but a leaking fuel cell, followed by an electrical fault, put us out of the race before it had even started. Then it was across the Atlantic for the final three races of the season in Canada, the USA and Mexico.

At Ste Jovite I managed my best finish of the year with a fifth place, despite being delayed by a pit stop with a misfire, but a flywheel detached itself on my car at Watkins Glen – where Derek Bell had a one-off drive for the team and finished sixth – and I rounded off the season with a rather disappointing eighth place in Mexico City.

While there were quite a lot of pressures involved in running a business and still attempting to be a professional driver, it was certainly a welcome relief after 1969. That had been such a dreadful year that I was half tempted to walk away from the whole thing.

On reflection, I should not have been so enthusiastic and carried away by the Honda project. I should have thought more as John Surtees, Formula 1 driver and potential Grand Prix winner, rather than trying to become part of the 'dream team'. My move to Honda was motivated in part by the terrible hurt that I had experienced over the Ferrari affair; I wanted to go somewhere to be part of a team which would come up and eclipse Ferrari.

What I should possibly have done was to have talked to the oil companies, swallowed some of my pride and spoken to Chapman or Brabham, or somebody like that. Interestingly, Shell wanted me to go back to Ferrari, but I didn't want to do that, although I did accept an invitation to drive a Ferrari 512S in the 1000-km races at Monza, Spa and the Nürburgring during the spring of 1970.

At Monza I finished third, partnered by Peter Schetty, at Spa I was second with Jacky Ickx and at the Nürburgring third with Nino Vaccarella. I was very disappointed in the 512S. The Porsche 917 made it look silly and, again, much as Jacky Ickx may have been a very good, forceful and fast driver, the car just wasn't sorted.

The Ferrari 512S simply didn't handle. You drove it despite its chassis performance. Moreover, by this time Forghieri had become quite full of himself and there wasn't any balancing factor within the team. They didn't have a driver who could really communicate what it was doing. The drivers took a deep breath and used a lot of courage, but it was quite ludicrous to make the drivers compensate for a problem which could have been removed.

I found that, even though the 512S was supposed to have a bit of an edge in sheer power over the Porsche, you couldn't use the power available because it just wasn't a predictable motor car. Aerodynamically, it was very badly balanced. At Spa, for example, they could have got it going a whole lot quicker just by some sensible, rational development work. It was slow down the straight because we had to put such large rear flaps on the end to cure its handling imbalance.

On the F1 front for the 1971 season, Brooke Bond Oxo came in with sponsorship of £22,000. We ran under the Brooke Bond Oxo Rob Walker banner, a gentlemanly gesture on the part of Brooke Bond who had first become involved the previous year with Rob's team. They said that, in fairness, he should have his name involved, which would ensure he sustained his interest in F1 by being linked with our team.

We also spoke to Mike Kranefuss, the head of Ford's competitions department in Cologne, who agreed to provide a couple of Cosworth V8s in return for Rolf Stommelen driving the second car. For 1971 we developed the F1 design into the TS9 and fielded the TS8 F5000 car for Mike Hailwood in the British championship with quite considerable success.

The Surtees TS9 proved similarly competitive from the outset of the new season, effectively keeping up the promise displayed by the TS7. Basically, it was a sound and straightforward car, but we did have a lot of minor problems surrounding the fuel and lubrication systems.

The year started well with Stommelen taking pole position for the Argentine Grand Prix, a non-championship event on this occasion. Rolf won the first heat, but in the second he was eliminated in a collision with Chris Amon's Matra. We came closest to victory at Kyalami, where I was running ahead of Mario Andretti's Ferrari when my gearbox lost its oil and Mario inherited his first Grand Prix win.

I finished third in the Race of Champions at Brands Hatch, but we missed the Questor Grand Prix at California's Ontario Motor Speedway and I retired in the Oulton Park Spring Cup. At Barcelona I got entangled in a first-corner collision, but at Monaco Rolf and I kept going to the end, finishing sixth and seventh respectively.

At Zandvoort I wound up fifth in the Dutch Grand Prix, but Rolf was disqualified after receiving a push-start following a spin. We were fifth and sixth in the British Grand Prix at Silverstone, I was seventh at the Nürburgring and then had the satisfaction of winning the Oulton Park Gold Cup for the second successive year, and the third time overall in my career.

We brought Mike Hailwood into the F1 team at Monza where he took the TS9 through to a strong fourth place, just over a tenth of a second behind Peter Gethin's winning BRM, while I concentrated on the development of the new TS9B prototype. Rolf crashed his car badly in practice when a tyre came off its rim and was unable to take the start.

The season was completed in North America: I took seventh at Mosport Park, while both Mike and I had a lot of problems in the final race at Watkins Glen. Consequently, neither of us was classified in the final results.

I don't think anybody would disagree that Team Surtees was right on the competitive pace, particularly during 1972 when we used the TS9B, a side-radiator version of the 1971 car. For example, Jackie Stewart would be the first to admit that there was no way he could have stayed with Mike in the South African Grand Prix at Kyalami. Mike was scrambling all over his Tyrrell, looking for a way past, when a tenpenny bolt broke in the rear suspension. At the Silverstone International Trophy, Mike had overtaken Fittipaldi's Lotus 72 and was pulling away until a radiator cap failed through the nickel becoming unsoldered – a chance in a million.

Partly, of course, this all came down to budgets, or shortage of them. With respect to the others, Team Surtees was one of the best training grounds for F1 personnel. We couldn't afford established managers or engineers; a lot of our team members were very green indeed when they started with us and, no doubt, problems like that broken bolt in the suspension stemmed from that. The power of money would prevent that sort of thing from happening today.

To be honest, I wasn't totally satisfied with our second driver Tim Schenken's performances in the TS9B during 1972. We had thought of pursuing a programme which meant that I would carry on driving full-time. Then Tim came along just at the time when things were frankly starting to get a little bit on top of me. I was rather concerned that I wouldn't be able to put the necessary time into the driving and looking after the team's interests.

If I could have been sure of getting a top-class man who could have looked after the basic running of the team, then I would have thought again. But such a man was not available so I had to make the decision to cut back myself. We had talked to Tim in the past and I thought that there was a good chance he would fit into the team quite well. We had the up-and-at-them approach of Mike and perhaps Tim developing his driving talents along slightly different lines: a good front-runner of obvious potential, but of a rather more subdued nature.

Tim proved himself capable of producing a good performance at times but didn't fit in exactly as I had hoped, and I felt he would be better served if he could get a position in a single-car team where he could be sure of total attention.

Also, the problems with my health were nibbling away. As things turned out, I gradually wound down my own competitive driving because the pressure of trying to run the company as well meant that I could no longer be so dedicated to the business behind the wheel. I thought, 'Well, I'll drive when it serves a purpose,' so I continued to do a lot of testing on the cars and, by the end of '72, I had restricted my F1 involvement to testing the new TS14, which was the prototype 1973 car, fitted with the mandatory deformable structures protecting the fuel tanks.

I think, on reflection, that part of the weight that I felt in running the business was connected with another factor which I misinterpreted. I did have this other health problem that was not resolved until the late 1970s. Later in the mid-Seventies, when I was looking after the team, the periods that I could really stay totally active on my legs became shorter. I also became prone to an increased number of skin problems and more general aches and pains than I should have done and my ability to concentrate through a full working day became impaired.

I gradually reduced my competitive driving during the course of 1972. On 23 July at Imola I emerged the aggregate winner of the Shell Grand Prix, a round of the European Formula 2 Championship held over two 28-lap heats of the challenging circuit near Bologna. In addition, I was very satisfied to have won the F2 Japanese Grand Prix at Mount Fuji with our little TS10 powered by the first of Brian Hart's 2-litre engines. It was 24 years since I had climbed aboard my father's sidecar for my first competitive outing in the Trent Park speed trials at Cockfosters.

During that time, I had seen motor racing, and particularly Formula 1, change a great deal. Not all of that, in my view, was for the better. In particular, I feel I must return to the manner in which Spa was changed as a result of Jackie Stewart's accident there in the 1966 Belgian Grand Prix.

The Grand Prix Drivers' Association, which was basically run by Jo Bonnier, began to have a little more say on safety matters and, after that '66 race, Stewart developed some very firm ideas about race track safety. I must say that, during 1991, when I heard that the

Princess Royal had presented Jackie with a Labatt's safety award, I allowed myself a little smile, wondering who on earth had judged that!

I remember sitting in meeting after meeting where the virtues of guard rails were continuously extolled. Yet I think, had there been a guard rail at the point where Jackie crashed at Spa, he wouldn't have escaped with such light injuries.

Guard rails have their place, but position them on curves where there is a chance of a car hitting them at right angles and they can be lethal. Also springing from the business at Spa was the first remodelling of the Nürburgring at the end of 1970. I find it interesting to recall that such demands on track authorities were often produced by meetings where Bonnier and Stewart virtually held the floor alone.

With all the rhetoric, Graham Hill and others often dozed off and were just prodded awake in time for the vote. Jack Brabham and Dan Gurney could be quite outspoken but had very limited time available, while some of the younger drivers were a little uncertain as to what to do, finding it difficult to speak out against the so-called stars. So it was often Bonnier, Hill and Stewart who effectively passed these resolutions.

I remember raising the point that guard rails were absolute murder for motor cycle racers, but the response was virtually nil. They also showed no real interest in developments such as those John Hugenholtz had introduced at Zandvoort. Sure enough, there were problems with gravel traps and catch fencing, but I think history has shown that that was the best way to proceed.

I also recall our young driver Helmut Koinigg suffering a tyre failure in the 1974 United States Grand Prix at Watkins Glen and being killed when he hit an inadequately secured guard rail. I hated the indiscriminate fitting of guard rails all round circuits. In my view it was not of unqualified benefit to the sport, a retrograde step.

In the end, the people who should have received all the safety awards were the constructors, because the safety standards that have come about in motor sport are largely due to their efforts, not those of the drivers.

Back on the circuits in the early 1970s, Team Surtees was facing an uphill struggle. At times our lads were working four consecutive nights. Our total budget in 1971 to run a two-car team was less than £50,000, and less than £70,000 the following year with the TS9B. The first time we ever looked like getting the budget to enable us to build the right groundwork for the team was when Bang and Olufsen came along.

It's my assessment that Team Surtees might still have been in racing today if we'd never got involved with them. At that point, I felt, we were standing on the springboard to considerable success. On the strength of the Bang and Olufsen contract we embarked on building a new factory, acquired some new engines . . . and we didn't get paid after the first instalment. Our total contract was for £110,000. The deal had been arranged with the company's Belgian representative, Mr de Dryver. One side condition was that we should test his son, Bernard, and see if he was suitable to run in one of our Formula 2 cars. Well, we did, at Goodwood, and after he had returned to the pits on more than one occasion with a radiator stuffed full of grass and other obvious signs of excursions from the track which he firmly denied, we advised his father that, one, he certainly wasn't ready for Formula 2 and, two, we thought he should find a different career. After this, no contract monies arrived and all we got after a lengthy legal experience was our legal costs of something like £25,000. We just didn't have the funds to keep up the court action. We never fully recovered from that episode because we'd got involved with quite big loans.

Partly as a consequence, perhaps, of all the stress, my health problems came to a head in 1978 when I had to fly home from both Long Beach and Canada without ever having been to the track. Finally, Professor Naylor, the specialist at St Thomas's, suggested that I come in for tests to get to the bottom of what the problem was. So I went in and spent another 12 weeks in there and they finally pin-pointed the trouble.

By this stage we were working on the Surtees TS21, Ken Sears spending a lot of time in the University of Southampton wind tunnel. We began making a few components but, with me laid up in hospital, there was no way I could chase sponsors or put any deals together. But I did have meetings with Keke Rosberg and René Arnoux, who'd driven the last couple of races in 1978 for us, about the possibilities for the following year.

Arnoux came along and said, 'Look, I've got an offer from Renault, but if you are racing I will stay with you.' I had to turn round and tell him that we had been compromising ourselves for a number of years employing drivers who, frankly, we wouldn't normally employ purely to keep things together. We were not doing justice either to the team or to myself. I was only prepared to continue if we could get together a feasible and sound financial package.

But there was no way I could put the package together in time. I called René in and said, 'Sorry, but we're out.' Meanwhile, Peter Briggs, who had worked with us on the F1 and F2 side, and who later took over my Honda dealership in Edenbridge, asked if he could run a couple of the TS20s in the Aurora national championship.

We grafted the prototype TS21 side pods onto one of the cars and the young American Gordon Smiley, who was sadly killed at Indianapolis in 1982, went out and won at Silverstone in it. This was the last race Team Surtees ever competed in, and his lap times were good enough to have put him on the third row of the grid for the 1979 British Grand Prix.

I had been approached by, of all people, Jack Oliver to buy the team's position in the Formula One Constructors' Association. The last thing I wanted to do was to allow Team Surtees to go into liquidation; somehow or other, we were going to pay what we owed. This was the immediate worry.

So I went to FOCA and explained the situation to Bernard Ecclestone. Bernard discussed it with the other FOCA members and said, yes, we could do it, but not with Oliver. They wanted me to sell what was termed our position and benefits to Frank Williams and, with the funds realised from that, we basically managed to save Team Surtees. The company eventually paid every single creditor by 1984, six years after we last raced in a Grand Prix.

Epilogue

So here we are at the end of the story, or at least the story as far as John Surtees the active racing competitor is concerned. The detailed story of Team Surtees is another tale for another day, but suffice it to say that that period taught me a great deal about the frustrations of going racing and not being able to follow the path you believe in because of totally commercial considerations.

We produced some very competitive cars, but the team was never able to realise its full potential. I am confident that we knew what was required but all too often it was compromise, compromise, with each of us who was involved being called upon at times to do more than was either fair or humanly possible for purely financial reasons.

Apart from the one disastrous sponsorship arrangement we made which was never fulfilled by the persons concerned, our sponsors, none of whom came in with large budgets, stayed loyal and openly stated their satisfaction. We gave an opportunity to and helped develop some superb drivers; it's a pity that in some cases the team was prevented from reaping the benefit of its investment by their lack of respect for their written or spoken word. Luckily it wasn't all like that, but we had to swallow hard at times and take drivers who could pay and had enthusiasm but very little else. It takes just as much time, money and effort to prepare a car for someone like that – with no hope of any results.

The end came after I had had that period in hospital, away from the pressures, and been able to ask myself where we were going. The team had taken virtually everything I had ever earned in motor sport but, more importantly, I hadn't been able to do it as I believed it should be done.

It's strange that when I came out of hospital in 1978 and set out on the path to recovery, part of my occupational therapy involved working on the old bike pieces I had left. I went over to the Isle of Man and did a demonstration round the TT course on an MV Agusta, and this sparked off a desire to assemble all the pieces I had left over from my bike career, as well as collecting machines with which I had been associated.

As I look back on my career, I reflect on the way in which the sporting ethic has changed. Those who compete in any professional sport these days should feel very fortunate that they can earn such a high level of remuneration for doing something which, when they set out on their chosen path, they would have been happy to do just for the love of it. It is a privilege for anybody to actually earn a living from something which is their hobby.

In that connection, I always remember that my father, many of his friends and, indeed, I myself competed simply for the pleasure of taking part in a sport we loved. The sort of rewards which are available today often overshadow the real reason why today's competitors originally took part.

At the same time, I have had the pleasure of taking a close look at two Grand Prix teams over the past year or so. One of them was Ken Tyrrell's organisation, which of course was the first team I drove for in car racing, and it really heartened me to see the enthusiasm which still surrounds Ken and his efforts. Although he has been obliged to get involved in all the politics which affect F1, it was a great pleasure to see somebody who is as much a survivor as Ken, a man who has been at the very top and at the very bottom, yet still come through and survived.

The other team I visited was McLaren International, which is now run, of course, by Ron Dennis. I remember taking on his Rondel Racing Formula 2 team back at the end of 1971 when we were both chasing the same sponsorship – and I got the £20,000 which came from Matchbox. We brought home the bacon and won the European F2 Championship with Mike Hailwood driving for us the following year, battling against Rondel.

When I see the plain, down-to-earth, practical approach that Ron Dennis applies to his F1 team, together with an awareness of the need to employ the very best specialist skills which are available, the reason McLaren have gained their current level of success becomes very obvious. He has pursued the same sort of logical path which I would have been happy to see Team Surtees follow had we had the necessary resources at our disposal.

By contrast, I also had the opportunity of looking at Ferrari closely, both at the time when Mr Ferrari died, when I was given the privilege of looking round the race shop, and again subsequently. One cannot help being aware of the tremendous potential which exists at Maranello; all that is lacking is a sense of direction. Somehow they have never really grasped the fundamental principle that you should all aim for the same objective. And if you are going racing, that is to win. There is no room for personal battles; you should stand up and be counted.

I hope that Mr Agnelli, who has recently cleared out the management of his football team and put in older and more experienced people, may think carefully on this, for Italy deserves a successful Ferrari.

I thoroughly enjoyed my racing career, on two wheels and four, although I would have made obvious changes to the way in which John Surtees, Racing Driver, tackled things. But I think that John Surtees the individual would still have followed the example of Frank Sinatra's song and 'done it my way'. I may not have done myself justice with some of the projects I became involved with, but it's all been worthwhile.

The motor cycling side I wouldn't have changed for the world, and, on the whole, I don't think I would have changed a great deal of my life, although, if I had been blessed with the knowledge I have now, I might well have sorted out the Ferrari problem a lot more easily than I did. But I wouldn't have missed my time at Maranello, much as it could be infuriating and frustrating at times. There is something very special about Italy and its attitude to motor sport and, although I will always be slightly saddened by the thought of what I am sure we could have achieved, a piece of me will always be back there.

The achievements of Mr Kume and Mr Kawamoto at Honda are well known and it was an honour to work with them when they were on the early stages of the ladder.

I naturally had enormous admiration for what Mr Honda had achieved – as I had for Mr Ferrari. I believe both of them in their own way sabotaged my career at different times through decisions they made which they were not technically qualified to make, but just look at what they achieved and the special place in motoring history they occupy.

The Agusta brothers obviously played a significant part in my life, as did Phil Vincent, Joe Craig, Reg Parnell, Tony Vandervell, Ken Tyrrell, Eric Broadley and Yoshio Nakamura, and I should not forget Colin Chapman, who placed such faith in me. I have had the pleasure of knowing and competing against the very best riders and drivers in the world during my career in racing.

Last but not least, I have a very special place in my memories for the engineers, mechanics and helpers who have been such an important part of the teams I have been with. In addition, I will never forget the support I received in the very early days in the form of the odd gallon of oil, a plug or a piece of chain which made all the difference to whether I went to the next race or not, and the subsequent happy relationship that I have been able to enjoy with all the representatives of accessory manufacturers – especially the tyre and fuel suppliers, without whose support racing wouldn't exist.

I suppose that you could say my career fell into four distinct phases. The Fifties was motor cycles, the Sixties was racing cars, the Seventies was building cars and the Eighties was spent tidying up the loose ends, my personal life and getting everything into its right perspective. One of the tasks was putting my old house in order – which became *our* house when I married Jane, who had been the sister on the ward at St Thomas's Hospital when I went back into hospital in 1978. Parenthood has also arrived – rather late in the day for me, perhaps – and we now have another team in action with three new models: Edwina, Leonora and Henry John!

In recent years I have had this wonderful opportunity to go back and touch base with a few of those names and people I can so strongly relate to. I remember Mrs Alice Caracciola, the widow of the great German driver, Rudolf Caracciola, coming up to me at the Nürburgring and saying, 'You remind me so much of Rudi, the way you drive the 'Ring,' and so it was with great pleasure that I was able to drive the Mercedes-Benz W125 and W154 with which he achieved so much success before the war, in addition to the Mercedes W196, the 300SLR and an Auto Union. I even managed to win a fourth Oulton Park Gold Cup, this time at the wheel of Anthony Bamford's Maserati 250F.

On two wheels, I have turned the clock back and ridden my Grey Flash and Black Lightning Vincents, and the MV works machines from 1956 through to the last four-cylinder made for Phil Read in '73. I have tested the Mike Hailwood four-cylinder Hondas, the superb single-cylinder Moto Guzzi and the astounding V8 that I was originally due to test back in '58, the Gilera four and the beautiful little Benelli fours, as well as reliving that boyhood dream by riding Georg Meier's supercharged BMW.

The future? Well, I'm hoping that one of my children may give me a helping hand because there are still about ten of the old Team Surtees cars which need to be put together one day, in addition to the balance of the motor cycles which I have collected and would like to see in action again before very much longer.

And if Henry John should one day say, 'Dad, I'd like some help to go motor cycle racing,' I would like to think I could give him as much help as my father gave me in those early years. To a large extent, of course, it will be his decision – or her decision, if it should be one of the girls! I just hope that some of the highs and lows that I have experienced in life will enable me to give them a helping hand in the right direction.

John Surtees's

Racing Record – Bikes

Compiled by Mick Woollett

John Surtees took part in his first race in 1948, when he rode in the sidecar of his father's Vincent at the Trent Park speed trials, but his serious racing career began the following year at the Eaton Bray grass track, where he raced an Excelsior-JAP.

In 1950 he had his first race on tarmac, riding a Triumph Tiger 70 at the newly surfaced Brands Hatch, and he soon scored his first win, taking a Vincent Grey Flash to victory at Aberdare later that season.

1951

Place	Race	Circuit	Date	Machine	Comment
2	1000 cc	Thruxton	26 Mar	Vincent	*non-experts race*
3	1000 cc	Boreham	30 Apr	Vincent	
1	500 cc	Brands Hatch	3 June	Vincent	
1	1000 cc	Brands Hatch	3 June	Vincent	
1	Handicap	Brands Hatch	3 June	Vincent	
6	350 cc	Boreham	21 July	Norton	
5	500 cc	Boreham	21 July	Vincent	
6	1000 cc	Boreham	21 July	Vincent	
2	500 cc	Thruxton	6 Aug	Vincent	*beaten only by Duke*
2	1000 cc	Thruxton	6 Aug	Vincent	*beaten only by Duke*
3	350 cc	Boreham	1 Sep	Norton	
1	500 cc	Boreham	1 Sep	Vincent	
1	500 cc	Brands Hatch	16 Sep	Vincent	
3	1000 cc	Thruxton	29 Sep	Vincent	
1	500 cc	Brands Hatch	30 Sep	Vincent	

1952

1	1000 cc championship	Brands Hatch	12 Apr	Vincent	*record lap*
2	1000 cc	Brands Hatch	12 Apr	Vincent	
3	500 cc	Thruxton	14 Apr	Vincent	
1	1000 cc scratch	Brands Hatch	20 Apr	Vincent	
1	1000 cc invitation	Brands Hatch	20 Apr	Vincent	
1	1000 cc scratch	Brands Hatch	25 May	Vincent	
1	1000 cc invitation	Brands Hatch	25 May	Vincent	
2	350 cc	Brands Hatch	29 June	Norton	*crashed in 1000 cc race*
1	1000 cc scratch	Brands Hatch	13 July	Vincent	
1	1000 cc handicap	Brands Hatch	13 July	Vincent	
6	**500 cc ULSTER GP**	**Clady**	**16 Aug**	**Norton**	**first World Championship race**
5	500 cc	Boreham	23 Aug	Norton	
1	1000 cc	Brands Hatch	24 Aug	Vincent	
1	500 cc	Aberdare	30 Aug	Vincent	*record lap*
1	500 cc	Castle Combe	6 Sep	Norton	
4	500 cc	Scarborough	20 Sep	Norton	
1	350 cc	Thruxton	4 Oct	AJS	*lent works 7R*
1	500 cc	Thruxton	4 Oct	Norton	
2	350 cc	Brands Hatch	5 Oct	Norton	
1	1000 cc scratch	Brands Hatch	5 Oct	Norton	
1	Solo handicap	Brands Hatch	5 Oct	Norton	
1	500 cc scratch	Blandford	11 Oct	Norton	
1	500 cc invitation	Blandford	11 Oct	Norton	

1953

1	350 cc	Brands Hatch	3 Apr	Norton	*crashed in 500 cc race*
3	350 cc	Thruxton	6 Apr	Norton	
1	500 cc	Thruxton	6 Apr	Norton	
2	350 cc	Silverstone	18 Apr	Norton	
2	500 cc	Silverstone	18 Apr	Norton	
1	350 cc	Brands Hatch	19 Apr	Norton	
1	1000 cc scratch	Brands Hatch	19 Apr	Norton	
1	1000 cc invitation	Brands Hatch	19 Apr	Norton	
1	350 cc	Snetterton	2 May	Norton	*record lap*
1	500 cc	Snetterton	2 May	Norton	*record lap*
1	1000 cc	Snetterton	2 May	Norton	
1	350 cc	Aberdare	23 May	Norton	*record lap*
1	500 cc	Aberdare	23 May	Norton	*record lap*
1	1000 cc	Aberdare	23 May	Norton	*record lap*

1953 (continued)

1	350 cc	Brands Hatch	*24 May*	Norton	*record lap*
1	1000 cc scratch	Brands Hatch	*24 May*	Norton	*record lap*
1	1000 cc invitation	Brands Hatch	*24 May*	Norton	*record lap*
dns	**350 cc JUNIOR TT**	**Isle of Man**	**8 June**	**Norton**	
dns	**125 cc TT**	**Isle of Man**	**11 June**	**EMC**	***practice crash***
dns	**500 cc SENIOR TT**	**Isle of Man**	**12 June**	**Norton**	
1	350 cc	Ibsley	*11 July*	Norton	*record lap*
1	350 cc	Castle Combe	*18 July*	Norton	*record lap*
1	500 cc	Castle Combe	*18 July*	Norton	
1	350 cc	Brands Hatch	*19 July*	Norton	
1	1000 cc	Brands Hatch	*19 July*	Norton	
rtd	1000 cc invitation	Brands Hatch	*19 July*	Norton	*startline collision*
3	250 cc	Blandford	*3 Aug*	REG	
rtd	350 cc	Blandford	*3 Aug*	Norton	*engine trouble*
2	500 cc	Blandford	*3 Aug*	Norton	
dns		Crystal Palace	*22 Aug*		*did not race – practice crash*
1	500 cc	Aberdare	*29 Aug*	Norton	
3	350 cc	Scarborough	*19 Sep*	AJS	
rtd	500 cc	Scarborough	*19 Sep*	Norton	*crashed*
6	350 cc	Silverstone	*26 Sep*	Norton	
5	500 cc	Silverstone	*26 Sep*	Norton	

1954

3	350 cc	Silverstone	*10 Apr*	Norton	
1	1000 cc	Silverstone	*10 Apr*	Norton	
1	250 cc	Brands Hatch	*16 Apr*	REG	*first win on REG*
1	350 cc	Brands Hatch	*16 Apr*	Norton	
1	1000 cc	Brands Hatch	*16 Apr*	Norton	
1	250 cc	Crystal Palace	*19 Apr*	REG	*record lap*
1	350 cc	Crystal Palace	*19 Apr*	Norton	*record lap*
1	1000 cc	Crystal Palace	*19 Apr*	Norton	*record lap*
1	250 cc	Brands Hatch	*25 Apr*	REG	
1	350 cc	Brands Hatch	*25 Apr*	Norton	
1	1000 cc	Brands Hatch	*25 Apr*	Norton	
1	1000 cc invitation	Brands Hatch	*25 Apr*	Norton	*four wins in a day*
1	350 cc	Aberdare	*8 May*	Norton	
1	500 cc	Aberdare	*8 May*	Norton	
1	1000 cc	Aberdare	*8 May*	Norton	

1954 (continued)

1	250 cc	Brands Hatch	*9 May*	REG	
1	350 cc	Brands Hatch	*9 May*	Norton	
1	1000 cc	Brands Hatch	*9 May*	Norton	
1	1000 cc invitation	Brands Hatch	*9 May*	Norton	*seven wins over weekend*
1	350 cc	Oulton Park	*15 May*	Norton	
1	1000 cc	Oulton Park	*15 May*	Norton	
11	**350 cc JUNIOR TT**	**Isle of Man**	***14 June***	**Norton**	
15	**500 cc SENIOR TT**	**Isle of Man**	***18 June***	**Norton**	
rtd	**350 cc ULSTER GP**	**Dundrod**	***26 June***	**Norton**	***led race***
5	**500 cc ULSTER GP**	**Dundrod**	***26 June***	**Norton**	
1	250 cc	Cadwell Park	*4 July*	REG	
1	350 cc	Cadwell Park	*4 July*	Norton	
1	500 cc	Cadwell Park	*4 July*	Norton	
1	250 cc	Crystal Palace	*17 July*	REG	
1	350 cc	Crystal Palace	*17 July*	Norton	
rtd	500 cc	Crystal Palace	*17 July*	Norton	*water in carburettor*
1	250 cc	Brands Hatch	*18 July*	REG	
1	350 cc	Brands Hatch	*18 July*	Norton	
1	1000 cc	Brands Hatch	*18 July*	Norton	
1	250 cc	Castle Combe	*24 July*	REG	
1	350 cc	Castle Combe	*24 July*	Norton	
1	500 cc	Castle Combe	*24 July*	Norton	
1	350 cc	Snetterton	*1 Aug*	Norton	*record lap*
1	500 cc	Snetterton	*1 Aug*	Norton	*record lap*
2	350 cc	Thruxton	*2 Aug*	Norton	
1	500 cc	Thruxton	*2 Aug*	Norton	*record lap*
1	350 cc	Silverstone	*7 Aug*	Norton	
rtd	500 cc	Silverstone	*7 Aug*	Norton	*led race*
2	250 cc	Ibsley	*21 Aug*	Norton	*Ian Telfer's modified Manx*
1	350 cc	Ibsley	*21 Aug*	Norton	*record lap*
1	500 cc	Ibsley	*21 Aug*	Norton	*record lap*
1	350 cc	Brands Hatch	*22 Aug*	Norton	
1	1000 cc	Brands Hatch	*22 Aug*	Norton	
1	250 cc	Aberdare	*28 Aug*	Norton	*during this meeting Surtees*
1	350 cc	Aberdare	*28 Aug*	Norton	*won eight races*
1	500 cc	Aberdare	*28 Aug*	Norton	*(four heats, four finals)*
1	1000 cc	Aberdare	*28 Aug*	Norton	*and set a new lap record*
1	250 cc	Brands Hatch	*12 Sep*	Norton	
1	350 cc	Brands Hatch	*12 Sep*	Norton	
1	1000 cc	Brands Hatch	*12 Sep*	Norton	

1954 (continued)

1	350 cc	Scarborough	*18 Sep*	Norton	*lent works bike*
2	500 cc	Scarborough	*18 Sep*	Norton	*beaten by Duke (Gilera)*
1	350 cc	Cadwell Park	*19 Sep*	Norton	
1	500 cc	Cadwell Park	*19 Sep*	Norton	
1	500 cc invitation	Cadwell Park	*19 Sep*	Norton	
3	350 cc	Aintree	*25 Sep*	Norton	
2	1000 cc	Aintree	*25 Sep*	Norton	*lent works bike*
1	350 cc	Cadwell Park	*10 Oct*	Norton	
1	500 cc	Cadwell Park	*10 Oct*	Norton	
1	350 cc	Brands Hatch	*17 Oct*	Norton	
1	1000 cc	Brands Hatch	*17 Oct*	Norton	*record lap*

1955

1	350 cc	Brough	*3 Apr*	Norton	
2	1000 cc	Brough	*3 Apr*	Norton	*crashed and remounted*
1	250 cc	Brands Hatch	*8 Apr*	NSU	*first race on NSU*
1	350 cc	Brands Hatch	*8 Apr*	Norton	*record lap*
1	1000 cc	Brands Hatch	*8 Apr*	Norton	*record lap*
1	250 cc	Snetterton	*10 Apr*	NSU	
1	350 cc	Snetterton	*10 Apr*	Norton	
1	500 cc	Snetterton	*10 Apr*	Norton	*record lap*
1	250 cc	Crystal Palace	*11 Apr*	NSU	*equalled record lap*
1	350 cc	Crystal Palace	*11 Apr*	Norton	*record lap*
1	1000 cc	Crystal Palace	*11 Apr*	Norton	
1	1000 cc invitation	Crystal Palace	*11 Apr*	Norton	*record lap*
1	250 cc (five-lap)	Silverstone	*23 Apr*	NSU	*record lap*
1	250 cc (ten-lap)	Silverstone	*23 Apr*	NSU	*record lap*
1	350 cc	Silverstone	*23 Apr*	Norton	
2	500 cc	Silverstone	*23 Apr*	Norton	
1	250 cc	Brands Hatch	*24 Apr*	NSU	
1	350 cc	Brands Hatch	*24 Apr*	Norton	
1	1000 cc	Brands Hatch	*24 Apr*	Norton	
2	350 cc	Mettet	*1 May*	Norton	*first Continental race*
2	500 cc	Mettet	*1 May*	Norton	
1	250 cc	Oulton Park	*7 May*	NSU	
1	350 cc	Oulton Park	*7 May*	Norton	*record lap*
1	1000 cc	Oulton Park	*7 May*	Norton	*record lap*

1955 (continued)

1	250 cc	Aberdare	*14 May*	NSU	
1	350 cc	Aberdare	*14 May*	Norton	
1	500 cc	Aberdare	*14 May*	Norton	
1	1000 cc	Aberdare	*14 May*	Norton	
1	250 cc	Brands Hatch	*15 May*	NSU	
1	350 cc	Brands Hatch	*15 May*	Norton	*record lap*
1	1000 cc	Brands Hatch	*15 May*	Norton	*record lap*
4	**350 cc JUNIOR TT**	**Isle of Man**	***6 June***	**Norton**	
29	**500 cc SENIOR TT**	**Isle of Man**	***10 June***	**Norton**	***ran out of fuel last lap, pushed home***
1	250 cc	Crystal Palace	*18 June*	NSU	*record lap*
1	350 cc	Crystal Palace	*18 June*	Norton	
1	500 cc	Crystal Palace	*18 June*	Norton	
rtd	**250 cc GERMAN GP**	**Nürburgring**	***26 June***	**NSU**	***crashed***
3	**350 cc GERMAN GP**	**Nürburgring**	***26 June***	**Norton**	
rtd	**500 cc GERMAN GP**	**Nürburgring**	***26 June***	**BMW**	***lent works machine; misfire***
1	350 cc	Scarborough	*1 July*	Norton	
1	500 cc	Scarborough	*2 July*	Norton	
1	250 cc	Castle Combe	*9 July*	NSU	
1	350 cc	Castle Combe	*9 July*	Norton	
1	500 cc	Castle Combe	*9 July*	Norton	
2	350 cc	Hedemora	*23 July*	Norton	
2	500 cc	Hedemora	*23 July*	Norton	
1	250 cc	Thruxton	*1 Aug*	NSU	*record lap*
2	350 cc	Thruxton	*1 Aug*	Norton	
1	500 cc	Thruxton	*1 Aug*	Norton	*beat Guzzi team*
1	250 cc	Snetterton	*2 Aug*	NSU	
1	350 cc	Snetterton	*2 Aug*	Norton	
1	500 cc	Snetterton	*2 Aug*	Norton	
3	**350 cc ULSTER GP**	**Dundrod**	***11 Aug***	**Norton**	***held Thursday***
1	**250 cc ULSTER GP**	**Dundrod**	***13 Aug***	**NSU**	***first World Championship win***
1	250 cc	Ibsley	*20 Aug*	NSU	*record lap*
1	350 cc	Ibsley	*20 Aug*	Norton	*record lap*
1	500 cc	Ibsley	*20 Aug*	Norton	*record lap*
1	250 cc	Brands Hatch	*21 Aug*	NSU	
1	350 cc	Brand Hatch	*21 Aug*	Norton	
1	1000 cc	Brands Hatch	*21 Aug*	Norton	
1	250 cc	Aberdare	*27 Aug*	NSU	
1	350 cc	Aberdare	*27 Aug*	Norton	
1	500 cc	Aberdare	*27 Aug*	Norton	
1	1000 cc	Aberdare	*27 Aug*	Norton	
rtd	**250 cc ITALIAN GP**	**Monza**	***4 Sep***	**NSU**	***seized piston***

1955 (continued)

1	250 cc	Snetterton	10 Sep	NSU	
rtd	350 cc	Snetterton	10 Sep	Norton	*crashed*
1	500 cc	Snetterton	10 Sep	Norton	*record lap*
1	250 cc	Cadwell Park	11 Sep	NSU	
1	500 cc	Cadwell Park	11 Sep	Norton	
1	350 cc	Scarborough	16 Sep	Norton	*record lap*
2	500 cc	Scarborough	17 Sep	Norton	
1	250 cc	Brands Hatch	18 Sep	NSU	*record lap*
1	1000 cc	Brands Hatch	18 Sep	Norton	
1	350 cc	Aintree	24 Sep	Norton	*record lap*
2	500 cc	Aintree	24 Sep	Norton	*beaten by Duke (Gilera)*
1	Open handicap	Aintree	24 Sep	Norton	*rode 350 cc*
1	250 cc	Brough	25 Sep	NSU	*record lap*
1	350 cc	Brough	25 Sep	Norton	*record lap*
1	1000 cc	Brough	25 Sep	Norton	
1	250 cc	Silverstone	1 Oct	NSU	*supporting race*
1	350 cc	Silverstone	1 Oct	Norton	*record lap*
1	500 cc	Silverstone	1 Oct	Norton	*beat Duke (Gilera)*
1	350 cc	Brands Hatch	2 Oct	Norton	
1	1000 cc	Brands Hatch	2 Oct	Norton	*beat Duke (Gilera)*
1	1000 cc invitation	Brands Hatch	2 Oct	Norton	*record lap*

1956

1	250 cc	Crystal Palace	2 Apr	MV Agusta	*first race on MV Agusta (203 cc)*
1	500 cc	Crystal Palace	2 Apr	MV Agusta	
1	250 cc	Snetterton	8 Apr	MV Agusta	*203 cc*
1	500 cc	Snetterton	8 Apr	MV Agusta	*record lap*
1	250 cc	Silverstone	14 Apr	MV Agusta	*203 cc*
1	250 cc invitation	Silverstone	14 Apr	MV Agusta	*203 cc*
1	1000 cc	Silverstone	14 Apr	MV Agusta	
1	500 cc	Mettet	29 Apr	MV Agusta	
1	500 cc	Floreffe	6 May	MV Agusta	
dsq	**350 cc JUNIOR TT**	**Isle of Man**	**4 June**	**MV Agusta**	***ran out of petrol last lap when leading***
1	**500 cc SENIOR TT**	**Isle of Man**	**8 June**	**MV Agusta**	
2	**350 cc DUTCH TT**	**Assen**	**30 June**	**MV Agusta**	
1	**500 cc DUTCH TT**	**Assen**	**30 June**	**MV Agusta**	***record lap***
1	**350 cc BELGIAN GP**	**Spa-Francorchamps**	**8 July**	**MV Agusta**	
1	**500 cc BELGIAN GP**	**Spa-Francorchamps**	**8 July**	**MV Agusta**	
rtd	**350 cc GERMAN GP**	**Solitude**	**21 July**	**MV Agusta**	***crashed and broke arm***

500 cc World Champion

1957

1	500 cc	Barcelona	7 Apr	MV Agusta	
1	250 cc	Brands Hatch	19 Apr	MV Agusta	
2	1000 cc	Brands Hatch	19 Apr	MV Agusta	*beaten by Alan Trow (Norton)*
2	1000 cc invitation	Brands Hatch	19 Apr	MV Agusta	*beaten by Alan Trow (Norton)*
rtd	250 cc	Oulton Park	22 Apr	MV Agusta	*crashed*
rtd	500 cc	Oulton Park	22 Apr	MV Agusta	*gearbox*
2	350 cc	Mettet	5 May	MV Agusta	
rtd	500 cc	Mettet	5 May	MV Agusta	*handling problems*
rtd	**350 cc GERMAN GP**	**Hockenheim**	**19 May**	**MV Agusta**	***engine trouble***
rtd	**500 cc GERMAN GP**	**Hockenheim**	**19 May**	**MV Agusta**	***engine trouble***
4	**350 cc JUNIOR TT**	**Isle of Man**	**3 June**	**MV Agusta**	
2	**500 cc SENIOR TT**	**Isle of Man**	**7 June**	**MV Agusta**	
1	250 cc	Oulton Park	10 June	NSU	
1	350 cc	Oulton Park	10 June	Norton	
2	500 cc	Oulton Park	10 June	Norton	
1	250 cc	Scarborough	15 June	NSU	
rtd	500 cc	Scarborough	15 June	Norton	*crashed*
rtd	**350 cc DUTCH TT**	**Assen**	**29 June**	**MV Agusta**	***suspension***
1	**500 cc DUTCH TT**	**Assen**	**29 June**	**MV Agusta**	
rtd	**350 cc BELGIAN GP**	**Spa-Francorchamps**	**7 July**	**MV Agusta**	***overheating***
rtd	**500 cc BELGIAN GP**	**Spa-Francorchamps**	**7 July**	**MV Agusta**	***holed piston***
2	250 cc	Oulton Park	3 Aug	NSU	
1	350 cc	Oulton Park	3 Aug	Norton	
1	1000 cc	Oulton Park	3 Aug	MV Agusta	*record lap*
1	350 cc	Thruxton	5 Aug	Norton	
1	500 cc	Thruxton	5 Aug	MV Agusta	
rtd	**350 cc ULSTER GP**	**Dundrod**	**10 Aug**	**MV Agusta**	***engine trouble***
rtd	**500 cc ULSTER GP**	**Dundrod**	**10 Aug**	**MV Agusta**	***engine trouble after breaking absolute lap record held by Mike Hawthorn (Jaguar D-type)***
1	250 cc	Crystal Palace	17 Aug	NSU	*record lap*
1	350 cc	Crystal Palace	17 Aug	Norton	*record lap*
1	500 cc	Crystal Palace	17 Aug	Norton	*record lap*
rtd	**350 cc ITALIAN GP**	**Monza**	**1 Sep**	**MV Agusta**	***engine trouble***
4	**500 cc ITALIAN GP**	**Monza**	**1 Sep**	**MV Agusta**	
rtd	350 cc	Scarborough	14 Sep	Norton	*retired when leading*
1	500 cc	Scarborough	14 Sep	Norton	
1	250 cc	Silverstone	21 Sep	MV Agusta	*record lap*
1	350 cc	Silverstone	21 Sep	Norton	*record lap*
1	500 cc	Silverstone	21 Sep	MV Agusta	

1957 (continued)

1	250 cc	Aintree	*28 Sep*	MV Agusta	
2*	350 cc	Aintree	*28 Sep*	Norton	*later disqualified; only allowed to*
1	500 cc	Aintree	*28 Sep*	MV Agusta	*compete in two races*
1	350 cc	Oulton Park	*5 Oct*	Norton	*record lap*
1	500 cc	Oulton Park	*5 Oct*	MV Agusta	*record lap*
2	350 cc	Brands Hatch	*12 Oct*	Norton	*beaten by Minter*
1	1000 cc	Brands Hatch	*12 Oct*	Norton	
1	1000 cc invitation	Brands Hatch	*12 Oct*	Norton	

1958

1	500 cc	Imola	*7 Apr*	MV Agusta	
1	500 cc	Barcelona	*20 Apr*	MV Agusta	
1	350 cc	Mettet	*4 May*	MV Agusta	
1	500 cc	Mettet	*4 May*	MV Agusta	
1	**350 cc JUNIOR TT**	**Isle of Man**	***2 June***	**MV Agusta**	
1	**500 cc SENIOR TT**	**Isle of Man**	***6 June***	**MV Agusta**	
1	**350 cc DUTCH TT**	**Assen**	***28 June***	**MV Agusta**	
1	**500 cc DUTCH TT**	**Assen**	***28 June***	**MV Agusta**	
1	**350 cc BELGIAN GP**	**Spa-Francorchamps**	***6 July***	**MV Agusta**	
1	**500 cc BELGIAN GP**	**Spa-Francorchamps**	***6 July***	**MV Agusta**	*record lap 120.17 mph*
1	**350 cc GERMAN GP**	**Nürburgring**	***20 July***	**MV Agusta**	*record lap*
1	**500 cc GERMAN GP**	**Nürburgring**	***20 July***	**MV Agusta**	
1	**350 cc ULSTER GP**	**Dundrod**	***9 Aug***	**MV Agusta**	
1	**500 cc ULSTER GP**	**Dundrod**	***9 Aug***	**MV Agusta**	
1	**350 cc ITALIAN GP**	**Monza**	***14 Sep***	**MV Agusta**	
1	**500 cc ITALIAN GP**	**Monza**	***14 Sep***	**MV Agusta**	
1	350 cc	Aintree	*27 Sep*	MV Agusta	*record lap*
1	500 cc	Aintree	*27 Sep*	MV Agusta	
1	Open handicap	Aintree	*27 Sep*	MV Agusta	
1	1000 cc	Mallory Park	*28 Sep*	MV Agusta	*'Race of the Year'*
1	350 cc	Oulton Park	*4 Oct*	MV Agusta	
1	500 cc	Oulton Park	*4 Oct*	MV Agusta	
1	350 cc	Brands Hatch	*12 Oct*	MV Agusta	
8	1000 cc	Brands Hatch	*12 Oct*	MV Agusta	*plug trouble, first defeat of year*
2	1000 cc invitation	Brands Hatch	*12 Oct*	MV Agusta	

350 cc & 500 cc World Champion

1959

1	500 cc	Imola	*12 Apr*	MV Agusta	*record lap*
1	350 cc	Silverstone	*18 Apr*	MV Agusta	*record lap*
rtd	500 cc	Silverstone	*18 Apr*	MV Agusta	*crashed*
1	**350 cc FRENCH GP**	**Clermont-Ferrand**	***17 May***	**MV Agusta**	
1	**500 cc FRENCH GP**	**Clermont-Ferrand**	***17 May***	**MV Agusta**	
1	**350 cc JUNIOR TT**	**Isle of Man**	***1 June***	**MV Agusta**	
1	**500 cc SENIOR TT**	**Isle of Man**	***6 June***	**MV Agusta**	***second successive Junior/ Senior TT double***
1	**350 cc GERMAN GP**	**Hockenheim**	***14 June***	**MV Agusta**	
1	**500 cc GERMAN GP**	**Hockenheim**	***14 June***	**MV Agusta**	
1	**500 cc DUTCH TT**	**Assen**	***27 June***	**MV Agusta**	*record lap*
1	**500 cc BELGIAN GP**	**Spa-Francorchamps**	***5 July***	**MV Agusta**	*record lap, 120.39 mph*
1	**350 cc SWEDISH GP**	**Kristianstad**	***26 July***	**MV Agusta**	
1	**350 cc ULSTER GP**	**Dundrod**	***8 Aug***	**MV Agusta**	
1	**500 cc ULSTER GP**	**Dundrod**	***8 Aug***	**MV Agusta**	*record lap*
1	**350 cc ITALIAN GP**	**Monza**	***6 Sep***	**MV Agusta**	
1	**500 cc ITALIAN GP**	**Monza**	***6 Sep***	**MV Agusta**	*record lap, 119.14 mph*
1	500 cc	Madrid	*11 Oct*	MV Agusta	*record lap*

350 cc & 500 cc World Champion

1960

1	500 cc	Cesenatico	*18 Apr*	MV Agusta	
1	500 cc	Imola	*25 Apr*	MV Agusta	
3	**350 cc FRENCH GP**	**Clermont-Ferrand**	***22 May***	**MV Agusta**	*pit stop to change plugs, record lap*
1	**500 cc FRENCH GP**	**Clermont-Ferrand**	***22 May***	**MV Agusta**	*record lap*
2	**350 cc JUNIOR TT**	**Isle of Man**	***15 June***	**MV Agusta**	*slowed by gearbox trouble, record lap*
1	**500 cc SENIOR TT**	**Isle of Man**	***17 June***	**MV Agusta**	*record lap, 104.08 mph*
1	**350 cc DUTCH TT**	**Assen**	***25 June***	**MV Agusta**	*record lap*
rtd	**500 cc DUTCH TT**	**Assen**	***25 June***	**MV Agusta**	*crashed; record lap*
1	**500 cc BELGIAN GP**	**Spa-Francorchamps**	***3 July***	**MV Agusta**	*record lap, 122.60 mph*
1	**500 cc GERMAN GP**	**Solitude**	***24 July***	**MV Agusta**	
1	**350 cc ULSTER GP**	**Dundrod**	***6 Aug***	**MV Agusta**	
2	**500 cc ULSTER GP**	**Dundrod**	***6 Aug***	**MV Agusta**	*broken gear pedal; record lap*
rtd	**350 cc ITALIAN GP**	**Monza**	***11 Sep***	**MV Agusta**	*loose exhaust pipe*
1	**500 cc ITALIAN GP**	**Monza**	***11 Sep***	**MV Agusta**	

350 cc & 500 cc World Champion

John Surtees's
Racing Record – Cars

Compiled by Alan Henry, Peter Lovering and Steve Small

1960

Place	Race	Circuit/Date	Car	Comment
	FORMULA 1			
rtd	International Trophy	Silverstone, *14 May*	Lotus 18-Climax 4	*oil leak*
rtd	**MONACO GP**	**Monte Carlo, *29 May***	**Lotus 18-Climax 4**	**transmission**
2	**BRITISH GP**	**Silverstone, *16 July***	**Lotus 18-Climax 4**	
6	Silver City Trophy	Brands Hatch, *1 Aug*	Lotus 18-Climax 4	
rtd	**PORTUGUESE GP**	**Oporto, *14 Aug***	**Lotus 18-Climax 4**	**split radiator**
rtd	**US GP**	**Riverside, *20 Nov***	**Lotus 18-Climax 4**	**crashed, lap 4**
	FORMULA 2			
2	F2 race	Oulton Park, *2 Apr*	Cooper-Climax 4	
4	Aintree 200	Aintree, *30 Apr*	Cooper-Climax 4	
rtd	Solitude GP	Solitude, *24 July*	Porsche F2	*spun off*
rtd	Kentish 100	Brands Hatch, *27 Aug*	Lotus 18-Climax 4	*collision with Duke*
rtd	Lombank Trophy	Snetterton, *17 Sep*	Lotus 18-Climax 4	*engine*
	FORMULA JUNIOR			
2	Formula Junior race	Goodwood, *19 Mar*	Cooper-Austin	
rtd	Formula Junior race	Oulton Park, *2 Apr*	Cooper-Austin	*engine*
2	Formula Junior race	Silverstone, *14 May*	Cooper-Austin	
4	John Davy Trophy	Brands Hatch, *1 Aug*	Cooper-Austin	
4	Formula Junior race	Snetterton, *17 Sep*	Lotus 18-Ford	
rtd	Formula Junior race	Oulton Park, *24 Sep*	Lotus 18-Ford	*gearbox*

1961

FORMULA 1

3	Lombank Trophy	Snetterton, *26 Mar*	Cooper T53-Climax 4	
1	Glover Trophy	Goodwood, *3 Apr*	Cooper T53-Climax 4	
rtd	Brussels GP	Heysel, *9 Apr*	Cooper T53-Climax 4	*accident, heat 2*
4	Aintree 200	Aintree, *22 Apr*	Cooper T53-Climax 4	
rtd	Syracuse GP	Syracuse, *25 Apr*	Cooper T53-Climax 4	*fuel pump*
11cl	**MONACO GP**	**Monte Carlo, *14 May***	**Cooper T53-Climax 4**	***head gasket***
7	**DUTCH GP**	**Zandvoort, *22 May***	**Cooper T53-Climax 4**	
rtd	Silver City Trophy	Brands Hatch, *3 June*	Cooper T53-Climax 4	*crash*
5	**BELGIAN GP**	**Spa-Francorchamps, *18 June***	**Cooper T53-Climax 4**	
rtd	**FRENCH GP**	**Reims, *2 July***	**Cooper T53-Climax 4**	***collision***
rtd	**BRITISH GP**	**Aintree, *15 July***	**Cooper T53-Climax 4**	***differential***
5	**GERMAN GP**	**Nürburgring, *6 Aug***	**Cooper T53-Climax 4**	
3	Kannonloppet	Karlskoga, *20 Aug*	Cooper T53-Climax 4	
rtd	Danish GP	Roskilde, *26-27 Aug*	Cooper T53-Climax 4	*cam follower, heat 3*
rtd	Modena GP	Modena, *3 Sep*	Cooper T53-Climax 4	*engine*
rtd	**ITALIAN GP**	**Monza, *10 Sep***	**Cooper T53-Climax 4**	***suspension***
10	Flugplatzrennen	Zeltweg, *17 Sep*	Cooper T56-Climax 4	
rtd	Gold Cup	Oulton Park, *23 Sep*	Cooper T53-Climax 4	*engine*
rtd	**US GP**	**Watkins Glen, *8 Oct***	**Cooper T53-Climax 4**	***engine***

INTERCONTINENTAL FORMULA – 2½ litres

5	International Trophy	Silverstone, *6 May*	Vanwall	
2	British Empire Trophy	Silverstone, *8 July*	Cooper T53-Climax 4	
rtd	Guards Trophy	Brands Hatch, *7 Aug*	Cooper T53-Climax 4	*spun off*

TASMAN RACES

| rtd | New Zealand GP | Ardmore, *7 Jan* | Lotus 18-Climax 4 | *transmission* |
| rtd | Lady Wigram Trophy | Christchurch, *21 Jan* | Lotus 18-Climax 4 | *engine* |

1962

FORMULA 1

rtd	Brussels GP	Heysel, *1 Apr*	Lola Mk 4-Climax 4	*engine, heat 2*
rtd	Lombank Trophy	Snetterton, *14 Apr*	Lola Mk 4-Climax 4	*overheating*
rtd	Lavant Cup	Goodwood, *23 Apr*	Lola Mk 4-Climax 4	*collision with Seifert*
rtd	Glover Trophy	Goodwood, *23 Apr*	Lola Mk 4-Climax V8	*engine*
rtd	Aintree 200	Aintree, *28 Apr*	Lola Mk 4-Climax V8	*valvegear*
3	International Trophy	Silverstone, *12 May*	Lola Mk 4-Climax V8	
rtd	**DUTCH GP**	**Zandvoort, *20 May***	**Lola Mk 4-Climax V8**	***broken wishbone/crash***
4	**MONACO GP**	**Monte Carlo, *3 June***	**Lola Mk 4-Climax V8**	
1	1000 Guineas	Mallory Park, *11 June*	Lola Mk 4-Climax V8	

1962 (continued)

5	**BELGIAN GP**	**Spa-Francorchamps, *17 June***	**Lola Mk 4-Climax V8**	
rtd	Reims GP	Reims, *1 July*	Lola Mk 4-Climax V8	*valve spring*
5	**FRENCH GP**	**Rouen, *8 July***	**Lola Mk 4-Climax V8**	**collision with T. Taylor at finish**
2	**BRITISH GP**	**Aintree, *21 July***	**Lola Mk 4-Climax V8**	
2	**GERMAN GP**	**Nürburgring, *5 Aug***	**Lola Mk 4-Climax V8**	
rtd	Kannonloppet	Karlskoga, *12 Aug*	Lola Mk 4-Climax V8	*valve spring*
rtd	Danish GP	Roskilde, *25-26 Aug*	Lola Mk 4-Climax V8	*ignition, heat 3*
rtd	Gold Cup	Oulton Park, *1 Sep*	Lola Mk 4-Climax V8	*valve*
rtd	**ITALIAN GP**	**Monza, *16 Sep***	**Lola Mk 4-Climax V8**	**piston**
rtd	**US GP**	**Watkins Glen, *7 Oct***	**Lola Mk 4-Climax V8**	**crankcase plug**
rtd	Mexican GP	Mexico City, *4 Nov*	Lotus 24-Climax V8	*hired Brabham's car*
3	Rand GP	Kyalami, *15 Dec*	Lola Mk 4-Climax V8	
rtd	**SOUTH AFRICAN GP**	**East London, *29 Dec***	**Lola Mk 4-Climax V8**	**valve**
	TASMAN RACES			
2	New Zealand GP	Ardmore, *6 Jan*	Cooper T53-Climax 4 2.7	
3	Vic Hudson Memorial	Levin, *13 Jan*	Cooper T53-Climax 4 2.7	
3	Lady Wigram Trophy	Christchurch, *20 Jan*	Cooper T53-Climax 4 2.7	
rtd	International 100	Warwick Farm, *4 Feb*	Cooper T53-Climax 4 2.7	
1	S. Pacific Trophy	Longford, *5 Mar*	Cooper T53-Climax 4 2.7	
	SPORTS CARS			
3	Sports Car race	Mallory Park, *11 June*	Ferrari 250GTO	
3	Scott Brown Trophy	Snetterton, *15 July*	Ferrari 250GTO	
3	Peco Trophy	Brands Hatch, *6 Aug*	Ferrari 250GTO	
rtd	Tourist Trophy	Goodwood, *18 Aug*	Ferrari 250GTO	*spun off avoiding Clark*
2	Paris 1000 Km	Montlhéry, *21 Oct*	Ferrari 250GTO	*/Parkes*

1963

	FORMULA 1			
rtd	International Trophy	Silverstone, *11 May*	Ferrari 156	*oil leak*
4	**MONACO GP**	**Monte Carlo, *26 May***	**Ferrari 156**	
rtd	**BELGIAN GP**	**Spa-Francorchamps, *9 June***	**Ferrari 156**	**injection feed pipe**
3	**DUTCH GP**	**Zandvoort, *23 June***	**Ferrari 156**	
rtd	**FRENCH GP**	**Reims, *30 June***	**Ferrari 156**	**fuel pump**
2	**BRITISH GP**	**Silverstone, *20 July***	**Ferrari 156**	
1	**GERMAN GP**	**Nürburgring, *4 Aug***	**Ferrari 156**	
1	Mediterranean GP	Enna, *18 Aug*	Ferrari 156	
rtd	**ITALIAN GP**	**Monza, *8 Sep***	**Ferrari 156**	**piston**
9cl	**US GP**	**Watkins Glen, *6 Oct***	**Ferrari 156**	**broken valve spring**

1963 (continued)

dsq **MEXICAN GP**	**Mexico City, *27 Oct***	**Ferrari 156**	***excluded, push-start***
1 Rand GP	Kyalami, *14 Dec*	Ferrari 156	*1st both heats*
rtd **SOUTH AFRICAN GP**	**East London, *28 Dec***	**Ferrari 156**	***con rod***
TASMAN RACES			
1 New Zealand GP	Pukekohe, *5 Jan*	Lola Mk 4-Climax 4 2.7	
rtd Vic Hudson Memorial	Levin, *12 Jan*	Lola Mk4-Climax 4 2.7	*gearbox*
rtd Lady Wigram Trophy	Christchurch, *19 Jan*	Lola Mk 4-Climax 4 2.7	*gearbox*
rtd Teretonga Int. Trophy	Invercargill, *26 Jan*	Lola Mk 4-Climax 4 2.7	*flat battery*
2 Australian GP	Warwick Farm, *10 Feb*	Lola Mk 4-Climax 4 2.7	*despite blistered feet*
1 Lakeside Int. Trophy	Lakeside, *17 Feb*	Lola Mk 4-Climax 4 2.7	
SPORTS CARS			
1 Sebring 12 Hours	Sebring, *23 Mar*	Ferrari 250P	*/Scarfiotti*
rtd Targa Florio	Madonie Piccolo, *5 May*	Ferrari 250P	*accident/Vaccarella*
1 Nürburgring 1000 Km	Nürburgring, *19 May*	Ferrari 250P	*/Mairesse*
rtd Le Mans 24 Hours	Le Mans, *15-16 June*	Ferrari 250P	*fire in car/Mairesse*
rtd Tourist Trophy	Goodwood, *24 Aug*	Ferrari 250GTO	
rtd Canadian GP	Mosport Park, *28 Sep*	Ferrari 250P	*overheating clutch*
4 Times GP	Riverside, *13 Oct*	Ferrari 250P	

1964

FORMULA 1			
1 Syracuse GP	Syracuse, *12 Apr*	Ferrari 158	
rtd International Trophy	Silverstone, *2 May*	Ferrari 156	*fuel pump*
rtd **MONACO GP**	**Monte Carlo, *10 May***	**Ferrari 158**	***gearbox***
2 **DUTCH GP**	**Zandvoort, *24 May***	**Ferrari 158**	
rtd **BELGIAN GP**	**Spa-Francorchamps, *14 June***	**Ferrari 158**	***piston***
rtd **FRENCH GP**	**Rouen, *28 June***	**Ferrari 158**	***oil pipe***
3 **BRITISH GP**	**Brands Hatch, *11 July***	**Ferrari 158**	
2 Solitude GP	Solitude, *19 July*	Ferrari 158	
1 **GERMAN GP**	**Nürburgring, *2 Aug***	**Ferrari 158**	
rtd **AUSTRIAN GP**	**Zeltweg, *23 Aug***	**Ferrari 158**	***broken suspension***
1 **ITALIAN GP**	**Monza, *6 Sep***	**Ferrari 158**	
2 **US GP**	**Watkins Glen, *4 Oct***	**Ferrari 158**	
2 **MEXICAN GP**	**Mexico City, *25 Oct***	**Ferrari 158**	
World Champion			
SPORTS CARS			
3 Sebring 12 Hours	Sebring, *22 Mar*	Ferrari 330P	*/Bandini*
rtd Nürburgring 1000 Km	Nürburgring, *31 May*	Ferrari 275P	*lost wheel/Bandini*

1964 (continued)

3	Le Mans 24 Hours	Le Mans, *20-21 June*	Ferrari 330P	*/Bandini*
2	Reims 12 Hours	Reims, *5 July*	Ferrari 275LM	*/Bandini*
rtd	Tourist Trophy	Goodwood, *29 Aug*	Ferrari 250GTO	*crashed, concussed*

1965

	FORMULA 1			
2	**SOUTH AFRICAN GP**	**East London, *1 Jan***	**Ferrari 158**	
rtd	Race of Champions	Brands Hatch, *13 Mar*	Ferrari 158	*fuel injection, heat 2*
2	Syracuse GP	Syracuse, *4 Apr*	Ferrari 158	
2	International Trophy	Silverstone, *15 May*	Ferrari 158	
4cl	**MONACO GP**	**Monte Carlo, *30 May***	**Ferrari 158**	***out of fuel last lap***
rtd	**BELGIAN GP**	**Spa-Francorchamps, *13 June***	**Ferrari 158**	***engine***
3	**FRENCH GP**	**Clermont-Ferrand, *27 June***	**Ferrari 158**	
3	**BRITISH GP**	**Silverstone, *10 July***	**Ferrari 1512**	
7	**DUTCH GP**	**Zandvoort, *18 July***	**Ferrari 1512**	
rtd	**GERMAN GP**	**Nürburgring, *1 Aug***	**Ferrari 1512**	***gearbox***
rtd	**ITALIAN GP**	**Monza, *12 Sep***	**Ferrari 1512**	***clutch***
	FORMULA 2			
rtd	London Trophy	Crystal Palace, *2 June*	Cooper-BMC	*engine, heat 1*
dns	Reims GP	Reims, *4 July*	Cooper-BMC	*engine*
rtd	British Eagle Trophy	Brands Hatch, *30 Aug*	Lola T60-Cosworth	*spun off*
1	Gold Cup	Oulton Park, *18 Sep*	Lola T60-Cosworth	
	SPORTS CARS			
rtd	Daytona 24 Hours	Daytona, *28 Feb*	Ferrari 330P2	*tyre/P. Rodriguez*
2	Sports Car race	Silverstone, *20 Mar*	Lola T70-Chevrolet	
2	Monza 1000 Km	Monza, *25 Apr*	Ferrari 330P2	*/Scarfiotti*
rtd	Tourist Trophy	Oulton Park, *1 May*	Lola T70-Chevrolet	*steering*
7cl	Sports Car race	Silverstone, *15 May*	Lola T70-Chevrolet	*transmission*
1	Nürburgring 1000 Km	Nürburgring, *25 May*	Ferrari 330P2	*/Scarfiotti*
1	Player's 200	Mosport Park, *4 June*	Lola T70-Chevrolet	
rtd	Le Mans 24 Hours	Le Mans, *19-20 June*	Ferrari 330P2	*gearbox/Scarfiotti*
2	Reims 12 Hours	Reims, *3-4 July*	Ferrari 365P2	*/Parkes*
rtd	Martini Trophy	Silverstone, *24 July*	Lola T70-Chevrolet	*engine*
1	Guards Int. Trophy	Brands Hatch, *30 Aug*	Lola T70-Chevrolet	
1	Player's Quebec	Ste Jovite, *19 Sep*	Lola T70-Chevrolet	
dns	Canadian GP	Mosport Park, *25 Sep*	Lola T70-Chevrolet	*practice accident*

1966

FORMULA 1

1	Syracuse GP	Syracuse, *1 May*	Ferrari 312	
2	International Trophy	Silverstone, *4 May*	Ferrari 312	
rtd	**MONACO GP**	**Monte Carlo, *22 May***	**Ferrari 312**	*seized differential*
1	**BELGIAN GP**	**Spa-Francorchamps, *12 June***	**Ferrari 312**	
rtd	**FRENCH GP**	**Reims, *3 July***	**Cooper T81-Maserati**	*fuel system*
rtd	**BRITISH GP**	**Brands Hatch, *16 July***	**Cooper T81-Maserati**	*transmission*
rtd	**DUTCH GP**	**Zandvoort, *24 July***	**Cooper T81-Maserati**	*ignition*
2	**GERMAN GP**	**Nürburgring, *7 Aug***	**Cooper T81-Maserati**	
rtd	**ITALIAN GP**	**Monza, *4 Sep***	**Cooper T81-Maserati**	*fuel tank*
3	**US GP**	**Watkins Glen, *2 Oct***	**Cooper T81-Maserati**	
1	**MEXICAN GP**	**Mexico City, *23 Oct***	**Cooper T81-Maserati**	

FORMULA 2

rtd	Reims GP	Reims, *2 July*	Matra MS5-Cosworth	*fuel pump*
7	Rouen GP	Rouen, *10 July*	Matra MS5-Cosworth	
rtd	Kannonloppet	Karlskoga, *21 Aug*	Lola T62-Cosworth	*halfshaft*

SPORTS CARS

1	Monza 1000 Km	Monza, *25 Apr*	Ferrari 330P3	*/Parkes*
rtd	Nürburgring 1000 Km	Nürburgring, *5 June*	Ferrari 330P3	*clutch and suspension /Parkes*
1	Wills Trophy	Croft, *14 Aug*	Lola T70-Chevrolet	
1	Guards Trophy	Brands Hatch, *29 Aug*	Lola T70-Chevrolet	
1	Player's Quebec	Ste Jovite, *11 Sep*	Lola T70-Chevrolet	
rtd	Bridgehampton GP	Bridgehampton, *18 Sep*	Lola T70-Chevrolet	*broken oil pipe*
rtd	Canadian GP	Mosport Park, *24 Sep*	Lola T70-Chevrolet	*accident*
rtd	Monterey GP	Laguna Seca, *16 Oct*	Lola T70-Chevrolet	*accident*
1	Riverside GP	Riverside, *30 Oct*	Lola T70-Chevrolet	
1	Stardust GP	Las Vegas, *13 Nov*	Lola T70-Chevrolet	

Can-Am Champion

1967

FORMULA 1

3	**SOUTH AFRICAN GP**	**Kyalami, *2 Jan***	**Honda RA273**	
rtd	Race of Champions	Brands Hatch, *12 Mar*	Honda RA273	*seized throttle slide*
3	Spring Cup	Oulton Park, *15 Apr*	Honda RA273	
rtd	**MONACO GP**	**Monte Carlo, *7 May***	**Honda RA273**	*piston*
rtd	**DUTCH GP**	**Zandvoort, *4 June***	**Honda RA273**	*throttle slide*
rtd	**BELGIAN GP**	**Spa-Francorchamps, *18 June***	**Honda RA273**	*engine*
6	**BRITISH GP**	**Silverstone, *15 July***	**Honda RA273**	
4	**GERMAN GP**	**Nürburgring, *6 Aug***	**Honda RA273**	

1967 (continued)

1	**ITALIAN GP**	**Monza,** *10 Sep*	**Honda RA300**	
rtd	**US GP**	**Watkins Glen,** *1 Oct*	**Honda RA300**	*flat battery*
4	**MEXICAN GP**	**Mexico City,** *22 Oct*	**Honda RA300**	
	FORMULA 2			
rtd	Guards 100	Snetterton, *24 Mar*	Lola T100-Cosworth	*jamming throttle*
3	Wills Trophy	Silverstone, *27 Mar*	Lola T100-Cosworth	
2	Eifelrennen	Nürburgring, *23 Apr*	Lola T100-BMW	
1	Guards Trophy	Mallory Park, *14 May*	Lola T100-Cosworth	
1	Grand Prix du Limbourg	Zolder, *21 May*	Lola T100-Cosworth	
7	BUA International Trophy	Crystal Palace, *29 May*	Lola T100-Cosworth	
3	Reims GP	Reims, *25 June*	Lola T100-Cosworth	
rtd	Guards Trophy	Brands Hatch, *28 Aug*	Lola T100-Cosworth	*oil filter sealing ring*
	SPORTS CARS			
rtd	Nürburgring 1000 Km	Nürburgring, *28 May*	Lola T70-Aston Martin V8	*broken rear wishbone /Hobbs*
rtd	Le Mans 24 Hours	Le Mans, *10-11 June*	Lola T70-Aston Martin V8	*piston/Hobbs*
rtd	Reims 12 Hours	Reims, *25 June*	Lola T70 GT Mk 2-Chevrolet	*crankshaft*
rtd	BOAC 1000 Km	Brands Hatch, *30 July*	Lola T70 GT Mk 2-Chevrolet	*piston*
3	Can-Am race	Elkhart Lake, *3 Sep*	Lola T70 Mk3-Chevrolet	
4	Chevron GP	Bridgehampton, *17 Sep*	Lola T70 Mk 3-Chevrolet	
rtd	Player's 200	Mosport Park, *23 Sep*	Lola T70 Mk 3-Chevrolet	*engine*
rtd	Monterey GP	Laguna Seca, *15 Oct*	Lola T70 Mk 3-Chevrolet	*collision*
rtd	Los Angeles Times GP	Riverside, *29 Oct*	Lola T70 Mk 3-Chevrolet	
1	Stardust GP	Las Vegas, *12 Nov*	Lola T70 Mk 3-Chevrolet	
	INDIANAPOLIS CARS			
rtd	Rex Mays 300	Riverside, *26 Nov*	Lola T90-Offenhauser	*misfire*

1968

	FORMULA 1			
8	**SOUTH AFRICAN GP**	**Kyalami,** *1 Jan*	**Honda RA300**	
rtd	**SPANISH GP**	**Jarama,** *12 May*	**Honda RA301**	*gear linkage selector belt*
rtd	**MONACO GP**	**Monte Carlo,** *26 May*	**Honda RA301**	*gearbox*
rtd	**BELGIAN GP**	**Spa-Francorchamps,** *9 June*	**Honda RA301**	*rear wishbone*
rtd	**DUTCH GP**	**Zandvoort,** *23 June*	**Honda RA301**	*battery/alternator*
2	**FRENCH GP**	**Rouen,** *7 July*	**Honda RA301**	
5	**BRITISH GP**	**Brands Hatch,** *20 July*	**Honda RA301**	
rtd	**GERMAN GP**	**Nürburgring,** *4 Aug*	**Honda RA301**	*engine*

1968 (continued)

rtd	**ITALIAN GP**	**Monza,** *8 Sep*	**Honda RA301**	*crashed avoiding Amon*
rtd	**CANADIAN GP**	**Ste Jovite,** *22 Sep*	**Honda RA301**	*gearbox*
3	**US GP**	**Watkins Glen,** *6 Oct*	**Honda RA301**	
rtd	**MEXICAN GP**	**Mexico City,** *3 Nov*	**Honda RA301**	*overheating*
	SPORTS CARS			
rtd	Can-Am race	Bridgehampton, *15 Sep*	Lola T160-Chevrolet	*pushrod*
rtd	Los Angeles Times GP	Riverside, *24 Oct*	Lola T160-Chevrolet	*water pump*

1969

	FORMULA 1			
rtd	**SOUTH AFRICAN GP**	**Kyalami,** *1 Mar*	**BRM P138**	*engine*
5	**SPANISH GP**	**Barcelona,** *4 May*	**BRM P138**	
rtd	**MONACO GP**	**Monte Carlo,** *18 May*	**BRM P138**	*gearbox*
9	**DUTCH GP**	**Zandvoort,** *21 June*	**BRM P138**	
rtd	**BRITISH GP**	**Silverstone,** *19 July*	**BRM P139**	*suspension*
dns	**GERMAN GP**	**Nürburgring,** *3 Aug*	**BRM P139**	*car withdrawn*
11	**ITALIAN GP**	**Monza,** *7 Sep*	**BRM P139**	
rtd	**CANADIAN GP**	**Mosport Park,** *20 Sep*	**BRM P139**	*engine*
3	**US GP**	**Watkins Glen,** *5 Oct*	**BRM P139**	
rtd	**MEXICAN GP**	**Mexico City,** *19 Oct*	**BRM P139**	*gearbox*
	SPORTS CARS			
3	Labatt's Blue Trophy	Mosport Park, *1 June*	McLaren M12-Chevrolet	
rtd	Labatt's Trophy	Ste Jovite, *15 June*	McLaren M12-Chevrolet	*bodywork*
12	Can-Am race	Watkins Glen, *13 July*	McLaren M12-Chevrolet	
4	Klondike 200	Edmonton, *27 July*	Chaparral 2H-Chevrolet	
5	Buckeye Can-Am	Lexington, *17 Aug*	Chaparral 2H-Chevrolet	
rtd	Can-Am race	Elkhart Lake, *31 Aug*	Chaparral 2H-Chevrolet	*transmission*
rtd	Inver House Scotch Can-Am	Bridgehampton, *14 Sep*	McLaren M12-Chevrolet	*engine*

1970

	FORMULA 1			
rtd	**SOUTH AFRICAN GP**	**Kyalami,** *7 Mar*	**McLaren M7C-Cosworth**	*engine*
rtd	Race of Champions	Brands Hatch, *22 Mar*	McLaren M7C-Cosworth	*throttle*
rtd	**SPANISH GP**	**Jarama,** *19 Apr*	**McLaren M7C-Cosworth**	*gearbox*
6	**DUTCH GP**	**Zandvoort,** *21 June*	**McLaren M7C-Cosworth**	
rtd	**BRITISH GP**	**Brands Hatch,** *18 July*	**Surtees TS7-Cosworth**	*oil pressure*
9cl	**GERMAN GP**	**Hockenheim,** *2 Aug*	**Surtees TS7-Cosworth**	*engine*

1970 (continued)

rtd	AUSTRIAN GP	Österreichring, *16 Aug*	Surtees TS7-Cosworth	*engine*
rtd	ITALIAN GP	Monza, *6 Sep*	Surtees TS7-Cosworth	*electrics*
5	CANADIAN GP	Ste Jovite, *19 Sep*	Surtees TS7-Cosworth	
rtd	US GP	Watkins Glen, *4 Oct*	Surtees TS7-Cosworth	*engine*
8	MEXICAN GP	Mexico City, *25 Oct*	Surtees TS7-Cosworth	
	SPORTS CARS			
3	Monza 1000 Km	Monza, *25 Apr*	Ferrari 512S	*/Schetty*
4	Spa 1000 Km	Spa-Francorchamps, *17 May*	Ferrari 512S	*/Ickx*
3	Nürburgring 1000 Km	Nürburgring, *31 May*	Ferrari 512S	*/Vaccarella*
	TOURING CARS			
rtd	Ford Capri 3000 GT race	Brands Hatch, *24 May*	Ford Capri	*collision*

1971

	FORMULA 1			
rtd	SOUTH AFRICAN GP	Kyalami, *6 Mar*	Surtees TS7-Cosworth	*gearbox oil pipe*
3	Race of Champions	Brands Hatch, *21 Mar*	Surtees TS9-Cosworth	
rtd	International Trophy	Oulton Park, *9 Apr*	Surtees TS9-Cosworth	*engine*
11	SPANISH GP	Barcelona, *18 Apr*	Surtees TS9-Cosworth	
11cl	International Trophy	Silverstone, *8 May*	Surtees TS9-Cosworth	*4th heat 1/rtd heat 2*
7	MONACO GP	Monte Carlo, *23 May*	Surtees TS9-Cosworth	
3	Rindt Memorial	Hockenheim, *13 June*	Surtees TS9-Cosworth	
5	DUTCH GP	Zandvoort, *20 June*	Surtees TS9-Cosworth	
8	FRENCH GP	Paul Ricard, *4 July*	Surtees TS9-Cosworth	
6	BRITISH GP	Silverstone, *17 July*	Surtees TS9-Cosworth	
7	GERMAN GP	Nürburgring, *1 Aug*	Surtees TS9-Cosworth	
rtd	AUSTRIAN GP	Österreichring, *15 Aug*	Surtees TS9-Cosworth	*engine*
1	Gold Cup	Oulton Park, *21 Aug*	Surtees TS9-Cosworth	
rtd	ITALIAN GP	Monza, *5 Sep*	Surtees TS9-Cosworth	*engine*
11	CANADIAN GP	Mosport Park, *19 Sep*	Surtees TS9-Cosworth	
17	US GP	Watkins Glen, *3 Oct*	Surtees TS9-Cosworth	
6	Victory Race	Brands Hatch, *24 Oct*	Surtees TS9-Cosworth	
	F5000			
rtd	Australian GP	Warwick Farm, *14 Feb*	Surtees TS8-Chevrolet	*broken driveshaft*
	TOURING CARS			
11	Paul Ricard 12 Hours	Paul Ricard, *12 Sep*	Ford Capri	*/G. Hill*

1972

FORMULA 1

3	International Trophy	Silverstone, *23 Apr*	Surtees TS9B-Cosworth	
rtd	**ITALIAN GP**	**Monza, *10 Sep***	**Surtees TS14-Cosworth**	***fuel vaporisation***
dns	**US GP**	**Watkins Glen, *8 Oct***	**Surtees TS14-Cosworth**	***engine shortage***

FORMULA 2

rtd	John Player British F2 race	Oulton Park, *31 Mar*	Surtees TS10-Hart	*electrics*
rtd	Esso Uniflo Trophy	Thruxton, *3 Apr*	Surtees TS10-Hart	*electrics*
1	Japanese Grand Prix	Mount Fuji, *3 May*	Surtees TS10-Hart	
rtd	Greater London Trophy	Crystal Palace, *29 May*	Surtees TS10-Hart	*engine, qualifying heat 1*
rtd	Rouen GP	Rouen, *25 June*	Surtees TS10-Hart	*clutch, qualifying heat 2*
1	Shell Trophy	Imola, *23 July*	Surtees TS10-Hart	*4th heat 1, 3rd heat 2*
rtd	John Player British F2 race	Oulton Park, *16 Sep*	Surtees TS10-Hart	*electrics*